Welfare Reform and Pensions Act 1999

CHAPTER 30

ARRANGEMENT OF SECTIONS

Welfare Reform and Pensions Act 1999

1999 CHAPTER 30

An Act to make provision about pensions and social security; to make provision for reducing under-occupation of dwellings by housing benefit claimants; to authorise certain expenditure by the Secretary of State having responsibility for social security; and for connected purposes.   [11th November 1999]

BE IT ENACTED by the Queen's most Excellent Majesty, by and with the advice and consent of the Lords Spiritual and Temporal, and Commons, in this present Parliament assembled, and by the authority of the same, as follows:—

PART I

STAKEHOLDER PENSION SCHEMES

1.—(1) A pension scheme is a stakeholder pension scheme for the purposes of this Part if it is registered as such a scheme under section 2 and each of the following is fulfilled, namely—

> Meaning of "stakeholder pension scheme".

    (a) the conditions set out in subsections (2) to (9); and

    (b) such other conditions as may be prescribed.

(2) The first condition is that the scheme is established under a trust or in such other way as may be prescribed.

(3) The second condition is that the provisions made by the instruments establishing the scheme comply with such requirements as may be prescribed.

(4) The third condition is that, subject to such exceptions as may be prescribed, the benefits provided by the scheme are money purchase benefits within the meaning given by section 181 of the Pension Schemes Act 1993 ("the 1993 Act").

> 1993 c. 48.

(5) The fourth condition is that the scheme complies with such requirements as may be prescribed as regards the extent to which, and the circumstances in which—

(a) any payment made to the scheme by or on behalf of a member of the scheme,

(b) any income or capital gain arising from the investment of such a payment, or

(c) the value of rights under the scheme,

may be used to defray the administrative expenses of the scheme, to pay commission or in any other way which does not result in the provision of benefits for or in respect of members.

(6) The fifth condition is that the scheme complies with such of the requirements of regulations under section 113 of the 1993 Act (disclosure of information about schemes to members etc.) as are applicable to it.

(7) The sixth condition is that, subject to such minimum contribution levels and other restrictions as may be prescribed, members of the scheme may make such contributions to the scheme as they think appropriate.

(8) The seventh condition is that, except in so far as is necessary to ensure that the scheme has tax-exemption or tax-approval (within the meaning of the 1993 Act), the scheme accepts transfer payments in respect of members' rights under—

(a) other pension schemes;

1988 c. 1.

(b) contracts and schemes approved under Chapter III of Part XIV of the Income and Corporation Taxes Act 1988 (retirement annuity contracts);

(c) annuities and insurance policies purchased or transferred for the purpose of giving effect to rights under pension schemes; and

(d) annuities purchased or entered into for the purpose of discharging liability in respect of pension credits under section 29(1)(b) or under corresponding Northern Ireland legislation.

(9) The eighth condition is that the scheme has such exemption or approval as is mentioned in subsection (8).

Registration of stakeholder pension schemes.

2.—(1) The Occupational Pensions Regulatory Authority ("the Authority") shall keep a register of stakeholder pension schemes.

(2) Subject to subsection (3), the Authority shall register a pension scheme under this section if the trustees of the scheme, or any person or persons prescribed in relation to the scheme—

(a) make an application for the purpose and pay such fee as the Authority may determine; and

(b) declare that each of the following is fulfilled in relation to the scheme, namely—

(i) the conditions set out in subsections (2) to (9) of section 1; and

(ii) such other conditions as may be prescribed under subsection (1) of that section.

(3) Where the Authority are satisfied on reasonable grounds that any of those conditions is not fulfilled in relation to a pension scheme, the Authority may—

(a) refuse to register the scheme; or

(b) where the scheme is registered under this section, remove it from the register.

(4) Section 3 (prohibition orders) and section 10 (civil penalties) of the Pensions Act 1995 ("the 1995 Act") apply to any trustee of a pension scheme which is or has been registered under this section, and section 10 of that Act applies to any person prescribed in relation to such a scheme, if—

1995 c. 26.

    (a) he fails to take all such steps as are reasonable to secure that each of those conditions is fulfilled in relation to the scheme or (as the case may be) while the scheme was so registered he failed to take all such steps as were reasonable to secure that each of those conditions was so fulfilled; or

    (b) where the scheme was registered on his application, any of those conditions was not fulfilled in relation to the scheme at the time of the application.

(5) Any person who, in applying for registration of a pension scheme under this section, knowingly or recklessly provides the Authority with information which is false or misleading in a material particular shall be liable—

    (a) on summary conviction, to a fine not exceeding the statutory maximum;

    (b) on conviction on indictment, to imprisonment or a fine or both.

(6) Section 115 of the 1995 Act (offences by bodies corporate or Scottish partnerships) applies in relation to an offence under subsection (5) as it applies in relation to an offence under Part I of that Act.

(7) The Secretary of State may by regulations make provision—

    (a) for the register, or extracts from the register, or for copies of the register or of extracts from the register, to be open to inspection by, and

    (b) for copies of the register, or of extracts from it, to be supplied to,

such persons, in such manner, at such times, on payment of such fees, and subject to such other terms and conditions, as may be prescribed.

3.—(1) Except in so far as regulations otherwise provide, it shall be the duty of an employer of relevant employees to comply with the requirements set out below.

Duty of employers to facilitate access to stakeholder pension schemes.

(2) The first requirement is that the employer shall ensure that at all times there is at least one scheme designated by him for the purposes of this subsection which is registered under section 2 and offers membership to all his relevant employees (whether or not any other scheme registered under that section which does not offer membership to all those employees is for the time being designated by him for those purposes).

Before designating a scheme for the purposes of this subsection the employer shall consult with his relevant employees and any organisations representing them.

(3) The second requirement is that the employer shall supply his relevant employees with—

    (a) the name and address of the designated scheme or, as the case may be, of each of the designated schemes; and

    (b) such other information as may be prescribed.

(4) The third requirement is that the employer shall allow representatives of the designated scheme or schemes reasonable access to his relevant employees for the purpose of supplying them with information about the scheme or schemes.

(5) The fourth requirement is that, subject to such exceptions and qualifications as may be prescribed, the employer shall, if he is requested to do so by a relevant employee of his who is a member of a qualifying scheme—

(a) deduct the employee's contributions to the scheme from his remuneration; and

(b) pay them to the trustees or managers of the scheme or, if regulations so provide, to a prescribed person.

(6) The fifth requirement is that the employer shall, if any scheme designated by him for the purposes of subsection (2) ceases to be registered under section 2, withdraw his designation of the scheme (but this requirement is not to be taken as implying that he cannot withdraw his designation of a scheme in other circumstances).

(7) Section 10 of the 1995 Act (civil penalties) applies to an employer who fails to comply with any of the requirements set out above.

(8) An employer is not, whether before designating a scheme for the purposes of subsection (2) or at any time while a scheme is designated by him for those purposes, under any duty—

(a) to make any enquiries, or act on any information, about the scheme for any purpose not connected with—

(i) ascertaining whether the scheme is for the time being registered under section 2,

(ii) ascertaining the persons to whom it offers membership, or

(iii) enabling him to comply with subsection (3), or

(b) in particular, to investigate or monitor, or make any judgment as to, the past, present or future performance of the scheme.

(9) In this section—

"employer" means any employer, whether or not resident or incorporated in any part of the United Kingdom;

"qualifying scheme", in relation to an employer, means—

(a) the designated scheme or one of the designated schemes; or

(b) if regulations so provide, any other stakeholder pension scheme;

"relevant employees", in relation to an employer, means all employees of his employed in Great Britain and also, in the case of an employer resident or incorporated in any part of Great Britain, all employees of his employed outside the United Kingdom, but with the exception, in the case of any employer, of any employees of his—

(a) whose employment qualifies them for membership of an occupational pension scheme of the employer;

(b) whose earnings fall below the lower earnings limit as defined in section 181 of the 1993 Act; or

(c) who are of such other description as may be prescribed.

4.—(1) Any person appearing to the Authority to be a person who holds, or is likely to hold, information which is relevant to the issue whether an employer is complying, or has complied, with the requirements under—

    (a) section 3, or

    (b) corresponding Northern Ireland legislation,

must, if required to do so by the Authority by notice in writing, produce any document which is so relevant.

(2) To comply with subsection (1) the document must be produced in such a manner, at such a place and within such a period as may be specified in the notice.

(3) Section 100 of the 1995 Act shall have effect as if references to section 98(1) or 99(1)(b) of that Act included references to subsection (1) or section 5(1)(b).

(4) Sections 101 to 103 of that Act shall have effect as if references which are or include references to section 98 or 99 of that Act included references to this section or section 5.

(5) In this section and section 5 "document" includes information recorded in any form, and any reference to production of a document, in relation to information recorded otherwise than in legible form, is to producing a copy of the information in legible form.

Obtaining information with respect to compliance with section 3 and corresponding Northern Ireland legislation.

5.—(1) An inspector may, for the purposes of investigating whether an employer is complying, or has complied, with the requirements under section 3 or corresponding Northern Ireland legislation, at any reasonable time enter premises liable to inspection and, while there—

    (a) may make such examination and inquiry as may be necessary for such purposes,

    (b) may require any person on the premises to produce, or secure the production of, any document relevant to compliance with those requirements for his inspection, and

    (c) may, as to any matter relevant to compliance with those requirements, examine, or require to be examined, either alone or in the presence of another person, any person on the premises whom he has reasonable cause to believe to be able to give information relevant to that matter.

(2) Premises are liable to inspection for the purposes of this section if the inspector has reasonable grounds to believe that—

    (a) employees of the employer are employed there,

    (b) documents relevant to the administration of the employer's business are being kept there, or

    (c) the administration of the employer's business, or work connected with that administration, is being carried out there,

unless the premises are a private dwelling-house not used by, or by permission of, the occupier for the purposes of a trade or business.

Powers of inspection for securing compliance with section 3 and corresponding Northern Ireland legislation.

(3) An inspector applying for admission to any premises for the purposes of this section must, if so required, produce his certificate of appointment.

(4) In this section "inspector" means a person appointed by the Authority as an inspector.

Application of
certain
enactments.
1996 c. 18.

6.—(1) Sections 46 and 102 of the Employment Rights Act 1996 (occupational pension scheme trustees: protection from unfair dismissal and other detriment) shall apply in relation to an employee who is (or is a director of a company which is) a trustee of a scheme designated by his employer under section 3(2) as they apply in relation to an employee who is (or is a director of a company which is) a trustee of a relevant occupational pension scheme which relates to his employment.

(2) Section 58 of that Act (occupational pension scheme trustees: time off) shall apply to the employer in relation to a designated scheme as it applies to the employer in relation to a relevant occupational pension scheme.

(3) Schedule 1 (application of the 1993 and 1995 Acts to registered schemes) shall have effect.

(4) In this section "relevant occupational pension scheme" has the meaning given by section 46 of the Employment Rights Act 1996.

Reduced rates of
contributions etc:
power to specify
different
percentages.

7.—(1) An order under section 42B(2) of the 1993 Act (determination and alteration of reduced rates of Class 1 contributions, and rebates, for members of money purchase contracted-out schemes) may specify different percentages in respect of earners by reference to whether the money purchase contracted-out scheme of which the earner is a member is or is not for the time being registered under section 2.

(2) An order under section 45A(2) of that Act (determination and alteration of minimum contributions to be paid to appropriate personal pension schemes) may—

(a) specify different percentages in respect of earners by reference to whether the appropriate personal pension scheme of which the earner is a member is or is not for the time being registered under section 2; and

(b) specify different percentages in respect of earners by reference to the time when the earner first became a member of the scheme.

(3) This section is without prejudice to section 182 of that Act (orders and regulations: general provisions).

Interpretation and
application of
Part I.
1993 c. 48.
1995 c. 26.

8.—(1) In this Part—

"the 1993 Act" means the Pension Schemes Act 1993;

"the 1995 Act" means the Pensions Act 1995;

"the Authority" means the Occupational Pensions Regulatory Authority;

"designated scheme", in relation to an employer, means a scheme designated by him for the purposes of section 3(2);

"occupational pension scheme" and "personal pension scheme" have the meanings given by section 1 of the 1993 Act;

"pension scheme" means an occupational pension scheme or a personal pension scheme;

"prescribed" means prescribed by regulations made by the Secretary of State;

"stakeholder pension scheme" shall be construed in accordance with section 1.

(2) The Secretary of State may by regulations make provision for a stakeholder pension scheme which—

(a) is of a prescribed description, and

(b) would (apart from the regulations) be an occupational pension scheme,

to be treated for all purposes, or for such purposes as may be prescribed, as if it were a personal pension scheme and not an occupational pension scheme.

(3) This Part applies to a pension scheme managed by or on behalf of the Crown as it applies to other pension schemes; and, accordingly, references in this Part to a person in his capacity as a trustee or manager of, or person prescribed in relation to, a pension scheme include the Crown, or a person acting on behalf of the Crown, in that capacity.

(4) This Part applies to persons employed by or under the Crown in like manner as if such persons were employed by a private person; and references in this Part to a person in his capacity as an employer include the Crown, or a person acting on behalf of the Crown, in that capacity.

(5) Subsections (3) and (4) do not apply to any provision of this Part under or by virtue of which a person may be prosecuted for an offence; but such a provision applies to persons in the public service of the Crown as it applies to other persons.

(6) Nothing in this Part applies to Her Majesty in Her private capacity (within the meaning of the Crown Proceedings Act 1947).

1947 c. 44.

Part II

Pensions: general

Payments by employers to pension schemes

9. In Part VI of the Pension Schemes Act 1993 (further requirements for protection of scheme members), after section 111 there shall be inserted—

Monitoring of employers' payments to personal pension schemes.
1993 c. 48.

"Monitoring of employers' payments to personal pension schemes.

111A.—(1) This section applies where—

(a) an employee is a member of a personal pension scheme; and

(b) direct payment arrangements exist between the employee and his employer.

(2) In this section "direct payment arrangements" means arrangements under which contributions fall to be paid by or on behalf of the employer towards the scheme—

(a) on the employer's own account (but in respect of the employee); or

(b) on behalf of the employee out of deductions from the employee's earnings.

(3) The employer must secure that there is prepared, maintained and from time to time revised a record of the direct payment arrangements which complies with subsection (4).

(4) The record must—

    (a) show the rates and due dates of contributions payable under the direct payment arrangements, and

    (b) satisfy prescribed requirements.

(5) The employer must, within the prescribed period after the preparation or any revision of the record, send a copy of the record or (as the case may be) of the revised record to the trustees or managers of the scheme.

(6) Except in prescribed circumstances, the trustees or managers of the scheme must, where any contribution shown by the record to be payable under the direct payment arrangements has not been paid on or before its due date, give notice of that fact, within the prescribed period, to the Regulatory Authority and the employee.

(7) The trustees or managers of the scheme must before the end of prescribed intervals send the employee a statement setting out the amounts and dates of the payments made under the direct payment arrangements during a prescribed period.

(8) If—

    (a) the employer fails to take all such steps as are reasonable to secure compliance with subsection (3) or (5), or

    (b) a contribution payable under the direct payment arrangements is not paid to the trustees or managers of the scheme on or before its due date,

1995 c. 26.

section 10 of the Pensions Act 1995 (power of the Regulatory Authority to impose civil penalties) applies to the employer.

(9) If subsection (6) or (7) is not complied with, section 10 of the Pensions Act 1995 applies to any trustee or manager of the scheme who has failed to take all such steps as are reasonable to secure compliance.

(10) If—

    (a) subsection (6) or (7) is not complied with, and

    (b) the scheme—

        (i) is established under a trust, and

(ii) is or has been registered under section 2 of the Welfare Reform and Pensions Act 1999 (stakeholder schemes),

section 3 of the Pensions Act 1995 (power of the Regulatory Authority to remove trustees) applies to any trustee of the scheme who has failed to take all such steps as are reasonable to secure compliance.   1995 c. 26.

(11) A person shall not be required by virtue of subsection (8)(b) above to pay a penalty under section 10 of the Pensions Act 1995 in respect of a failure if in respect of that failure he has been—

> (a) required to pay a penalty under that section by virtue of section 3(7) of the Welfare Reform and Pensions Act 1999 (failures in respect of stakeholder pensions), or
>
> (b) convicted of an offence under subsection (12) below.

(12) A person is guilty of an offence if he is knowingly concerned in the fraudulent evasion of the direct payment arrangements so far as they are arrangements for the payment by him or any other person of any such contribution towards the scheme as is mentioned in subsection (2)(b).

(13) A person guilty of an offence under subsection (12) is liable—

> (a) on summary conviction, to a fine not exceeding the statutory maximum; and
>
> (b) on conviction on indictment, to imprisonment for a term not exceeding seven years or a fine or both.

(14) No prosecution shall be brought against the Crown for an offence under subsection (12), but that subsection applies to persons in the public service of the Crown as to other persons.

(15) In this section "due date", in relation to a contribution payable under the direct payment arrangements, means—

> (a) if the contribution falls to be paid on the employer's own account, the latest day under the arrangements for paying it;
>
> (b) if the contribution falls to be paid on behalf of the employee, the last day of a prescribed period.

(16) Regulations may provide for this section to apply with such modifications as may be prescribed in a case where—

(a) the direct payment arrangements give effect to a requirement arising under subsection (5) of section 3 of the Welfare Reform and Pensions Act 1999 (deduction and payment of employee's contributions to stakeholder scheme), and

(b) in accordance with regulations under that subsection, that requirement is for the employer to pay contributions to a person prescribed by such regulations (instead of to the trustees or managers of the scheme).

(17) Nothing in this section shall be taken as varying the provisions of the direct payment arrangements or as affecting their enforceability.

Obtaining information for purposes of section 111A and corresponding Northern Ireland legislation.

111B.—(1) Any person appearing to the Regulatory Authority to be a person who holds, or is likely to hold, information which is relevant to the issue—

(a) whether any provision made by or under section 111A is being, or has been, complied with by an employer or the trustees or managers of a personal pension scheme,

(b) whether, in the case of any direct payment arrangements existing between an employee and his employer, there has been such a failure to pay a contribution as is mentioned in subsection (8)(b) of that section, or

(c) whether an offence has been committed under subsection (12) of that section in relation to any such arrangements,

must, if required to do so by the Regulatory Authority by notice in writing, produce any document which is so relevant.

(2) To comply with subsection (1) the document must be produced in such a manner, at such a place and within such a period as may be specified in the notice.

(3) An inspector may, for the purposes of investigating any of the matters set out in subsection (1)(a) to (c), at any reasonable time enter premises liable to inspection and, while there—

(a) may make such examination and inquiry as may be necessary for such purposes,

(b) may require any person on the premises to produce for his inspection, or secure the production for his inspection of, any document relevant—

(i) to compliance with any provision made by or under section 111A, or with the direct payment arrangements, or

(ii) to the issue whether an offence has been committed under subsection (12) of that section in relation to those arrangements, and

(c) may, as to any matter so relevant, examine, or require to be examined, either alone or in the presence of another person, any person on the premises whom he has reasonable cause to believe to be able to give information relevant to that matter.

(4) An inspector applying for admission to any premises in pursuance of subsection (3) must, if so required, produce his certificate of appointment.

(5) For the purposes of subsection (3) premises are liable to inspection if the inspector has reasonable grounds to believe that—

(a) employees of the employer are employed there,

(b) documents relevant to the administration of—

(i) the employer's business,

(ii) the direct payment arrangements, or

(iii) the scheme to which those arrangements relate,

are kept there, or

(c) either of the following is being carried out there, namely—

(i) the administration of the employer's business, the arrangements or the scheme, or

(ii) work connected with the administration of the employer's business, the arrangements or the scheme,

unless the premises are a private dwelling-house not used by, or by permission of, the occupier for the purposes of a trade or business.

(6) Section 100 of the Pensions Act 1995 (warrants) shall have effect as if references to section 98(1) or 99(1)(b) of that Act included references to subsection (1) or (3)(b). 1995 c. 26.

(7) Sections 101 to 103 of that Act (penalties, savings and reports) shall have effect as if references which are or include references to section 98 or 99 of that Act included references to this section.

(8) In this section—

"direct payment arrangements" has the same meaning as in section 111A;

"document" includes information recorded in any form, and any reference to production of a document, in relation to information recorded otherwise than in legible form, is to producing a copy of the information in legible form;

"inspector" means a person appointed by the Regulatory Authority as an inspector.

(9) References in this section to, or to any provision of, section 111A include references to corresponding provisions of Northern Ireland legislation; and in this

section as it has effect in relation to those corresponding provisions, "employee" and "employer" have the meaning they have for the purposes of those provisions."

Late payments by employers to occupational pension schemes.
1995 c. 26.

10.—(1) For section 49(8) of the Pensions Act 1995 (offence where deduction from earnings not paid in timely fashion to occupational pension scheme) there shall be substituted—

"(8) Where on making a payment of any earnings in respect of any employment there is deducted any amount corresponding to any contribution payable on behalf of an active member of an occupational pension scheme, the amount deducted is to be paid, within a prescribed period, to the trustees or managers of the scheme.

(9) If in any case there is a failure to comply with subsection (8)—

(a) section 10 applies to the employer; and

(b) except in prescribed circumstances, the trustees or managers must give notice of the failure, within the prescribed period, to the Authority and the member.

(10) If in any case subsection (9)(b) is not complied with—

(a) section 3 applies to any trustee who has failed to take all such steps as are reasonable to secure compliance; and

(b) section 10 applies to any trustee or manager who has failed to take all such steps.

(11) If any person is knowingly concerned in the fraudulent evasion of the obligation imposed by subsection (8) in any case, he is guilty of an offence.

(12) A person guilty of an offence under subsection (11) is liable—

(a) on summary conviction, to a fine not exceeding the statutory maximum; and

(b) on conviction on indictment, to imprisonment for a term not exceeding seven years or a fine or both.

(13) A person shall not be required by virtue of subsection (9)(a) above to pay a penalty under section 10 in respect of a failure if in respect of that failure he has been—

(a) required to pay a penalty under that section by virtue of section 3(7) of the Welfare Reform and Pensions Act 1999 (failures in respect of stakeholder pensions), or

(b) convicted of an offence under subsection (11) above."

(2) In section 88(3) of that Act (civil penalty where contributions by or on behalf of employer to occupational pension scheme not paid by due date), after "by or on behalf of the employer" there shall be inserted "on the employer's own account".

Pensions and bankruptcy

11.—(1) Where a bankruptcy order is made against a person on a petition presented after the coming into force of this section, any rights of his under an approved pension arrangement are excluded from his estate.

(2) In this section "approved pension arrangement" means—

    (a) an exempt approved scheme;

    (b) a relevant statutory scheme;

    (c) a retirement benefits scheme set up by a government outside the United Kingdom for the benefit, or primarily for the benefit, of its employees;

    (d) a retirement benefits scheme which is being considered for approval under Chapter I of Part XIV of the Taxes Act;

    (e) a contract or scheme which is approved under Chapter III of that Part (retirement annuities);

    (f) a personal pension scheme which is approved under Chapter IV of that Part;

    (g) an annuity purchased for the purpose of giving effect to rights under a scheme falling within any of paragraphs (a) to (c) and (f);

    (h) any pension arrangements of any description which may be prescribed by regulations made by the Secretary of State.

(3) The reference in subsection (1) to rights under an approved pension arrangement does not include rights under a personal pension scheme approved under Chapter IV of Part XIV of the Taxes Act unless those rights arise by virtue of approved personal pension arrangements.

(4) Subsection (5) applies if—

    (a) at the time when a bankruptcy order is made against a person a retirement benefits scheme is being considered for approval under Chapter I of Part XIV of the Taxes Act, and

    (b) the decision of the Commissioners of Inland Revenue is that approval is not to be given to the scheme.

(5) Any rights of that person under the scheme shall (without any conveyance, assignment or transfer) vest in his trustee in bankruptcy, as part of his estate, immediately on—

    (a) the Commissioners' decision being made, or

    (b) (if later) the trustee's appointment taking effect or, in the case of the official receiver, his becoming trustee.

(6) Subsection (7) applies if, at any time after a bankruptcy order is made against a person, the Commissioners of Inland Revenue give notice—

    (a) withdrawing their approval under Chapter I of Part XIV of the Taxes Act from a retirement benefits scheme, or

    (b) withdrawing their approval under Chapter IV of that Part from a personal pension scheme or from any approved personal pension arrangements,

and the date specified as being that from which the approval is withdrawn ("the withdrawal date") is a date not later than that on which the bankruptcy order is made.

(7) Any rights of that person under the scheme or arising by virtue of the arrangements, and any rights of his under any related annuity, shall (without any conveyance, assignment or transfer) vest in his trustee in bankruptcy, as part of his estate, immediately on—

    (a) the giving of the notice, or

    (b) (if later) the trustee's appointment taking effect or, in the case of the official receiver, his becoming trustee.

(8) In subsection (7) "related annuity" means an annuity purchased on or after the withdrawal date for the purpose of giving effect to rights under the scheme or (as the case may be) to rights arising by virtue of the arrangements.

(9) Where under subsection (5) or (7) any rights vest in a person's trustee in bankruptcy, the trustee's title to them has relation back to the commencement of the person's bankruptcy; but where any transaction is entered into by the trustees or managers of the scheme in question—

    (a) in good faith, and

    (b) without notice of the making of the decision mentioned in subsection (4)(b) or (as the case may be) the giving of the notice mentioned in subsection (6),

the trustee in bankruptcy is not in respect of that transaction entitled by virtue of this subsection to any remedy against them or any person whose title to any property derives from them.

(10) Without prejudice to section 83, regulations under subsection (2)(h) may, in the case of any description of arrangements prescribed by the regulations, make provision corresponding to any provision made by subsections (4) to (9).

(11) In this section—

    (a) "exempt approved scheme", "relevant statutory scheme" and "retirement benefits scheme" have the same meaning as in Chapter I of Part XIV of the Taxes Act;

    (b) "approved personal pension arrangements" and "personal pension scheme" have the same meaning as in Chapter IV of that Part;

    (c) "estate", in relation to a person against whom a bankruptcy order is made, means his estate for the purposes of Parts VIII to XI of the Insolvency Act 1986;

1986 c. 45.

    (d) "the Taxes Act" means the Income and Corporation Taxes Act 1988.

1988 c. 1.

(12) For the purposes of this section a person shall be treated as having a right under an approved pension arrangement where—

    (a) he is entitled to a credit under section 29(1)(b) as against the person responsible for the arrangement (within the meaning of Chapter I of Part IV), and

    (b) the person so responsible has not discharged his liability in respect of the credit.

12.—(1) The Secretary of State may by regulations make provision for or in connection with enabling rights of a person under an unapproved pension arrangement to be excluded, in the event of a bankruptcy order being made against that person, from his estate for the purposes of Parts VIII to XI of the Insolvency Act 1986.

Effect of bankruptcy on pension rights: unapproved arrangements.
1986 c. 45.

(2) Regulations under this section may, in particular, make provision—

(a) for rights under an unapproved pension arrangement to be excluded from a person's estate—

(i) by an order made on his application by a prescribed court, or

(ii) in accordance with a qualifying agreement made between him and his trustee in bankruptcy;

(b) for the court's decision whether to make such an order in relation to a person to be made by reference to—

(i) future likely needs of him and his family, and

(ii) whether any benefits (by way of a pension or otherwise) are likely to be received by virtue of rights of his under other pension arrangements and (if so) the extent to which they appear likely to be adequate for meeting any such needs;

(c) for the prescribed persons in the case of any pension arrangement to provide a person or his trustee in bankruptcy on request with information reasonably required by that person or trustee for or in connection with the making of such applications and agreements as are mentioned in paragraph (a).

(3) In this section—

"prescribed" means prescribed by regulations under this section;

"qualifying agreement" means an agreement entered into in such circumstances, and satisfying such requirements, as may be prescribed;

"unapproved pension arrangement" means a pension arrangement which—

(a) is not an approved pension arrangement within the meaning of section 11, and

(b) is of a prescribed description.

(4) For the purposes of this section a person shall be treated as having a right under an unapproved pension arrangement where—

(a) he is entitled to a credit under section 29(1)(b) as against the person responsible for the arrangement (within the meaning of Chapter I of Part IV), and

(b) the person so responsible has not discharged his liability in respect of the credit.

Sections 11 and
12: application to
Scotland.

13.—(1) This section shall have effect for the purposes of the application of sections 11 and 12 to Scotland.

(2) A reference to—

1980 c. 46.

(a) the making of a bankruptcy order against a person is a reference to the award of sequestration on his estate or the making of the appointment on his estate of a judicial factor under section 41 of the Solicitors (Scotland) Act 1980;

1985 c. 66.

(b) the estate of a person is a reference to his estate for the purposes of the Bankruptcy (Scotland) Act 1985 or of the Solicitors (Scotland) Act 1980, as the case may be;

(c) assignment is a reference to assignation;

(d) a person's trustee in bankruptcy is a reference to his permanent trustee or judicial factor, as the case may be;

(e) the commencement of a person's bankruptcy is a reference to the date of sequestration (within the meaning of section 12(4) of the Bankruptcy (Scotland) Act 1985) or of the judicial factor's appointment taking effect, as the case may be.

(3) For paragraph (b) of each of subsections (5) and (7) of section 11 there shall be substituted—

"(b) if later, the date of sequestration (within the meaning of section 12(4) of the Bankruptcy (Scotland) Act 1985) or of the judicial factor's appointment taking effect, as the case may be."

No forfeiture on
bankruptcy of
rights under
pension schemes.
1993 c. 48.

14.—(1) In the Pension Schemes Act 1993, after section 159 there shall be inserted—

"No forfeiture
on bankruptcy
of rights under
personal pension
schemes.

159A.—(1) A person's rights under a personal pension scheme cannot be forfeited by reference to his bankruptcy.

(2) For the purposes of this section—

(a) a person shall be treated as having a right under a personal pension scheme where—

(i) he is entitled to a credit under section 29(1)(b) of the Welfare Reform and Pensions Act 1999 (sharing of rights on divorce etc.),

(ii) he is so entitled as against the person responsible for the scheme (within the meaning of Chapter I of Part IV of that Act), and

(iii) the person so responsible has not discharged his liability in respect of the credit; and

(b) forfeiture shall be taken to include any manner of deprivation or suspension."

(2) In section 159(6) of that Act (application of section 159 to Scotland), after "this section" there shall be inserted "and section 159A".

(3) In section 92(2) of the Pensions Act 1995 (exceptions to the rule preventing forfeiture of rights under occupational pension schemes), paragraph (b) (which allows forfeiture of such rights by reference to a scheme member's bankruptcy) shall cease to have effect.

1995 c. 26.

15. For sections 342A to 342C of the Insolvency Act 1986 there shall be substituted—

Excessive pension contributions made by persons who have become bankrupt.
1986 c. 45.

"Recovery of excessive pension contributions.

342A.—(1) Where an individual who is adjudged bankrupt—

    (a) has rights under an approved pension arrangement, or

    (b) has excluded rights under an unapproved pension arrangement,

the trustee of the bankrupt's estate may apply to the court for an order under this section.

(2) If the court is satisfied—

    (a) that the rights under the arrangement are to any extent, and whether directly or indirectly, the fruits of relevant contributions, and

    (b) that the making of any of the relevant contributions ("the excessive contributions") has unfairly prejudiced the individual's creditors,

the court may make such order as it thinks fit for restoring the position to what it would have been had the excessive contributions not been made.

(3) Subsection (4) applies where the court is satisfied that the value of the rights under the arrangement is, as a result of rights of the individual under the arrangement or any other pension arrangement having at any time become subject to a debit under section 29(1)(a) of the Welfare Reform and Pensions Act 1999 (debits giving effect to pension-sharing), less than it would otherwise have been.

(4) Where this subsection applies—

    (a) any relevant contributions which were represented by the rights which became subject to the debit shall, for the purposes of subsection (2), be taken to be contributions of which the rights under the arrangement are the fruits, and

    (b) where the relevant contributions represented by the rights under the arrangement (including those so represented by virtue of paragraph (a)) are not all excessive contributions, relevant contributions which are represented by the rights under the arrangement otherwise than by virtue of paragraph (a) shall be treated as excessive contributions before any which are so represented by virtue of that paragraph.

(5) In subsections (2) to (4) "relevant contributions" means contributions to the arrangement or any other pension arrangement—

(a) which the individual has at any time made on his own behalf, or

(b) which have at any time been made on his behalf.

(6) The court shall, in determining whether it is satisfied under subsection (2)(b), consider in particular—

(a) whether any of the contributions were made for the purpose of putting assets beyond the reach of the individual's creditors or any of them, and

(b) whether the total amount of any contributions—

(i) made by or on behalf of the individual to pension arrangements, and

(ii) represented (whether directly or indirectly) by rights under approved pension arrangements or excluded rights under unapproved pension arrangements,

is an amount which is excessive in view of the individual's circumstances when those contributions were made.

(7) For the purposes of this section and sections 342B and 342C ("the recovery provisions"), rights of an individual under an unapproved pension arrangement are excluded rights if they are rights which are excluded from his estate by virtue of regulations under section 12 of the Welfare Reform and Pensions Act 1999.

(8) In the recovery provisions—

"approved pension arrangement" has the same meaning as in section 11 of the Welfare Reform and Pensions Act 1999;

"unapproved pension arrangement" has the same meaning as in section 12 of that Act.

Orders under section 342A.

342B.—(1) Without prejudice to the generality of section 342A(2), an order under section 342A may include provision—

(a) requiring the person responsible for the arrangement to pay an amount to the individual's trustee in bankruptcy,

(b) adjusting the liabilities of the arrangement in respect of the individual,

(c) adjusting any liabilities of the arrangement in respect of any other person that derive, directly or indirectly, from rights of the individual under the arrangement,

(d) for the recovery by the person responsible for the arrangement (whether by deduction from any amount which that person is ordered to pay or otherwise) of costs incurred by that person in complying in the bankrupt's case with any requirement under section 342C(1) or in giving effect to the order.

(2) In subsection (1), references to adjusting the liabilities of the arrangement in respect of a person include (in particular) reducing the amount of any benefit or future benefit to which that person is entitled under the arrangement.

(3) In subsection (1)(c), the reference to liabilities of the arrangement does not include liabilities in respect of a person which result from giving effect to an order or provision falling within section 28(1) of the Welfare Reform and Pensions Act 1999 (pension sharing orders and agreements).

(4) The maximum amount which the person responsible for an arrangement may be required to pay by an order under section 342A is the lesser of—

    (a) the amount of the excessive contributions, and

    (b) the value of the individual's rights under the arrangement (if the arrangement is an approved pension arrangement) or of his excluded rights under the arrangement (if the arrangement is an unapproved pension arrangement).

(5) An order under section 342A which requires the person responsible for an arrangement to pay an amount ("the restoration amount") to the individual's trustee in bankruptcy must provide for the liabilities of the arrangement to be correspondingly reduced.

(6) For the purposes of subsection (5), liabilities are correspondingly reduced if the difference between—

    (a) the amount of the liabilities immediately before the reduction, and

    (b) the amount of the liabilities immediately after the reduction,

is equal to the restoration amount.

(7) An order under section 342A in respect of an arrangement—

    (a) shall be binding on the person responsible for the arrangement, and

    (b) overrides provisions of the arrangement to the extent that they conflict with the provisions of the order.

Orders under section 342A: supplementary.

342C.—(1) The person responsible for—

    (a) an approved pension arrangement under which a bankrupt has rights,

    (b) an unapproved pension arrangement under which a bankrupt has excluded rights, or

(c) a pension arrangement under which a bankrupt has at any time had rights,

shall, on the bankrupt's trustee in bankruptcy making a written request, provide the trustee with such information about the arrangement and rights as the trustee may reasonably require for, or in connection with, the making of applications under section 342A.

(2) Nothing in—

1993 c. 48.
1995 c. 26.

(a) any provision of section 159 of the Pension Schemes Act 1993 or section 91 of the Pensions Act 1995 (which prevent assignment and the making of orders that restrain a person from receiving anything which he is prevented from assigning),

(b) any provision of any enactment (whether passed or made before or after the passing of the Welfare Reform and Pensions Act 1999) corresponding to any of the provisions mentioned in paragraph (a), or

(c) any provision of the arrangement in question corresponding to any of those provisions,

applies to a court exercising its powers under section 342A.

(3) Where any sum is required by an order under section 342A to be paid to the trustee in bankruptcy, that sum shall be comprised in the bankrupt's estate.

(4) Regulations may, for the purposes of the recovery provisions, make provision about the calculation and verification of—

(a) any such value as is mentioned in section 342B(4)(b);

(b) any such amounts as are mentioned in section 342B(6)(a) and (b).

(5) The power conferred by subsection (4) includes power to provide for calculation or verification—

(a) in such manner as may, in the particular case, be approved by a prescribed person; or

(b) in accordance with guidance—

(i) from time to time prepared by a prescribed person, and

(ii) approved by the Secretary of State.

(6) References in the recovery provisions to the person responsible for a pension arrangement are to—

(a) the trustees, managers or provider of the arrangement, or

(b) the person having functions in relation to the arrangement corresponding to those of a trustee, manager or provider.

(7) In this section and sections 342A and 342B—

"prescribed" means prescribed by regulations;

"the recovery provisions" means this section and sections 342A and 342B;

"regulations" means regulations made by the Secretary of State.

(8) Regulations under the recovery provisions may—

(a) make different provision for different cases;

(b) contain such incidental, supplemental and transitional provisions as appear to the Secretary of State necessary or expedient.

(9) Regulations under the recovery provisions shall be made by statutory instrument subject to annulment in pursuance of a resolution of either House of Parliament."

16. For sections 36A to 36C of the Bankruptcy (Scotland) Act 1985 there shall be substituted—

Excessive pension contributions made by persons who have become bankrupt: Scotland.
1985 c. 66.

"Recovery of excessive pension contributions.

36A.—(1) Where a debtor's estate has been sequestrated and he—

(a) has rights under an approved pension arrangement, or

(b) has excluded rights under an unapproved pension arrangement,

the permanent trustee may apply to the court for an order under this section.

(2) If the court is satisfied—

(a) that the rights under the arrangement are to any extent, and whether directly or indirectly, the fruits of relevant contributions, and

(b) that the making of any of the relevant contributions ("the excessive contributions") has unfairly prejudiced the debtor's creditors,

the court may make such order as it thinks fit for restoring the position to what it would have been had the excessive contributions not been made.

(3) Subsection (4) applies where the court is satisfied that the value of the rights under the arrangement is, as a result of rights of the debtor under the arrangement or any other pension arrangement having at any time become subject to a debit under section 29(1)(a) of the Welfare Reform and Pensions Act 1999 (debits giving effect to pension-sharing), less than it would otherwise have been.

(4) Where this subsection applies—

(a) any relevant contributions which were represented by the rights which became subject to the debit shall, for the purposes of subsection (2), be taken to be contributions of which the rights under the arrangement are the fruits, and

(b) where the relevant contributions represented by the rights under the arrangement (including those so represented by virtue of paragraph (a)) are not all excessive contributions, relevant contributions which are represented by the rights under the arrangement otherwise than by virtue of paragraph (a) shall be treated as excessive contributions before any which are so represented by virtue of that paragraph.

(5) In subsections (2) to (4) "relevant contributions" means contributions to the arrangement or any other pension arrangement—

(a) which the debtor has at any time made on his own behalf, or

(b) which have at any time been made on his behalf.

(6) The court shall, in determining whether it is satisfied under subsection (2)(b), consider in particular—

(a) whether any of the contributions were made for the purpose of putting assets beyond the reach of the debtor's creditors or any of them, and

(b) whether the total amount of any contributions—

(i) made by or on behalf of the debtor to pension arrangements, and

(ii) represented (whether directly or indirectly) by rights under approved pension arrangements or excluded rights under unapproved pensions arrangements,

is an amount which is excessive in view of the debtor's circumstances when those contributions were made.

(7) For the purposes of this section and sections 36B and 36C ("the recovery provisions"), rights of a debtor under an unapproved pension arrangement are excluded rights if they are rights which are excluded from his estate by virtue of regulations under section 12 of the Welfare Reform and Pensions Act 1999.

(8) In the recovery provisions—

"approved pension arrangement" has the same meaning as in section 11 of the Welfare Reform and Pensions Act 1999;

"unapproved pension arrangement" has the same meaning as in section 12 of that Act.

Orders under section 36A.

36B.—(1) Without prejudice to the generality of section 36A(2) an order under section 36A may include provision—

(a) requiring the person responsible for the arrangement to pay an amount to the permanent trustee,

(b) adjusting the liabilities of the arrangement in respect of the debtor,

(c) adjusting any liabilities of the arrangement in respect of any other person that derive, directly or indirectly, from rights of the debtor under the arrangement,

(d) for the recovery by the person responsible for the arrangement (whether by deduction from any amount which that person is ordered to pay or otherwise) of costs incurred by that person in complying in the debtor's case with any requirement under section 36C(1) or in giving effect to the order.

(2) In subsection (1), references to adjusting the liabilities of the arrangement in respect of a person include (in particular) reducing the amount of any benefit or future benefit to which that person is entitled under the arrangement.

(3) In subsection (1)(c), the reference to liabilities of the arrangement does not include liabilities in respect of a person which result from giving effect to an order or provision falling within section 28(1) of the Welfare Reform and Pensions Act 1999 (pension sharing orders and agreements).

(4) The maximum amount which the person responsible for an arrangement may be required to pay by an order under section 36A is the lesser of—

(a) the amount of the excessive contributions, and

(b) the value of the debtor's rights under the arrangement (if the arrangement is an approved pension arrangement) or of his excluded rights under the arrangement (if the arrangement is an unapproved pension arrangement).

(5) An order under section 36A which requires the person responsible for an arrangement to pay an amount ("the restoration amount") to the permanent trustee must provide for the liabilities of the arrangement to be correspondingly reduced.

(6) For the purposes of subsection (5), liabilities are correspondingly reduced if the difference between—

(a) the amount of the liabilities immediately before the reduction, and

(b) the amount of the liabilities immediately after the reduction,

is equal to the restoration amount.

(7) An order under section 36A in respect of an arrangement—

(a) shall be binding on the person responsible for the arrangement; and

(b) overrides provisions of the arrangement to the extent that they conflict with the provisions of the order.

Orders under section 36A: supplementary.

36C.—(1) The person responsible for—

(a) an approved pension arrangement under which a debtor has rights,

(b) an unapproved pension arrangement under which a debtor has excluded rights, or

(c) a pension arrangement under which a debtor has at any time had rights,

shall, on the permanent trustee making a written request, provide the permanent trustee with such information about the arrangement and rights as the permanent trustee may reasonably require for, or in connection with, the making of applications under section 36A.

(2) Nothing in—

1993 c. 48.
1995 c. 26.

(a) any provision of section 159 of the Pensions Schemes Act 1993 or section 91 of the Pensions Act 1995 (which prevent assignation and the making of orders that restrain a person from receiving anything which he is prevented from assigning),

(b) any provision of any enactment (whether passed or made before or after the passing of the Welfare Reform and Pensions Act 1999) corresponding to any of the provisions mentioned in paragraph (a), or

(c) any provision of the arrangement in question corresponding to any of those provisions,

applies to a court exercising its powers under section 36A.

(3) Where any sum is required by an order under section 36A to be paid to the permanent trustee, that sum shall be comprised in the debtor's estate.

(4) Regulations may, for the purposes of the recovery provisions, make provision about the calculation and verification of—

(a) any such value as is mentioned in section 36B(4)(b);

(b) any such amounts as are mentioned in section 36B(6)(a) and (b).

(5) The power conferred by subsection (4) includes power to provide for calculation or verification—

(a) in such manner as may, in the particular case, be approved by a prescribed person; or

(b) in accordance with guidance—

(i) from time to time prepared by a prescribed person, and

(ii) approved by the Secretary of State.

(6) References in the recovery provisions to the person responsible for a pension arrangement are to—

(a) the trustees, managers or provider of the arrangement, or

(b) the person having functions in relation to the arrangement corresponding to those of a trustee, manager or provider.

(7) In this section and sections 36A and 36B—

"the recovery provisions" means this section and sections 36A and 36B;

"regulations" means regulations made by the Secretary of State.

(8) Regulations under the recovery provisions may contain such incidental, supplemental and transitional provisions as appear to the Secretary of State necessary or expedient."

Miscellaneous

17.—(1) In subsection (1)(d) of section 81 of the Pensions Act 1995 (compensation not payable by the Pensions Compensation Board unless assets of salary-related trust scheme worth less than 90 per cent. of its liabilities), for "90 per cent. of the amount of the liabilities of the scheme" there shall be substituted "the protection level".

Compensating occupational pension schemes. 1995 c. 26.

(2) After subsection (2) of that section there shall be inserted—

"(2A) In subsection (1)(d) "the protection level" means the aggregate of—

(a) the amount of the liabilities of the scheme to, or in respect of, its pensioner members and such other of its members as fall within a prescribed class or description,

(b) 90 per cent. of the amount of the liabilities of the scheme to, or in respect of, any other members of the scheme, and

(c) the amount of the liabilities of the scheme which are not liabilities to, or in respect of, its members;

and references in this subsection to liabilities to, or in respect of, members of the scheme are references to liabilities in respect of pensions or other benefits."

(3) Section 83 of that Act (amount of compensation) shall be amended as follows.

(4) In subsection (3)(a) (compensation not to exceed 90 per cent. of shortfall), the words "90 per cent. of" shall be omitted.

(5) In subsection (3)(b) (compensation not to cause value of salary-related trust scheme's assets to exceed 90 per cent. of amount of its liabilities), for the words from "90 per cent." onwards there shall be substituted "the aggregate of the protected liabilities."

(6) After subsection (3) there shall be added—

"(4) In subsection (3) "the protected liabilities" means—

(a) the amount on the settlement date of the liabilities of the scheme to, or in respect of, its pensioner members and such other of its members as fall within a prescribed class or description,

(b) 90 per cent. of the amount on that date of the liabilities of the scheme to, or in respect of, any other members of the scheme, and

(c) the amount on that date of the liabilities of the scheme which are not liabilities to, or in respect of, its members;

and references in this subsection to liabilities to, or in respect of, members of the scheme are to liabilities in respect of pensions or other benefits."

Miscellaneous amendments.

18. Schedule 2 (which contains amendments of the law relating to pensions) shall have effect.

PART III

PENSIONS ON DIVORCE ETC.

Pension sharing orders

Orders in England and Wales.
1973 c. 18.

19. Schedule 3 (which amends the Matrimonial Causes Act 1973 for the purpose of enabling the court to make pension sharing orders in connection with proceedings in England and Wales for divorce or nullity of marriage, and for supplementary purposes) shall have effect.

Orders in Scotland.
1985 c. 37.

20.—(1) The Family Law (Scotland) Act 1985 shall be amended as follows.

(2) In section 8(1) (orders for financial provision), after paragraph (b) there shall be inserted—

"(baa) a pension sharing order."

(3) In section 27 (interpretation), in subsection (1), there shall be inserted at the appropriate place—

""pension sharing order" is an order which—

(a) provides that one party's—

(i) shareable rights under a specified pension arrangement, or

(ii) shareable state scheme rights,

be subject to pension sharing for the benefit of the other party, and

(b) specifies the percentage value, or the amount, to be transferred;".

(4) In that section, after subsection (1) there shall be inserted—

"(1A) In subsection (1), in the definition of "pension sharing order"—

(a) the reference to shareable rights under a pension arrangement is to rights in relation to which pension sharing is available under Chapter I of Part IV of the Welfare Reform and Pensions Act 1999, or under corresponding Northern Ireland legislation, and

(b) the reference to shareable state scheme rights is to rights in relation to which pension sharing is available under Chapter II of Part IV of the Welfare Reform and Pensions Act 1999, or under corresponding Northern Ireland legislation."

Sections 25B to 25D of the Matrimonial Causes Act 1973

21. Schedule 4 (which amends the sections about pensions inserted in the Matrimonial Causes Act 1973 by section 166 of the Pensions Act 1995) shall have effect.

Amendments.
1973 c. 18.
1995 c. 26.

22.—(1) Part III of the Matrimonial and Family Proceedings Act 1984 (financial relief in England and Wales after overseas divorce etc.) shall be amended as follows.

Extension to overseas divorces etc.
1984 c. 42.

(2) In section 18 (matters to which the court is to have regard in exercising its powers to make orders for financial relief), after subsection (3) there shall be inserted—

"(3A) The matters to which the court is to have regard under subsection (3) above—

(a) so far as relating to paragraph (a) of section 25(2) of the 1973 Act, include any benefits under a pension arrangement which a party to the marriage has or is likely to have (whether or not in the foreseeable future), and

(b) so far as relating to paragraph (h) of that provision, include any benefits under a pension arrangement which, by reason of the dissolution or annulment of the marriage, a party to the marriage will lose the chance of acquiring."

(3) In that section, at the end there shall be added—

"(7) In this section—

(a) "pension arrangement" has the meaning given by section 25D(3) of the 1973 Act, and

(b) references to benefits under a pension arrangement include any benefits by way of pension, whether under a pension arrangement or not."

(4) In section 21 (application of provisions of Part II of the Matrimonial Causes Act 1973), the existing provision shall become subsection (1) and, in that subsection, after paragraph (b) there shall be inserted—

"(bd) section 25B(3) to (7B) (power, by financial provision order, to attach payments under a pension arrangement, or to require the exercise of a right of commutation under such an arrangement);

(be) section 25C (extension of lump sum powers in relation to death benefits under a pension arrangement);".

(5) In that section, after subsection (1) there shall be inserted—

"(2) Subsection (1)(bd) and (be) above shall not apply where the court has jurisdiction to entertain an application for an order for financial relief by reason only of the situation in England or Wales of a dwelling-house which was a matrimonial home of the parties.

(3) Section 25D(1) of the 1973 Act (effect of transfers on orders relating to rights under a pension arrangement) shall apply in relation to an order made under section 17 above by virtue of subsection (1)(bd) or (be) above as it applies in relation to an order made under section 23 of that Act by virtue of section 25B or 25C of the 1973 Act.

(4) The Lord Chancellor may by regulations make for the purposes of this Part of this Act provision corresponding to any provision which may be made by him under subsections (2) to (2B) of section 25D of the 1973 Act.

(5) Power to make regulations under this section shall be exercisable by statutory instrument which shall be subject to annulment in pursuance of a resolution of either House of Parliament."

Miscellaneous

Supply of pension information in connection with divorce etc.

23.—(1) The Secretary of State may by regulations—

(a) make provision imposing on the person responsible for a pension arrangement, or on the Secretary of State, requirements with respect to the supply of information relevant to any power with respect to—

1973 c. 18
1984 c. 42.

(i) financial relief under Part II of the Matrimonial Causes Act 1973 or Part III of the Matrimonial and Family Proceedings Act 1984 (England and Wales powers in relation to domestic and overseas divorce etc.),

1985 c. 37.

(ii) financial provision under the Family Law (Scotland) Act 1985 or Part IV of the Matrimonial and Family Proceedings Act 1984 (corresponding Scottish powers), or

S.I. 1978/1045 (N.I. 15).
S.I. 1989/677 (N.I. 4).

(iii) financial relief under Part III of the Matrimonial Causes (Northern Ireland) Order 1978 or Part IV of the Matrimonial and Family Proceedings (Northern Ireland) Order 1989 (corresponding Northern Ireland powers);

(b) make provision about calculation and verification in relation to the valuation of—

(i) benefits under a pension arrangement, or

(ii) shareable state scheme rights,

for the purposes of regulations under paragraph (a)(i) or (iii);

(c) make provision about calculation and verification in relation to—

(i) the valuation of shareable rights under a pension arrangement or shareable state scheme rights for the purposes of regulations under paragraph (a)(ii), so far as relating to the making of orders for financial provision (within the meaning of the Family Law (Scotland) Act 1985), or

1985 c. 37.

(ii) the valuation of benefits under a pension arrangement for the purposes of such regulations, so far as relating to the making of orders under section 12A of that Act;

(d) make provision for the purpose of enabling the person responsible for a pension arrangement to recover prescribed charges in respect of providing information in accordance with regulations under paragraph (a).

(2) Regulations under subsection (1)(b) or (c) may include provision for calculation or verification in accordance with guidance from time to time prepared by a person prescribed by the regulations.

(3) Regulations under subsection (1)(d) may include provision for the application in prescribed circumstances, with or without modification, of any provision made by virtue of section 41(2).

(4) In subsection (1)—

(a) the reference in paragraph (c)(i) to shareable rights under a pension arrangement is to rights in relation to which pension sharing is available under Chapter I of Part IV, or under corresponding Northern Ireland legislation, and

(b) the references to shareable state scheme rights are to rights in relation to which pension sharing is available under Chapter II of Part IV, or under corresponding Northern Ireland legislation.

24. The Secretary of State may by regulations make provision for the purpose of enabling the person responsible for a pension arrangement to recover prescribed charges in respect of complying with—

Charges by pension arrangements in relation to earmarking orders.

1973 c. 18.

(a) an order under section 23 of the Matrimonial Causes Act 1973 (financial provision orders in connection with divorce etc.), so far as it includes provision made by virtue of section 25B or 25C of that Act (powers to include provision about pensions),

(b) an order under section 12A(2) or (3) of the Family Law (Scotland) Act 1985 (powers in relation to pensions lump sums when making a capital sum order), or

(c) an order under Article 25 of the Matrimonial Causes (Northern Ireland) Order 1978, so far as it includes provision made by virtue of Article 27B or 27C of that Order (Northern Ireland powers corresponding to those mentioned in paragraph (a)).

S.I. 1978/1045 (N.I. 15).

Supplementary

25.—(1) If any amendment by the Family Law Act 1996 of Part II or IV of the Matrimonial Causes Act 1973 comes into force before the day on which any provision of this Part comes into force, the Lord Chancellor may by order make such consequential amendment of that provision as he thinks fit.

Power to make consequential amendments of Part III.

1996 c. 27.

PART III

(2) No order under this section may be made unless a draft of the order has been laid before and approved by resolution of each House of Parliament.

Interpretation of Part III.

1993 c. 48.

26.—(1) In this Part—

"occupational pension scheme" has the same meaning as in the Pension Schemes Act 1993;

"pension arrangement" means

(a) an occupational pension scheme,

(b) a personal pension scheme,

(c) a retirement annuity contract,

(d) an annuity or insurance policy purchased, or transferred, for the purpose of giving effect to rights under an occupational pension scheme or a personal pension scheme, and

(e) an annuity purchased, or entered into, for the purpose of discharging liability in respect of a pension credit under section 29(1)(b) or under corresponding Northern Ireland legislation;

"personal pension scheme" has the same meaning as in the Pension Schemes Act 1993;

"prescribed" means prescribed by regulations made by the Secretary of State;

1988 c. 1.

"retirement annuity contract" means a contract or scheme approved under Chapter III of Part XIV of the Income and Corporation Taxes Act 1988;

"trustees or managers", in relation to an occupational pension scheme or a personal pension scheme, means—

(a) in the case of a scheme established under a trust, the trustees of the scheme, and

(b) in any other case, the managers of the scheme.

(2) References to the person responsible for a pension arrangement are—

(a) in the case of an occupational pension scheme or a personal pension scheme, to the trustees or managers of the scheme,

(b) in the case of a retirement annuity contract or an annuity falling within paragraph (d) or (e) of the definition of "pension arrangement" above, the provider of the annuity, and

(c) in the case of an insurance policy falling within paragraph (d) of the definition of that expression, the insurer.

Part IV

Pension sharing

Chapter I

Sharing of rights under pension arrangements

Pension sharing mechanism

27.—(1) Pension sharing is available under this Chapter in relation to a person's shareable rights under any pension arrangement other than an excepted public service pension scheme.

Scope of mechanism.

(2) For the purposes of this Chapter, a person's shareable rights under a pension arrangement are any rights of his under the arrangement, other than rights of a description specified by regulations made by the Secretary of State.

(3) For the purposes of subsection (1), a public service pension scheme is excepted if it is specified by order made by such Minister of the Crown or government department as may be designated by the Treasury as having responsibility for the scheme.

28.—(1) Section 29 applies on the taking effect of any of the following relating to a person's shareable rights under a pension arrangement—

Activation of pension sharing.

(a) a pension sharing order under the Matrimonial Causes Act 1973,

1973 c. 18.

(b) provision which corresponds to the provision which may be made by such an order and which—

(i) is contained in a qualifying agreement between the parties to a marriage, and

(ii) takes effect on the dissolution of the marriage under the Family Law Act 1996,

1996 c. 27.

(c) provision which corresponds to the provision which may be made by such an order and which—

(i) is contained in a qualifying agreement between the parties to a marriage or former marriage, and

(ii) takes effect after the dissolution of the marriage under the Family Law Act 1996,

(d) an order under Part III of the Matrimonial and Family Proceedings Act 1984 (financial relief in England and Wales in relation to overseas divorce etc.) corresponding to such an order as is mentioned in paragraph (a),

1984 c. 42.

(e) a pension sharing order under the Family Law (Scotland) Act 1985,

1985 c. 37.

(f) provision which corresponds to the provision which may be made by such an order and which—

(i) is contained in a qualifying agreement between the parties to a marriage,

(ii) is in such form as the Secretary of State may prescribe by regulations, and

(iii) takes effect on the grant, in relation to the marriage, of decree of divorce under the Divorce (Scotland) Act 1976 or of declarator of nullity,

1976 c. 39.

(g) an order under Part IV of the Matrimonial and Family Proceedings Act 1984 (financial relief in Scotland in relation to overseas divorce etc.) corresponding to such an order as is mentioned in paragraph (e),

(h) a pension sharing order under Northern Ireland legislation, and

(i) an order under Part IV of the Matrimonial and Family Proceedings (Northern Ireland) Order 1989 (financial relief in Northern Ireland in relation to overseas divorce etc.) corresponding to such an order as is mentioned in paragraph (h).

(2) For the purposes of subsection (1)(b) and (c), a qualifying agreement is one which—

(a) has been entered into in such circumstances as the Lord Chancellor may prescribe by regulations, and

(b) satisfies such requirements as the Lord Chancellor may so prescribe.

(3) For the purposes of subsection (1)(f), a qualifying agreement is one which—

(a) has been entered into in such circumstances as the Secretary of State may prescribe by regulations, and

(b) is registered in the Books of Council and Session.

(4) Subsection (1)(b) does not apply if—

(a) the pension arrangement to which the provision relates is the subject of a pension sharing order under the Matrimonial Causes Act 1973 in relation to the marriage, or

(b) there is in force a requirement imposed by virtue of section 25B or 25C of that Act (powers to include in financial provision orders requirements relating to benefits under pension arrangements) which relates to benefits or future benefits to which the party who is the transferor is entitled under the pension arrangement to which the provision relates.

(5) Subsection (1)(c) does not apply if—

(a) the marriage was dissolved by an order under section 3 of the Family Law Act 1996 (divorce not preceded by separation) and the satisfaction of the requirements of section 9(2) of that Act (settlement of future financial arrangements) was a precondition to the making of the order,

(b) the pension arrangement to which the provision relates—

(i) is the subject of a pension sharing order under the Matrimonial Causes Act 1973 in relation to the marriage, or

(ii) has already been the subject of pension sharing between the parties, or

(c) there is in force a requirement imposed by virtue of section 25B or 25C of that Act which relates to benefits or future benefits to which the party who is the transferor is entitled under the pension arrangement to which the provision relates.

(6) Subsection (1)(f) does not apply if there is in force an order under section 12A(2) or (3) of the Family Law (Scotland) Act 1985 which relates to benefits or future benefits to which the party who is the transferor is entitled under the pension arrangement to which the provision relates.

1985 c. 37.

(7) For the purposes of this section, an order or provision falling within subsection (1)(e), (f) or (g) shall be deemed never to have taken effect if the person responsible for the arrangement to which the order or provision relates does not receive before the end of the period of 2 months beginning with the relevant date—

    (a) copies of the relevant matrimonial documents, and

    (b) such information relating to the transferor and transferee as the Secretary of State may prescribe by regulations under section 34(1)(b)(ii).

(8) The relevant date for the purposes of subsection (7) is—

    (a) in the case of an order or provision falling within subsection (1)(e) or (f), the date of the extract of the decree or declarator responsible for the divorce or annulment to which the order or provision relates, and

    (b) in the case of an order falling within subsection (1)(g), the date of disposal of the application under section 28 of the Matrimonial and Family Proceedings Act 1984.

1984 c. 42.

(9) The reference in subsection (7)(a) to the relevant matrimonial documents is—

    (a) in the case of an order falling within subsection (1)(e) or (g), to copies of the order and the order, decree or declarator responsible for the divorce or annulment to which it relates, and

    (b) in the case of provision falling within subsection (1)(f), to—

        (i) copies of the provision and the order, decree or declarator responsible for the divorce or annulment to which it relates, and

        (ii) documentary evidence that the agreement containing the provision is one to which subsection (3)(a) applies.

(10) The sheriff may, on the application of any person having an interest, make an order—

    (a) extending the period of 2 months referred to in subsection (7), and

    (b) if that period has already expired, providing that, if the person responsible for the arrangement receives the documents and information concerned before the end of the period specified in the order, subsection (7) is to be treated as never having applied.

(11) In subsections (4)(b), (5)(c) and (6), the reference to the party who is the transferor is to the party to whose rights the provision relates.

29.—(1) On the application of this section—

    (a) the transferor's shareable rights under the relevant arrangement become subject to a debit of the appropriate amount, and

    (b) the transferee becomes entitled to a credit of that amount as against the person responsible for that arrangement.

Creation of pension debits and credits.

(2) Where the relevant order or provision specifies a percentage value to be transferred, the appropriate amount for the purposes of subsection (1) is the specified percentage of the cash equivalent of the relevant benefits on the valuation day.

(3) Where the relevant order or provision specifies an amount to be transferred, the appropriate amount for the purposes of subsection (1) is the lesser of—

(a) the specified amount, and

(b) the cash equivalent of the relevant benefits on the valuation day.

(4) Where the relevant arrangement is an occupational pension scheme and the transferor is in pensionable service under the scheme on the transfer day, the relevant benefits for the purposes of subsections (2) and (3) are the benefits or future benefits to which he would be entitled under the scheme by virtue of his shareable rights under it had his pensionable service terminated immediately before that day.

(5) Otherwise, the relevant benefits for the purposes of subsections (2) and (3) are the benefits or future benefits to which, immediately before the transfer day, the transferor is entitled under the terms of the relevant arrangement by virtue of his shareable rights under it.

(6) The Secretary of State may by regulations provide for any description of benefit to be disregarded for the purposes of subsection (4) or (5).

(7) For the purposes of this section, the valuation day is such day within the implementation period for the credit under subsection (1)(b) as the person responsible for the relevant arrangement may specify by notice in writing to the transferor and transferee.

(8) In this section—

"relevant arrangement" means the arrangement to which the relevant order or provision relates;

"relevant order or provision" means the order or provision by virtue of which this section applies;

"transfer day" means the day on which the relevant order or provision takes effect;

"transferor" means the person to whose rights the relevant order or provision relates;

"transferee" means the person for whose benefit the relevant order or provision is made.

Cash equivalents.   **30.**—(1) The Secretary of State may by regulations make provision about the calculation and verification of cash equivalents for the purposes of section 29.

(2) The power conferred by subsection (1) includes power to provide for calculation or verification—

(a) in such manner as may, in the particular case, be approved by a person prescribed by the regulations, or

(b) in accordance with guidance from time to time prepared by a person so prescribed.

Pension debits

31.—(1) Subject to subsection (2), where a person's shareable rights under a pension arrangement are subject to a pension debit, each benefit or future benefit—

Reduction of benefit.

    (a) to which he is entitled under the arrangement by virtue of those rights, and

    (b) which is a qualifying benefit,

is reduced by the appropriate percentage.

(2) Where a pension debit relates to the shareable rights under an occupational pension scheme of a person who is in pensionable service under the scheme on the transfer day, each benefit or future benefit—

    (a) to which the person is entitled under the scheme by virtue of those rights, and

    (b) which corresponds to a qualifying benefit,

is reduced by an amount equal to the appropriate percentage of the corresponding qualifying benefit.

(3) A benefit is a qualifying benefit for the purposes of subsections (1) and (2) if the cash equivalent by reference to which the amount of the pension debit is determined includes an amount in respect of it.

(4) The provisions of this section override any provision of a pension arrangement to which they apply to the extent that the provision conflicts with them.

(5) In this section—

"appropriate percentage", in relation to a pension debit, means—

        (a) if the relevant order or provision specifies the percentage value to be transferred, that percentage;

        (b) if the relevant order or provision specifies an amount to be transferred, the percentage which the appropriate amount for the purposes of subsection (1) of section 29 represents of the amount mentioned in subsection (3)(b) of that section;

"relevant order or provision", in relation to a pension debit, means the pension sharing order or provision on which the debit depends;

"transfer day", in relation to a pension debit, means the day on which the relevant order or provision takes effect.

32.—(1) The Pension Schemes Act 1993 shall be amended as follows.

Effect on contracted-out rights.
1993 c. 48.

(2) In section 10 (protected rights), in subsection (1), for "subsections (2) and (3)" there shall be substituted "the following provisions of this section", and at the end there shall be added—

"(4) Where, in the case of a scheme which makes such provision as is mentioned in subsection (2) or (3), a member's rights under the scheme become subject to a pension debit, his protected rights shall exclude the appropriate percentage of the rights which were his protected rights immediately before the day on which the pension debit arose.

(5) For the purposes of subsection (4), the appropriate percentage is—

(a) if the order or provision on which the pension debit depends specifies the percentage value to be transferred, that percentage;

(b) if the order or provision on which the pension debit depends specifies an amount to be transferred, the percentage which the appropriate amount for the purposes of subsection (1) of section 29 of the Welfare Reform and Pensions Act 1999 (lesser of specified amount and cash equivalent of transferor's benefits) represents of the amount mentioned in subsection (3)(b) of that section (cash equivalent of transferor's benefits)."

(3) After section 15 there shall be inserted—

"Reduction of guaranteed minimum in consequence of pension debit.

15A.—(1) Where—

(a) an earner has a guaranteed minimum in relation to the pension provided by a scheme, and

(b) his right to the pension becomes subject to a pension debit,

his guaranteed minimum in relation to the scheme is, subject to subsection (2), reduced by the appropriate percentage.

(2) Where the earner is in pensionable service under the scheme on the day on which the order or provision on which the pension debit depends takes effect, his guaranteed minimum in relation to the scheme is reduced by an amount equal to the appropriate percentage of the corresponding qualifying benefit.

(3) For the purposes of subsection (2), the corresponding qualifying benefit is the guaranteed minimum taken for the purpose of calculating the cash equivalent by reference to which the amount of the pension debit is determined.

(4) For the purposes of this section the appropriate percentage is—

(a) if the order or provision on which the pension debit depends specifies the percentage value to be transferred, that percentage;

(b) if the order or provision on which the pension debit depends specifies an amount to be transferred, the percentage which the appropriate amount for the purposes of subsection (1) of section 29 of the Welfare Reform and Pensions Act 1999 (lesser of specified amount and cash equivalent of transferor's benefits) represents of the amount mentioned in subsection (3)(b) of that section (cash equivalent of transferor's benefits)."

(4) In section 47 (entitlement to guaranteed minimum pensions for the purposes of the relationship with social security benefits), at the end there shall be added—

"(6) For the purposes of section 46, a person shall be treated as entitled to any guaranteed minimum pension to which he would have been entitled but for any reduction under section 15A."

(5) In section 181(1), there shall be inserted at the appropriate place—

""pension debit" means a debit under section 29(1)(a) of the Welfare Reform and Pensions Act 1999;".

Pension credits

33.—(1) A person subject to liability in respect of a pension credit shall discharge his liability before the end of the implementation period for the credit.

Time for discharge of liability.

(2) Where the trustees or managers of an occupational pension scheme have not done what is required to discharge their liability in respect of a pension credit before the end of the implementation period for the credit—

    (a) they shall, except in such cases as the Secretary of State may prescribe by regulations, notify the Regulatory Authority of that fact within such period as the Secretary of State may so prescribe, and

    (b) section 10 of the Pensions Act 1995 (power of the Regulatory Authority to impose civil penalties) shall apply to any trustee or manager who has failed to take all such steps as are reasonable to ensure that liability in respect of the credit was discharged before the end of the implementation period for it.

1995 c. 26.

(3) If trustees or managers to whom subsection (2)(a) applies fail to perform the obligation imposed by that provision, section 10 of the Pensions Act 1995 shall apply to any trustee or manager who has failed to take all reasonable steps to ensure that the obligation was performed.

(4) On the application of the trustees or managers of an occupational pension scheme who are subject to liability in respect of a pension credit, the Regulatory Authority may extend the implementation period for the credit for the purposes of this section if it is satisfied that the application is made in such circumstances as the Secretary of State may prescribe by regulations.

(5) In this section "the Regulatory Authority" means the Occupational Pensions Regulatory Authority.

34.—(1) For the purposes of this Chapter, the implementation period for a pension credit is the period of 4 months beginning with the later of—

"Implementation period".

    (a) the day on which the relevant order or provision takes effect, and

    (b) the first day on which the person responsible for the pension arrangement to which the relevant order or provision relates is in receipt of—

        (i) the relevant matrimonial documents, and

        (ii) such information relating to the transferor and transferee as the Secretary of State may prescribe by regulations.

(2) The reference in subsection (1)(b)(i) to the relevant matrimonial documents is to copies of—

    (a) the relevant order or provision, and

(b) the order, decree or declarator responsible for the divorce or annulment to which it relates,

and, if the pension credit depends on provision falling within subsection (1)(f) of section 28, to documentary evidence that the agreement containing the provision is one to which subsection (3)(a) of that section applies.

(3) Subsection (1) is subject to any provision made by regulations under section 41(2)(a).

(4) The Secretary of State may by regulations—

(a) make provision requiring a person subject to liability in respect of a pension credit to notify the transferor and transferee of the day on which the implementation period for the credit begins;

(b) provide for this section to have effect with modifications where the pension arrangement to which the relevant order or provision relates is being wound up;

(c) provide for this section to have effect with modifications where the pension credit depends on a pension sharing order and the order is the subject of an application for leave to appeal out of time.

(5) In this section—

"relevant order or provision", in relation to a pension credit, means the pension sharing order or provision on which the pension credit depends;

"transferor" means the person to whose rights the relevant order or provision relates;

"transferee" means the person for whose benefit the relevant order or provision is made.

Mode of discharge of liability.

35.—(1) Schedule 5 (which makes provision about how liability in respect of a pension credit may be discharged) shall have effect.

(2) Where the person entitled to a pension credit dies before liability in respect of the credit has been discharged—

(a) Schedule 5 shall cease to have effect in relation to the discharge of liability in respect of the credit, and

(b) liability in respect of the credit shall be discharged in accordance with regulations made by the Secretary of State.

Treatment of pension credit rights under schemes

Safeguarded rights.
1993 c. 48.

36. After section 68 of the Pension Schemes Act 1993 there shall be inserted—

"PART IIIA

SAFEGUARDED RIGHTS

Safeguarded rights.

68A.—(1) Subject to subsection (2), the safeguarded rights of a member of an occupational pension scheme or a personal pension scheme are such of his rights to future benefits under the scheme as are attributable (directly or indirectly) to a pension credit in respect of which the reference rights are, or include, contracted-out rights or safeguarded rights.

(2) If the rules of an occupational pension scheme or a personal pension scheme so provide, a member's safeguarded rights are such of his rights falling within subsection (1) as—

    (a) in the case of rights directly attributable to a pension credit, represent the safeguarded percentage of the rights acquired by virtue of the credit, and

    (b) in the case of rights directly attributable to a transfer payment, represent the safeguarded percentage of the rights acquired by virtue of the payment.

(3) For the purposes of subsection (2)(a), the safeguarded percentage is the percentage of the rights by reference to which the amount of the credit is determined which are contracted-out rights or safeguarded rights.

(4) For the purposes of subsection (2)(b), the safeguarded percentage is the percentage of the rights in respect of which the transfer payment is made which are contracted-out rights or safeguarded rights.

(5) In this section—

    "contracted-out rights" means such rights under, or derived from—

        (a) an occupational pension scheme contracted-out by virtue of section 9(2) or (3), or

        (b) an appropriate personal pension scheme,

    as may be prescribed;

    "reference rights", in relation to a pension credit, means the rights by reference to which the amount of the credit is determined.

Requirements relating to safeguarded rights.

68B. Regulations may prescribe requirements to be met in relation to safeguarded rights by an occupational pension scheme or a personal pension scheme.

Reserve powers in relation to non-complying schemes.

68C.—(1) This section applies to—

    (a) any occupational pension scheme, other than a public service pension scheme, and

    (b) any personal pension scheme.

(2) If any scheme to which this section applies does not comply with a requirement prescribed under section 68B and there are any persons who—

    (a) have safeguarded rights under the scheme, or

(b) are entitled to any benefit giving effect to such rights under the scheme,

the Inland Revenue may direct the trustees or managers of the scheme to take or refrain from taking such steps as they may specify in writing for the purpose of safeguarding the rights of persons falling within paragraph (a) or (b).

(3) A direction under subsection (2) shall be final and binding on the trustees or managers to whom the direction is given and any person claiming under them.

(4) An appeal on a point of law shall lie to the High Court or, in Scotland, the Court of Session from a direction under subsection (2) at the instance of the trustees or managers, or any person claiming under them.

(5) A direction under subsection (2) shall be enforceable—

(a) in England and Wales, in a county court, as if it were an order of that court, and

(b) in Scotland, by the sheriff, as if it were an order of the sheriff and whether or not the sheriff could himself have given such an order.

Power to control transfer or discharge of liability.

68D. Regulations may prohibit or restrict the transfer or discharge of any liability under an occupational pension scheme or a personal pension scheme in respect of safeguarded rights except in prescribed circumstances or on prescribed conditions."

Requirements relating to pension credit benefit.
1993 c. 48.

37. After section 101 of the Pension Schemes Act 1993 there shall be inserted—

"PART IVA

REQUIREMENTS RELATING TO PENSION CREDIT BENEFIT

CHAPTER I

PENSION CREDIT BENEFIT UNDER OCCUPATIONAL SCHEMES

Scope of Chapter I.

101A.—(1) This Chapter applies to any occupational pension scheme whose resources are derived in whole or part from—

(a) payments to which subsection (2) applies made or to be made by one or more employers of earners to whom the scheme applies, or

(b) such other payments by the earner or his employer, or both, as may be prescribed for different categories of scheme.

(2) This subsection applies to payments—

(a) under an actual or contingent legal obligation, or

(b) in the exercise of a power conferred, or the discharge of a duty imposed, on a Minister of the Crown, government department or any other person, being a power or duty which extends to the disbursement or allocation of public money.

Interpretation.

101B. In this Chapter—

"scheme" means an occupational pension scheme to which this Chapter applies;

"pension credit rights" means rights to future benefits under a scheme which are attributable (directly or indirectly) to a pension credit;

"pension credit benefit", in relation to a scheme, means the benefits payable under the scheme to or in respect of a person by virtue of rights under the scheme attributable (directly or indirectly) to a pension credit;

"normal benefit age", in relation to a scheme, means the earliest age at which a person who has pension credit rights under the scheme is entitled to receive a pension by virtue of those rights (disregarding any scheme rule making special provision as to early payment of pension on grounds of ill-health or otherwise).

Basic principle as to pension credit benefit.

101C.—(1) Normal benefit age under a scheme must be between 60 and 65.

(2) A scheme must not provide for payment of pension credit benefit in the form of a lump sum at any time before normal benefit age, except in such circumstances as may be prescribed.

Form of pension credit benefit and its alternatives.

101D.—(1) Subject to subsection (2) and section 101E, a person's pension credit benefit under a scheme must be—

(a) payable directly out of the resources of the scheme, or

(b) assured to him by such means as may be prescribed.

(2) Subject to subsections (3) and (4), a scheme may, instead of providing a person's pension credit benefit, provide—

(a) for his pension credit rights under the scheme to be transferred to another occupational pension scheme or a personal pension scheme with a view to acquiring rights for him under the rules of the scheme, or

(b) for such alternatives to pension credit benefit as may be prescribed.

(3) The option conferred by subsection (2)(a) is additional to any obligation imposed by Chapter II of this Part.

(4) The alternatives specified in subsection (2)(a) and (b) may only be by way of complete or partial substitute for pension credit benefit—

(a) if the person entitled to the benefit consents, or

(b) in such other cases as may be prescribed.

Discharge of liability where pension credit or alternative benefits secured by insurance policies or annuity contracts.

101E.—(1) A transaction to which section 19 applies discharges the trustees or managers of a scheme from their liability to provide pension credit benefit or any alternative to pension credit benefit for or in respect of a member of the scheme if and to the extent that—

(a) it results in pension credit benefit, or any alternative to pension credit benefit, for or in respect of the member being appropriately secured (within the meaning of that section),

(b) the transaction is entered into with the consent of the member or, if the member has died, of the member's widow or widower, and

(c) such requirements as may be prescribed are met.

(2) Regulations may provide that subsection (1)(b) shall not apply in prescribed circumstances.

CHAPTER II

TRANSFER VALUES

Power to give transfer notice.

101F.—(1) An eligible member of a qualifying scheme may by notice in writing require the trustees or managers of the scheme to use an amount equal to the cash equivalent of his pension credit benefit for such one or more of the authorised purposes as he may specify in the notice.

(2) In the case of a member of an occupational pension scheme, the authorised purposes are—

(a) to acquire rights allowed under the rules of an occupational pension scheme, or personal pension scheme, which is an eligible scheme,

(b) to purchase from one or more insurance companies such as are mentioned in section 19(4)(a), chosen by the member and willing to accept payment on account of the member from the trustees or managers, one or more annuities which satisfy the prescribed requirements, and

(c) in such circumstances as may be prescribed, to subscribe to other pension arrangements which satisfy prescribed requirements.

(3) In the case of a member of a personal pension scheme, the authorised purposes are—

(a) to acquire rights allowed under the rules of an occupational pension scheme, or personal pension scheme, which is an eligible scheme, and

(b) in such circumstances as may be prescribed, to subscribe to other pension arrangements which satisfy prescribed requirements.

(4) The cash equivalent for the purposes of subsection (1) shall—

    (a) in the case of a salary related occupational pension scheme, be taken to be the amount shown in the relevant statement under section 101H, and

    (b) in any other case, be determined by reference to the date the notice under that subsection is given.

(5) The requirements which may be prescribed under subsection (2) or (3) include, in particular, requirements of the Inland Revenue.

(6) In subsections (2) and (3), references to an eligible scheme are to a scheme—

    (a) the trustees or managers of which are able and willing to accept payment in respect of the member's pension credit rights, and

    (b) which satisfies the prescribed requirements.

(7) In this Chapter, "transfer notice" means a notice under subsection (1).

Restrictions on power to give transfer notice.

101G.—(1) In the case of a salary related occupational pension scheme, the power to give a transfer notice may only be exercised if—

    (a) the member has been provided with a statement under section 101H, and

    (b) not more than 3 months have passed since the date by reference to which the amount shown in the statement is determined.

(2) The power to give a transfer notice may not be exercised in the case of an occupational pension scheme if—

    (a) there is less than a year to go until the member reaches normal benefit age, or

    (b) the pension to which the member is entitled by virtue of his pension credit rights, or benefit in lieu of that pension, or any part of it has become payable.

(3) Where an eligible member of a qualifying scheme—

    (a) is entitled to make an application under section 95 to the trustees or managers of the scheme, or

    (b) would be entitled to do so, but for the fact that he has not received a statement under section 93A in respect of which the guarantee date is sufficiently recent,

he may not, if the scheme so provides, exercise the power to give them a transfer notice unless he also makes an application to them under section 95.

(4) The power to give a transfer notice may not be exercised if a previous transfer notice given by the member to the trustees or managers of the scheme is outstanding.

Salary related schemes: statements of entitlement.

101H.—(1) The trustees or managers of a qualifying scheme which is a salary related occupational pension scheme shall, on the application of an eligible member, provide him with a written statement of the amount of the cash equivalent of his pension credit benefit under the scheme.

(2) For the purposes of subsection (1), the amount of the cash equivalent shall be determined by reference to a date falling within—

> (a) the prescribed period beginning with the date of the application, and

> (b) the prescribed period ending with the date on which the statement under that subsection is provided to the applicant.

(3) Regulations may make provision in relation to applications under subsection (1) and may, in particular, restrict the making of successive applications.

1995 c. 26.

(4) If trustees or managers to whom subsection (1) applies fail to perform an obligation under that subsection, section 10 of the Pensions Act 1995 (power of the Regulatory Authority to impose civil penalties) shall apply to any trustee or manager who has failed to take all such steps as are reasonable to secure that the obligation was performed.

Calculation of cash equivalents.

101I. Cash equivalents for the purposes of this Chapter shall be calculated and verified in the prescribed manner.

Time for compliance with transfer notice.

101J.—(1) Trustees or managers of a qualifying scheme who receive a transfer notice shall comply with the notice—

> (a) in the case of an occupational pension scheme, within 6 months of the valuation date or, if earlier, by the date on which the member to whom the notice relates reaches normal benefit age, and

> (b) in the case of a personal pension scheme, within 6 months of the date on which they receive the notice.

(2) The Regulatory Authority may, in prescribed circumstances, extend the period for complying with the notice.

(3) If the Regulatory Authority are satisfied—

> (a) that there has been a relevant change of circumstances since they granted an extension under subsection (2), or

(b) that they granted an extension under that subsection in ignorance of a material fact or on the basis of a mistake as to a material fact,

they may revoke or reduce the extension.

(4) Where the trustees or managers of an occupational pension scheme have failed to comply with a transfer notice before the end of the period for compliance—

(a) they shall, except in prescribed cases, notify the Regulatory Authority of that fact within the prescribed period, and

(b) section 10 of the Pensions Act 1995 (power of the Regulatory Authority to impose civil penalties) shall apply to any trustee or manager who has failed to take all such steps as are reasonable to ensure that the notice was complied with before the end of the period for compliance.

1995 c. 26.

(5) If trustees or managers to whom subsection (4)(a) applies fail to perform the obligation imposed by that provision, section 10 of the Pensions Act 1995 shall apply to any trustee or manager who has failed to take all such steps as are reasonable to ensure that the obligation was performed.

(6) Regulations may—

(a) make provision in relation to applications under subsection (2), and

(b) provide that subsection (4) shall not apply in prescribed circumstances.

(7) In this section, "valuation date", in relation to a transfer notice given to the trustees or managers of an occupational pension scheme, means—

(a) in the case of a salary related scheme, the date by reference to which the amount shown in the relevant statement under section 101H is determined, and

(b) in the case of any other scheme, the date the notice is given.

Withdrawal of transfer notice.

101K.—(1) Subject to subsections (2) and (3), a person who has given a transfer notice may withdraw it by giving the trustees or managers to whom it was given notice in writing that he no longer requires them to comply with it.

(2) A transfer notice may not be withdrawn if the trustees or managers have already entered into an agreement with a third party to use the whole or part of the amount they are required to use in accordance with the notice.

(3) If the giving of a transfer notice depended on the making of an application under section 95, the notice may only be withdrawn if the application is also withdrawn.

Variation of the amount required to be used.

101L.—(1) Regulations may make provision for the amount required to be used under section 101F(1) to be increased or reduced in prescribed circumstances.

(2) Without prejudice to the generality of subsection (1), the circumstances which may be prescribed include—

(a) failure by the trustees or managers of a qualifying scheme to comply with a notice under section 101F(1) within 6 months of the date by reference to which the amount of the cash equivalent falls to be determined, and

(b) the state of funding of a qualifying scheme.

(3) Regulations under subsection (1) may have the effect of extinguishing an obligation under section 101F(1).

Effect of transfer on trustees' duties.

101M. Compliance with a transfer notice shall have effect to discharge the trustees or managers of a qualifying scheme from any obligation to provide the pension credit benefit of the eligible member who gave the notice.

Matters to be disregarded in calculations.

101N. In making any calculation for the purposes of this Chapter—

(a) any charge or lien on, and

(b) any set-off against,

the whole or part of a pension shall be disregarded.

Service of notices.

101O. A notice under section 101F(1) or 101K(1) shall be taken to have been given if it is delivered to the trustees or managers personally or sent by post in a registered letter or by recorded delivery service.

Interpretation of Chapter II.

101P.—(1) In this Chapter—

"eligible member", in relation to a qualifying scheme, means a member who has pension credit rights under the scheme;

"normal benefit age", in relation to an eligible member of a qualifying scheme, means the earliest age at which the member is entitled to receive a pension by virtue of his pension credit rights under the scheme (disregarding any scheme rule making special provision as to early payment of pension on grounds of ill-health or otherwise);

"pension credit benefit", in relation to an eligible member of a qualifying scheme, means the benefits payable under the scheme to or in respect of the member by virtue of rights under the scheme attributable (directly or indirectly) to a pension credit;

"pension credit rights", in relation to a qualifying scheme, means rights to future benefits under the scheme which are attributable (directly or indirectly) to a pension credit;

"qualifying scheme" means a funded occupational pension scheme and a personal pension scheme;

"transfer notice" has the meaning given by section 101F(7).

(2) For the purposes of this Chapter, an occupational pension scheme is salary related if—

(a) it is not a money purchase scheme, and

(b) it does not fall within a prescribed class.

(3) In this Chapter, references to the relevant statement under section 101H, in relation to a transfer notice given to the trustees or managers of a salary related occupational pension scheme, are to the statement under that section on which the giving of the notice depended.

(4) For the purposes of this section, an occupational pension scheme is funded if it meets its liabilities out of a fund accumulated for the purpose during the life of the scheme.

Power to modify Chapter II in relation to hybrid schemes.

101Q. Regulations may apply this Chapter with prescribed modifications to occupational pension schemes—

(a) which are not money purchase schemes, but

(b) where some of the benefits that may be provided are money purchase benefits."

38.—(1) In section 73 of the Pensions Act 1995 (treatment of rights on winding up of an occupational pension scheme to which section 56 of that Act (minimum funding requirement) applies), in subsection (3) (classification of liabilities), in paragraph (c) (accrued rights), at the end of sub-paragraph (i) there shall be inserted—

Treatment in winding up.
1995 c. 26.

"(ia) future pensions, or other future benefits, attributable (directly or indirectly) to pension credits (but excluding increases to pensions),".

(2) In the case of an occupational pension scheme which is not a scheme to which section 56 of the Pensions Act 1995 applies, rights attributable (directly or indirectly) to a pension credit are to be accorded in a winding up the same treatment—

(a) if they have come into payment, as the rights of a pensioner member, and

(b) if they have not come into payment, as the rights of a deferred member.

(3) Subsection (2) overrides the provisions of a scheme to the extent that it conflicts with them, and the scheme has effect with such modifications as may be required in consequence.

(4) In subsection (2)—

(a) "deferred member" and "pensioner member" have the same meanings as in Part I of the Pensions Act 1995,

(b) "pension credit" includes a credit under Northern Ireland legislation corresponding to section 29(1)(b), and

(c) references to rights attributable to a pension credit having come into payment are to the person to whom the rights belong having become entitled by virtue of the rights to the present payment of pension or other benefits.

Indexation

Public service
pension schemes.
1971 c. 56.

39.—(1) The Pensions (Increase) Act 1971 shall be amended as follows.

(2) In section 3 (qualifying conditions), after subsection (2) there shall be inserted—

"(2A) A pension attributable to the pensioner having become entitled to a pension credit shall not be increased unless the pensioner has attained the age of fifty-five years."

(3) In section 8, in subsection (1) (definition of "pension"), in paragraph (a), the words from "(either" to "person)" shall be omitted.

(4) In that section, in subsection (2) (when pension deemed for purposes of the Act to begin), after "pension", in the first place, there shall be inserted "which is not attributable to a pension credit", and after that subsection there shall be inserted—

"(2A) A pension which is attributable to a pension credit shall be deemed for purposes of this Act to begin on the day on which the order or provision on which the credit depends takes effect."

(5) In section 17(1) (interpretation)—

(a) for the definitions of "derivative pension" and "principal pension" there shall be substituted—

""derivative pension" means a pension which—

(a) is not payable in respect of the pensioner's own services, and

(b) is not attributable to the pensioner having become entitled to a pension credit;",

(b) after the definition of "pension" there shall be inserted—

""pension credit" means a credit under section 29(1)(b) of the Welfare Reform and Pensions Act 1999 or under corresponding Northern Ireland legislation;

"principal pension" means a pension which—

(a) is payable in respect of the pensioner's own services, or

(b) is attributable to the pensioner having become entitled to a pension credit;", and

(c) for the definition of "widow's pension" there shall be substituted—

""widow's pension" means a pension payable—

(a) in respect of the services of the pensioner's deceased husband, or

(b) by virtue of the pensioner's deceased husband having become entitled to a pension credit."

40.—(1) The Secretary of State may by regulations make provision for a pension to which subsection (2) applies to be increased, as a minimum, by reference to increases in the retail prices index, so far as not exceeding 5% per annum.

(2) This subsection applies to—

    (a) a pension provided to give effect to eligible pension credit rights of a member under a qualifying occupational pension scheme, and

    (b) a pension provided to give effect to safeguarded rights of a member under a personal pension scheme.

(3) In this section—

    "eligible", in relation to pension credit rights, means of a description prescribed by regulations made by the Secretary of State;

    "pension credit rights", in relation to an occupational pension scheme, means rights to future benefits under the scheme which are attributable (directly or indirectly) to a credit under section 29(1)(b) or under corresponding Northern Ireland legislation;

    "qualifying occupational pension scheme" means an occupational pension scheme which is not a public service pension scheme;

    "safeguarded rights" has the meaning given in section 68A of the Pension Schemes Act 1993.

Other pension schemes.

1993 c. 48.

Charges by pension arrangements

41.—(1) The Secretary of State may by regulations make provision for the purpose of enabling the person responsible for a pension arrangement involved in pension sharing to recover from the parties to pension sharing prescribed charges in respect of prescribed descriptions of pension sharing activity.

Charges in respect of pension sharing costs.

(2) Regulations under subsection (1) may include—

    (a) provision for the start of the implementation period for a pension credit to be postponed in prescribed circumstances;

    (b) provision, in relation to payments in respect of charges recoverable under the regulations, for reimbursement as between the parties to pension sharing;

    (c) provision, in relation to the recovery of charges by deduction from a pension credit, for the modification of Schedule 5;

    (d) provision for the recovery in prescribed circumstances of such additional amounts as may be determined in accordance with the regulations.

(3) For the purposes of regulations under subsection (1), the question of how much of a charge recoverable under the regulations is attributable to a party to pension sharing is to be determined as follows—

    (a) where the relevant order or provision includes provision about the apportionment of charges under this section, there is attributable to the party so much of the charge as is apportioned to him by that provision;

    (b) where the relevant order or provision does not include such provision, the charge is attributable to the transferor.

(4) For the purposes of subsection (1), a pension arrangement is involved in pension sharing if section 29 applies by virtue of an order or provision which relates to the arrangement.

(5) In that subsection, the reference to pension sharing activity is to activity attributable (directly or indirectly) to the involvement in pension sharing.

(6) In subsection (3)—

    (a) the reference to the relevant order or provision is to the order or provision which gives rise to the pension sharing, and

    (b) the reference to the transferor is to the person to whose rights that order or provision relates.

(7) In this section "prescribed" means prescribed in regulations under subsection (1).

Adaptation of statutory schemes

Extension of scheme-making powers.

42.—(1) Power under an Act to establish a pension scheme shall include power to make provision for the provision, by reference to pension credits which derive from rights under—

    (a) the scheme, or

    (b) a scheme in relation to which the scheme is specified as an alternative for the purposes of paragraph 2 of Schedule 5,

of benefits to or in respect of those entitled to the credits.

(2) Subsection (1) is without prejudice to any other power.

(3) Subsection (1) shall apply in relation to Acts whenever passed.

(4) No obligation to consult shall apply in relation to the making, in exercise of a power under an Act to establish a pension scheme, of provision of a kind authorised by subsection (1).

(5) Any provision of, or under, an Act which makes benefits under a pension scheme established under an Act a charge on, or payable out of—

    (a) the Consolidated Fund,

    (b) the Scottish Consolidated Fund, or

    (c) the Consolidated Fund of Northern Ireland,

shall be treated as including any benefits under the scheme which are attributable (directly or indirectly) to a pension credit which derives from rights to benefits charged on, or payable out of, that fund.

(6) In this section—

    "pension credit" includes a credit under Northern Ireland legislation corresponding to section 29(1)(b);

    "pension scheme" means a scheme or arrangement providing benefits, in the form of pensions or otherwise, payable on termination of service, or on death or retirement, to or in respect of persons to whom the scheme or arrangement applies.

43.—(1) The appropriate minister may by regulations amend the Sheriffs' Pensions (Scotland) Act 1961, the Judicial Pensions Act 1981 or the Judicial Pensions and Retirement Act 1993 for the purpose of—

(a) extending a pension scheme under the Act to include the provision, by reference to pension credits which derive from rights under—

(i) the scheme, or

(ii) a scheme in relation to which the scheme is specified as an alternative for the purposes of paragraph 2 of Schedule 5,

of benefits to or in respect of those entitled to the credits, or

(b) restricting the power of the appropriate minister to accept payments into a pension scheme under the Act, where the payments represent the cash equivalent of rights under another pension scheme which are attributable (directly or indirectly) to a pension credit.

(2) Regulations under subsection (1)—

(a) may make benefits provided by virtue of paragraph (a) of that subsection a charge on, and payable out of, the Consolidated Fund;

(b) may confer power to make subordinate legislation, including subordinate legislation which provides for calculation of the value of rights in accordance with guidance from time to time prepared by a person specified in the subordinate legislation.

(3) The appropriate minister for the purposes of subsection (1) is—

(a) in relation to a pension scheme whose ordinary members are limited to those who hold judicial office whose jurisdiction is exercised exclusively in relation to Scotland, the Secretary of State, and

(b) in relation to any other pension scheme, the Lord Chancellor.

(4) In this section—

"pension credit" includes a credit under Northern Ireland legislation corresponding to section 29(1)(b);

"pension scheme" means a scheme or arrangement providing benefits, in the form of pensions or otherwise, payable on termination of service, or on death or retirement, to or in respect of persons to whom the scheme or arrangement applies.

Power to extend
judicial pension
schemes.
1961 c. 42.
1981 c. 20.
1993 c. 8.

Supplementary

44.—(1) Nothing in any of the following provisions (restrictions on alienation of pension rights) applies in relation to any order or provision falling within section 28(1)—

(a) section 203(1) and (2) of the Army Act 1955, section 203(1) and (2) of the Air Force Act 1955, section 128G(1) and (2) of the Naval Discipline Act 1957 and section 159(4) and (4A) of the Pension Schemes Act 1993,

(b) section 91 of the Pensions Act 1995,

Disapplication of
restrictions on
alienation.
1955 c. 18.
1955 c. 19.
1957 c. 53.
1993 c. 48.
1995 c. 26.

(c) any provision of any enactment (whether passed or made before or after this Act is passed) corresponding to any of the enactments mentioned in paragraphs (a) and (b), and

(d) any provision of a pension arrangement corresponding to any of those enactments.

1978 c. 30.

(2) In this section, "enactment" includes an enactment comprised in subordinate legislation (within the meaning of the Interpretation Act 1978).

Information.

45.—(1) The Secretary of State may by regulations require the person responsible for a pension arrangement involved in pension sharing to supply to such persons as he may specify in the regulations such information relating to anything which follows from the application of section 29 as he may so specify.

1993 c. 48.

(2) Section 168 of the Pension Schemes Act 1993 (breach of regulations) shall apply as if this section were contained in that Act (otherwise than in Chapter II of Part VII).

(3) For the purposes of this section, a pension arrangement is involved in pension sharing if section 29 applies by virtue of an order or provision which relates to the arrangement.

Interpretation of Chapter I.

46.—(1) In this Chapter—

"implementation period", in relation to a pension credit, has the meaning given by section 34;

"occupational pension scheme" has the meaning given by section 1 of the Pension Schemes Act 1993;

"pension arrangement" means—

(a) an occupational pension scheme,

(b) a personal pension scheme,

(c) a retirement annuity contract,

(d) an annuity or insurance policy purchased, or transferred, for the purpose of giving effect to rights under an occupational pension scheme or a personal pension scheme, and

(e) an annuity purchased, or entered into, for the purpose of discharging liability in respect of a credit under section 29(1)(b) or under corresponding Northern Ireland legislation;

"pension credit" means a credit under section 29(1)(b);

"pension debit" means a debit under section 29(1)(a);

"pensionable service", in relation to a member of an occupational pension scheme, means service in any description or category of employment to which the scheme relates which qualifies the member (on the assumption that it continues for the appropriate period) for pension or other benefits under the scheme;

"personal pension scheme" has the meaning given by section 1 of the Pension Schemes Act 1993;

"retirement annuity contract" means a contract or scheme approved under Chapter III of Part XIV of the Income and Corporation Taxes Act 1988;

1988 c. 1.

"shareable rights" has the meaning given by section 27(2);

"trustees or managers", in relation to an occupational pension scheme or a personal pension scheme means—

> (a) in the case of a scheme established under a trust, the trustees of the scheme, and

> (b) in any other case, the managers of the scheme.

(2) In this Chapter, references to the person responsible for a pension arrangement are—

> (a) in the case of an occupational pension scheme or a personal pension scheme, to the trustees or managers of the scheme,

> (b) in the case of a retirement annuity contract or an annuity falling within paragraph (d) or (e) of the definition of "pension arrangement" in subsection (1), to the provider of the annuity, and

> (c) in the case of an insurance policy falling within paragraph (d) of the definition of that expression, to the insurer.

(3) In determining what is "pensionable service" for the purposes of this Chapter—

> (a) service notionally attributable for any purpose of the scheme is to be disregarded, and

> (b) no account is to be taken of any rules of the scheme by which a period of service can be treated for any purpose as being longer or shorter than it actually is.

CHAPTER II

SHARING OF STATE SCHEME RIGHTS

47.—(1) Pension sharing is available under this Chapter in relation to a person's shareable state scheme rights.

Shareable state scheme rights.

(2) For the purposes of this Chapter, a person's shareable state scheme rights are—

> (a) his entitlement, or prospective entitlement, to a Category A retirement pension by virtue of section 44(3)(b) of the Contributions and Benefits Act (earnings-related additional pension), and

> (b) his entitlement, or prospective entitlement, to a pension under section 55A of that Act (shared additional pension).

48.—(1) Section 49 applies on the taking effect of any of the following relating to a person's shareable state scheme rights—

Activation of benefit sharing.

> (a) a pension sharing order under the Matrimonial Causes Act 1973,

1973 c. 18.

> (b) provision which corresponds to the provision which may be made by such an order and which—

>> (i) is contained in a qualifying agreement between the parties to a marriage, and

>> (ii) takes effect on the dissolution of the marriage under the Family Law Act 1996,

1996 c. 27.

(c) provision which corresponds to the provision which may be made by such an order and which—

    (i) is contained in a qualifying agreement between the parties to a marriage or former marriage, and

    (ii) takes effect after the dissolution of the marriage under the Family Law Act 1996,

(d) an order under Part III of the Matrimonial and Family Proceedings Act 1984 (financial relief in England and Wales in relation to overseas divorce etc.) corresponding to such an order as is mentioned in paragraph (a),

(e) a pension sharing order under the Family Law (Scotland) Act 1985,

(f) provision which corresponds to the provision which may be made by such an order and which—

    (i) is contained in a qualifying agreement between the parties to a marriage,

    (ii) is in such form as the Secretary of State may prescribe by regulations, and

    (iii) takes effect on the grant, in relation to the marriage, of decree of divorce under the Divorce (Scotland) Act 1976 or of declarator of nullity,

(g) an order under Part IV of the Matrimonial and Family Proceedings Act 1984 (financial relief in Scotland in relation to overseas divorce etc.) corresponding to such an order as is mentioned in paragraph (e),

(h) a pension sharing order under Northern Ireland legislation, and

(i) an order under Part IV of the Matrimonial and Family Proceedings (Northern Ireland) Order 1989 (financial relief in Northern Ireland in relation to overseas divorce etc.) corresponding to such an order as is mentioned in paragraph (h).

(2) For the purposes of subsection (1)(b) and (c), a qualifying agreement is one which—

(a) has been entered into in such circumstances as the Lord Chancellor may prescribe by regulations, and

(b) satisfies such requirements as the Lord Chancellor may so prescribe.

(3) For the purposes of subsection (1)(f), a qualifying agreement is one which—

(a) has been entered into in such circumstances as the Secretary of State may prescribe by regulations, and

(b) is registered in the Books of Council and Session.

(4) Subsection (1)(b) does not apply if the provision relates to rights which are the subject of a pension sharing order under the Matrimonial Causes Act 1973 in relation to the marriage.

(5) Subsection (1)(c) does not apply if—

   (a) the marriage was dissolved by an order under section 3 of the Family Law Act 1996 (divorce not preceded by separation) and the satisfaction of the requirements of section 9(2) of that Act (settlement of future financial arrangements) was a precondition to the making of the order,

1996 c. 27.

   (b) the provision relates to rights which are the subject of a pension sharing order under the Matrimonial Causes Act 1973 in relation to the marriage, or

1973 c. 18.

   (c) shareable state scheme rights have already been the subject of pension sharing between the parties.

(6) For the purposes of this section, an order or provision falling within subsection (1)(e), (f) or (g) shall be deemed never to have taken effect if the Secretary of State does not receive before the end of the period of 2 months beginning with the relevant date—

   (a) copies of the relevant matrimonial documents, and

   (b) such information relating to the transferor and transferee as the Secretary of State may prescribe by regulations under section 34(1)(b)(ii).

(7) The relevant date for the purposes of subsection (6) is—

   (a) in the case of an order or provision falling within subsection (1)(e) or (f), the date of the extract of the decree or declarator responsible for the divorce or annulment to which the order or provision relates, and

   (b) in the case of an order falling within subsection (1)(g), the date of disposal of the application under section 28 of the Matrimonial and Family Proceedings Act 1984.

1984 c. 42.

(8) The reference in subsection (6)(a) to the relevant matrimonial documents is—

   (a) in the case of an order falling within subsection (1)(e) or (g), to copies of the order and the order, decree or declarator responsible for the divorce or annulment to which it relates, and

   (b) in the case of provision falling within subsection (1)(f), to—

      (i) copies of the provision and the order, decree or declarator responsible for the divorce or annulment to which it relates, and

      (ii) documentary evidence that the agreement containing the provision is one to which subsection (3)(a) applies.

(9) The sheriff may, on the application of any person having an interest, make an order—

   (a) extending the period of 2 months referred to in subsection (6), and

   (b) if that period has already expired, providing that, if the Secretary of State receives the documents and information concerned before the end of the period specified in the order, subsection (6) is to be treated as never having applied.

Creation of state
scheme pension
debits and credits.

49.—(1) On the application of this section—

    (a) the transferor becomes subject, for the purposes of Part II of the Contributions and Benefits Act (contributory benefits), to a debit of the appropriate amount, and

    (b) the transferee becomes entitled, for those purposes, to a credit of that amount.

(2) Where the relevant order or provision specifies a percentage value to be transferred, the appropriate amount for the purposes of subsection (1) is the specified percentage of the cash equivalent on the transfer day of the transferor's shareable state scheme rights immediately before that day.

(3) Where the relevant order or provision specifies an amount to be transferred, the appropriate amount for the purposes of subsection (1) is the lesser of—

    (a) the specified amount, and

    (b) the cash equivalent on the transfer day of the transferor's relevant state scheme rights immediately before that day.

(4) Cash equivalents for the purposes of this section shall be calculated in accordance with regulations made by the Secretary of State.

(5) In determining prospective entitlement to a Category A retirement pension for the purposes of this section, only tax years before that in which the transfer day falls shall be taken into account.

(6) In this section—

    "relevant order or provision" means the order or provision by virtue of which this section applies;

    "transfer day" means the day on which the relevant order or provision takes effect;

    "transferor" means the person to whose rights the relevant order or provision relates;

    "transferee" means the person for whose benefit the relevant order or provision is made.

Effect of state
scheme pension
debits and credits.

50.—(1) Schedule 6 (which amends the Contributions and Benefits Act for the purpose of giving effect to debits and credits under section 49(1)) shall have effect.

(2) Section 55C of that Act (which is inserted by that Schedule) shall have effect, in relation to incremental periods (within the meaning of that section) beginning on or after 6th April 2010, with the following amendments—

    (a) in subsection (3), for "period of enhancement" there is substituted "period of deferment",

    (b) in subsection (4), for "1/7th per cent." there is substituted "1/5th per cent.",

    (c) in subsection (7), for "period of enhancement", in both places, there is substituted "period of deferment", and

    (d) in subsection (9), the definition of "period of enhancement" (and the preceding "and") are omitted.

51. In this Chapter—

"shareable state scheme rights" has the meaning given by section 47(2); and

"tax year" has the meaning given by section 122(1) of the Contributions and Benefits Act.

PART V

WELFARE

CHAPTER I

SOCIAL SECURITY BENEFITS

Additional pensions

52.—(1) The Secretary of State may by regulations make such provision as is authorised by one or more of subsections (2) to (4).

(2) The regulations may provide for any prescribed provision of Part II of the Contributions and Benefits Act (contributory benefits) which relates to additional pension for widows or widowers to have effect, in relation to persons of any prescribed description, with such modifications as may be prescribed for securing—

    (a) that any such additional pension, or

    (b) in the case of any provision of Schedule 5 to that Act (increase of pension where entitlement is deferred), that any constituent element of an increase provided for by that Schedule,

is increased by such percentage as may be prescribed (which may be 100 per cent.).

(3) The regulations may amend (or further amend) any prescribed provision of Part II of the Contributions and Benefits Act falling within subsection (2) by substituting for any reference to the year 2000 (or any year previously substituted by virtue of this subsection) a reference to such later year as may be prescribed.

(4) The regulations may make provision for and in connection with—

    (a) the establishment, for a prescribed period, of a scheme for dealing with claims made by persons on the grounds that, in reliance on any incorrect or incomplete information provided by a government department with respect to the SERPS reduction (however that information came to their knowledge), they—

        (i) failed to take any, or any particular, relevant steps which they would have taken, or

        (ii) took any steps which they would not have taken,

    had they instead received correct and complete information with respect to that reduction; and

    (b) securing that, where persons have made successful claims under the scheme, surviving spouses of those persons (or, as the case may be, those persons themselves) will not be affected by the SERPS reduction.

(5) In subsection (4) "relevant steps", in relation to a person, means steps towards safeguarding the financial position of that person's spouse in the event of the spouse becoming that person's surviving spouse or (as

the case may be) towards safeguarding that person's own financial position in the event of that person becoming a surviving spouse (whether or not, in either case, that person was at any material time already married); and "the SERPS reduction" means—

    (a) (in the context of subsection (4)(a)) the operation of any of—

        (i) the provisions of section 19 of the Social Security Act 1986, or

        (ii) the provisions of Part II of the Contributions and Benefits Act reproducing the effect of those provisions;

    (b) (in the context of subsection (4)(b)) the operation of any of the provisions of the Contributions and Benefits Act mentioned in paragraph (a)(ii) above or of section 39C(4) or 48BB(7) of that Act.

(6) Regulations under subsection (4) may, in particular, make provision—

    (a) with respect to the time within which, and the manner in which, claims under the scheme are to be made;

    (b) for requiring claimants—

        (i) to supply such information in connection with their claims as may be prescribed or reasonably requested by any person for the purpose of dealing with their claims,

        (ii) to attend interviews at such time and place as may be reasonably specified by any person for that purpose;

    (c) for a claim to be disallowed where the claimant fails to comply with a requirement imposed by virtue of paragraph (a) or (b) above and does not show within the prescribed period that he had good cause for that failure;

    (d) prescribing—

        (i) matters which are or are not to be taken into account in determining whether a person does or does not have good cause for any failure to comply with any such requirement, or

        (ii) circumstances in which a person is or is not to be regarded as having or not having good cause for any such failure;

    (e) prescribing the conditions which must be satisfied in relation to any claim in order for it to be a successful claim under the scheme;

    (f) with respect to—

        (i) the manner in which decisions under the scheme are to be made (which may include authorising decisions of any prescribed description to be made by a computer), and

        (ii) the time within which, and the manner in which, such decisions are to be notified to claimants;

    (g) for provisions of Chapter II of Part I of the Social Security Act 1998 (social security decisions and appeals) to apply in relation to decisions under the scheme with such modifications as may be prescribed;

    (h) for provisions of Part II of the Contributions and Benefits Act to apply in relation to—

(i) surviving spouses of persons who have made successful claims under the scheme, or

(ii) persons who have themselves made such claims,

with such modifications as may be prescribed.

(7) If no regulations under this section are in force on 6th April 2000, then until such time as any such regulations come into force—

(a) any provisions of Part II of the Contributions and Benefits Act which (whether alone or together with other provisions) would otherwise result in a reduction of one-half in the amount payable by way of additional pension in cases where a person's spouse dies after 5th April 2000 shall be taken—

(i) as not applying, or

(ii) as providing for the full amount to be payable by way of additional pension,

as the case may require; and

(b) in Schedule 5 to that Act—

(i) any provision which is expressed to apply in relation to deaths occurring after that date shall not apply, and

(ii) any provision which (with or without any other limitation) is expressed to apply in relation to deaths occurring before 6th April 2000 shall be taken as applying also in relation to deaths occurring on or after that date.

(8) No regulations shall be made under this section unless a draft of the regulations has been laid before, and approved by a resolution of, each House of Parliament.

(9) In this section "prescribed" means prescribed by regulations under subsection (2), (3) or (4), as the case may be.

State maternity allowance

53.—(1) In section 35 of the Contributions and Benefits Act (state maternity allowance), for subsections (1) and (1A) there shall be substituted—

Extension of entitlement to state maternity allowance.

"(1) A woman shall be entitled to a maternity allowance, at the appropriate weekly rate determined under section 35A below, if—

(a) she has become pregnant and has reached, or been confined before reaching, the commencement of the 11th week before the expected week of confinement; and

(b) she has been engaged in employment as an employed or self-employed earner for any part of the week in the case of at least 26 of the 66 weeks immediately preceding the expected week of confinement; and

(c) (within the meaning of section 35A) her average weekly earnings are not less than the maternity allowance threshold; and

(d) she is not entitled to statutory maternity pay for the same week in respect of the same pregnancy."

(2) In subsection (3) of that section—

(a) for "Schedule 3, Part I, paragraph 3" there shall be substituted "section 35A below"; and

(b) for "and (c) above" there shall be substituted "above or in section 35A(2) or (3) below".

(3) After that section there shall be inserted—

"Appropriate weekly rate of maternity allowance.

35A.—(1) For the purposes of section 35(1) above the appropriate weekly rate is that specified in whichever of subsection (2) or (3) below applies.

(2) Where the woman's average weekly earnings are not less than the lower earnings limit for the relevant tax year, the appropriate weekly rate is a weekly rate equal to the lower rate of statutory maternity pay for the time being prescribed under section 166(3) below.

(3) Where the woman's average weekly earnings—

(a) are less than the lower earnings limit for the relevant tax year, but

(b) are not less than the maternity allowance threshold for that tax year,

the appropriate weekly rate is a weekly rate equivalent to 90 per cent. of her average weekly earnings or (if lower) the rate specified in subsection (2) above.

(4) For the purposes of this section a woman's "average weekly earnings" shall be taken to be the average weekly amount (as determined in accordance with regulations) of specified payments which—

(a) were made to her or for her benefit as an employed earner, or

(b) are (in accordance with regulations) to be treated as made to her or for her benefit as a self-employed earner,

during the specified period.

(5) Regulations may, for the purposes of subsection (4) above, provide—

(a) for the amount of any payments falling within paragraph (a) or (b) of that subsection to be calculated or estimated in such manner and on such basis as may be prescribed;

(b) for a payment made outside the specified period to be treated as made during that period where it was referable to that period or any part of it;

(c) for a woman engaged in employment as a self-employed earner to be treated as having received a payment in respect of a week—

(i) equal to the lower earnings limit in force on the last day of the week, if she paid a Class 2 contribution in respect of the week, or

(ii) equal to the maternity allowance threshold in force on that day, if she was excepted (under section 11(4) above) from liability for such a contribution in respect of the week;

(d) for aggregating payments made or treated as made to or for the benefit of a woman where, either in the same week or in different weeks, she was engaged in two or more employments (whether, in each case, as an employed earner or a self-employed earner).

(6) In this section—

(a) "the maternity allowance threshold", in relation to a tax year, means (subject to subsection (7) below) £30;

(b) "the relevant tax year" means the tax year in which the beginning of the period of 66 weeks mentioned in section 35(1)(b) above falls; and

(c) "specified" (except in subsections (7) and (8) below) means prescribed by or determined in accordance with regulations.

(7) The Secretary of State may, in relation to any tax year after 1999-2000, by order increase the amount for the time being specified in subsection (6)(a) above to such amount as is specified in the order.

(8) When deciding whether, and (if so) by how much, to increase the amount so specified the Secretary of State shall have regard to the movement, over such period as he thinks fit, in the general level of prices obtaining in Great Britain (estimated in such manner as he thinks fit); and the Secretary of State shall in each tax year carry out such a review of the amount so specified as he thinks fit."

(4) This section applies in relation to the payment of maternity allowance in cases where a woman's expected week of confinement (within the meaning of section 35 of the Contributions and Benefits Act) begins on or after 20th August 2000.

Benefits for widows and widowers

54.—(1) For section 36 of the Contributions and Benefits Act there shall be substituted—

Bereavement payments.

"Bereavement payment.

36.—(1) A person whose spouse dies on or after the appointed day shall be entitled to a bereavement payment if—

(a) either that person was under pensionable age at the time when the spouse died or the spouse was then not entitled to a Category A retirement pension under section 44 below; and

(b) the spouse satisfied the contribution condition for a bereavement payment specified in Schedule 3, Part I, paragraph 4.

(2) A bereavement payment shall not be payable to a person if that person and a person of the opposite sex to whom that person was not married were living together as husband and wife at the time of the spouse's death.

(3) In this section "the appointed day" means the day appointed for the coming into force of sections 54 to 56 of the Welfare Reform and Pensions Act 1999."

(2) In Schedule 4 to the Contributions and Benefits Act (rates of benefits etc.), for Part II there shall be substituted—

"PART II

BEREAVEMENT PAYMENT

Bereavement payment.   £2,000.00".

New allowances for bereaved spouses.

55.—(1) After section 36 of the Contributions and Benefits Act there shall be inserted—

"Cases in which sections 37 to 41 apply.

36A.—(1) Sections 37 to 39 and section 40 below apply only in cases where a woman's husband has died before the appointed day, and section 41 below applies only in cases where a man's wife has died before that day.

(2) Sections 39A to 39C below apply in cases where a person's spouse dies on or after the appointed day, but section 39A also applies (in accordance with subsection (1)(b) of that section) in cases where a man's wife has died before that day.

(3) In this section, and in sections 39A and 39B below, "the appointed day" means the day appointed for the coming into force of sections 54 to 56 of the Welfare Reform and Pensions Act 1999."

(2) After section 39 of the Contributions and Benefits Act there shall be inserted—

"Widowed parent's allowance.

39A.—(1) This section applies where—

(a) a person whose spouse dies on or after the appointed day is under pensionable age at the time of the spouse's death, or

(b) a man whose wife died before the appointed day—

(i) has not remarried before that day, and

(ii) is under pensionable age on that day.

(2) The surviving spouse shall be entitled to a widowed parent's allowance at the rate determined in accordance with section 39C below if the deceased spouse satisfied the contribution conditions for a widowed parent's allowance specified in Schedule 3, Part I, paragraph 5 and—

(a) the surviving spouse is entitled to child benefit in respect of a child falling within subsection (3) below; or

(b) the surviving spouse is a woman who either—

(i) is pregnant by her late husband, or

(ii) if she and he were residing together immediately before the time of his death, is pregnant in circumstances falling within section 37(1)(c) above.

(3) A child falls within this subsection if one of the conditions specified in section 81(2) below is for the time being satisfied with respect to the child and the child is either—

  (a) a son or daughter of the surviving spouse and the deceased spouse; or

  (b) a child in respect of whom the deceased spouse was immediately before his or her death entitled to child benefit; or

  (c) if the surviving spouse and the deceased spouse were residing together immediately before his or her death, a child in respect of whom the surviving spouse was then entitled to child benefit.

(4) The surviving spouse shall not be entitled to the allowance for any period after she or he remarries, but, subject to that, the surviving spouse shall continue to be entitled to it for any period throughout which she or he—

  (a) satisfies the requirements of subsection (2)(a) or (b) above; and

  (b) is under pensionable age.

(5) A widowed parent's allowance shall not be payable—

  (a) for any period falling before the day on which the surviving spouse's entitlement is to be regarded as commencing by virtue of section 5(1)(k) of the Administration Act; or

  (b) for any period during which the surviving spouse and a person of the opposite sex to whom she or he is not married are living together as husband and wife.

Bereavement allowance where no dependent children.

39B.—(1) This section applies where a person whose spouse dies on or after the appointed day is over the age of 45 but under pensionable age at the spouse's death.

(2) The surviving spouse shall be entitled to a bereavement allowance at the rate determined in accordance with section 39C below if the deceased spouse satisfied the contribution conditions for a bereavement allowance specified in Schedule 3, Part I, paragraph 5.

(3) A bereavement allowance shall be payable for not more than 52 weeks beginning with the date of the spouse's death or (if later) the day on which the surviving spouse's entitlement is to be regarded as commencing by virtue of section 5(1)(k) of the Administration Act.

(4) The surviving spouse shall not be entitled to the allowance for any period after she or he remarries, but, subject to that, the surviving spouse shall continue to be entitled to it until—

  (a) she or he attains pensionable age, or

(b) the period of 52 weeks mentioned in subsection (3) above expires,

whichever happens first.

(5) The allowance shall not be payable—

(a) for any period for which the surviving spouse is entitled to a widowed parent's allowance; or

(b) for any period during which the surviving spouse and a person of the opposite sex to whom she or he is not married are living together as husband and wife.

Rate of widowed parent's allowance and bereavement allowance.

39C.—(1) The weekly rate of a widowed parent's allowance shall be determined in accordance with the provisions of sections 44 to 45A below as they apply in the case of a Category A retirement pension, but subject, in particular, to the following provisions of this section and section 46(2) below.

(2) The weekly rate of a bereavement allowance shall be determined in accordance with the provisions of section 44 below as they apply in the case of a Category A retirement pension so far as consisting only of the basic pension referred to in subsection (3)(a) of that section, but subject, in particular, to the following provisions of this section.

(3) In the application of sections 44 to 45A or (as the case may be) section 44 below by virtue of subsection (1) or (2) above—

(a) where the deceased spouse was over pensionable age at his or her death, references in those sections to the pensioner shall be taken as references to the deceased spouse, and

(b) where the deceased spouse was under pensionable age at his or her death, references in those sections to the pensioner and the tax year in which he attained pensionable age shall be taken as references to the deceased spouse and the tax year in which he or she died.

(4) Where a widowed parent's allowance is payable to a person whose spouse dies after 5th April 2000, the additional pension falling to be calculated under sections 44 to 45A below by virtue of subsection (1) above shall be one half of the amount which it would be apart from this subsection.

(5) Where a bereavement allowance is payable to a person who was under the age of 55 at the time of the spouse's death, the weekly rate of the allowance shall be reduced by 7 per cent. of what it would be apart from this subsection multiplied by the number of years by which that person's age at that time was less than 55 (any fraction of a year being counted as a year)."

56. After section 48B of the Contributions and Benefits Act there shall be inserted—

"Category B
retirement
pension:
entitlement by
reference to
benefits under
section 39A or
39B.

48BB.—(1) Subsection (2) below applies where a person ("the pensioner") who has attained pensionable age—

    (a) was, immediately before attaining that age, entitled to a widowed parent's allowance in consequence of the death of his or her spouse; and

    (b) has not remarried.

(2) The pensioner shall be entitled to a Category B retirement pension by virtue of the contributions of the spouse, which shall be payable at the same weekly rate as the widowed parent's allowance.

(3) Subsections (4) to (10) below apply where a person ("the pensioner") who has attained pensionable age—

    (a) was in consequence of the death of his or her spouse either—

        (i) entitled to a bereavement allowance at any time prior to attaining that age, or

        (ii) entitled to a widowed parent's allowance at any time when over the age of 45 (but not immediately before attaining pensionable age); and

    (b) has not remarried.

(4) The pensioner shall be entitled to a Category B retirement pension by virtue of the contributions of the spouse.

(5) A Category B retirement pension payable by virtue of subsection (4) above shall be payable at a weekly rate corresponding to the weekly rate of the additional pension determined in accordance with the provisions of sections 44 to 45A above as they apply in relation to a Category A retirement pension, but subject, in particular, to the following provisions of this section and section 46(2) above.

(6) Where the spouse died under pensionable age, references in the provisions of sections 44 to 45A above, as applied by subsection (5) above, to the tax year in which the pensioner attained pensionable age shall be taken as references to the tax year in which the spouse died.

(7) Where the spouse dies after 5th April 2000, the pension payable by virtue of subsection (4) above shall (before making any reduction required by subsection (8) below) be one half of the amount which it would be apart from this subsection.

(8) Where the pensioner was under the age of 55 at the relevant time, the weekly rate of the pension shall be reduced by 7 per cent. of what it would be apart from this subsection multiplied—

(a) by the number of years by which the pensioner's age at that time was less than 55 (any fraction of a year being counted as a year), or

(b) by ten, if that number exceeds ten.

(9) In subsection (8) above "the relevant time" means—

(a) where the pensioner became entitled to a widowed parent's allowance in consequence of the death of the spouse, the time when the pensioner's entitlement to that allowance ended; and

(b) otherwise, the time of the spouse's death.

(10) The amount determined in accordance with subsections (5) to (9) above as the weekly rate of the pension payable to the pensioner by virtue of subsection (4) above shall be increased by such percentage as equals the overall percentage by which, had the pension been in payment as from the date of the spouse's death until the date when the pensioner attained pensionable age, that weekly rate would have been increased during that period by virtue of any orders under section 150 of the Administration Act (annual up-rating of benefits)."

Work-focused interviews

Claim or full entitlement to certain benefits conditional on work-focused interview.

57. After section 2 of the Administration Act there shall be inserted—

"Work-focused interviews

Claim or full entitlement to certain benefits conditional on work-focused interview.

2A.—(1) Regulations may make provision for or in connection with—

(a) imposing, as a condition falling to be satisfied by a person who—

(i) makes a claim for a benefit to which this section applies, and

(ii) is under the age of 60 at the time of making the claim,

a requirement to take part in a work-focused interview;

(b) imposing, at a time when—

(i) a person is under that age and entitled to such a benefit, and

(ii) any prescribed circumstances exist,

a requirement to take part in such an interview as a condition of that person continuing to be entitled to the full amount which is payable to him in respect of the benefit apart from the regulations.

(2) The benefits to which this section applies are—

    (a) income support;

    (b) housing benefit;

    (c) council tax benefit;

    (d) widow's and bereavement benefits falling within section 20(1)(e) and (ea) of the Contributions and Benefits Act (other than a bereavement payment);

    (e) incapacity benefit;

    (f) severe disablement allowance; and

    (g) invalid care allowance.

(3) Regulations under this section may, in particular, make provision—

    (a) for securing, where a person would otherwise be required to take part in interviews relating to two or more benefits—

        (i) that he is only required to take part in one interview, and

        (ii) that any such interview is capable of counting for the purposes of all those benefits;

    (b) for determining the persons by whom interviews are to be conducted;

    (c) conferring power on such persons or the designated authority to determine when and where interviews are to take place (including power in prescribed circumstances to determine that they are to take place in the homes of those being interviewed);

    (d) prescribing the circumstances in which persons attending interviews are to be regarded as having or not having taken part in them;

    (e) for securing that the appropriate consequences mentioned in subsection (4)(a) or (b) below ensue if a person who has been notified that he is required to take part in an interview—

        (i) fails to take part in the interview, and

        (ii) does not show, within the prescribed period, that he had good cause for that failure;

    (f) prescribing—

        (i) matters which are or are not to be taken into account in determining whether a person does or does not have good cause for any failure to comply with the regulations, or

        (ii) circumstances in which a person is or is not to be regarded as having or not having good cause for any such failure.

(4) For the purposes of subsection (3)(e) above the appropriate consequences of a failure falling within that provision are—

(a) where the requirement to take part in an interview applied by virtue of subsection (1)(a) above, that as regards any relevant benefit either—

(i) the person in question is to be regarded as not having made a claim for the benefit, or

(ii) if (in the case of an interview postponed in accordance with subsection (7)) that person has already been awarded the benefit, his entitlement to the benefit is to terminate immediately;

(b) where the requirement to take part in an interview applied by virtue of subsection (1)(b) above, that the amount payable to the person in question in respect of any relevant benefit is to be reduced by the specified amount until the specified time.

(5) Regulations under this section may, in relation to any such reduction, provide—

(a) for the amount of the reduction to be calculated in the first instance by reference to such amount as may be prescribed;

(b) for the amount as so calculated to be restricted, in prescribed circumstances, to the prescribed extent;

(c) where the person in question is entitled to two or more relevant benefits, for determining the extent, and the order, in which those benefits are to be reduced in order to give effect to the reduction required in his case.

(6) Regulations under this section may provide that any requirement to take part in an interview that would otherwise apply to a person by virtue of such regulations—

(a) is, in any prescribed circumstances, either not to apply or not to apply until such time as is specified;

(b) is not to apply if the designated authority determines that an interview—

(i) would not be of assistance to that person, or

(ii) would not be appropriate in the circumstances;

(c) is not to apply until such time as the designated authority determines, if that authority determines that an interview—

(i) would not be of assistance to that person, or

   (ii) would not be appropriate in the circumstances,

  until that time;

and the regulations may make provision for treating a person in relation to whom any such requirement does not apply, or does not apply until a particular time, as having complied with that requirement to such extent and for such purposes as are specified.

(7) Where—

 (a) a person is required to take part in an interview by virtue of subsection (1)(a), and

 (b) the interview is postponed by or under regulations made in pursuance of subsection (6)(a) or (c),

the time to which it is so postponed may be a time falling after an award of the relevant benefit to that person.

(8) In this section—

"the designated authority" means such of the following as may be specified, namely—

  (a) the Secretary of State,

  (b) a person providing services to the Secretary of State,

  (c) a local authority,

  (d) a person providing services to, or authorised to exercise any function of, any such authority;

"interview" (in subsections (3) to (7)) means a work-focused interview;

"relevant benefit", in relation to any person required to take part in a work-focused interview, means any benefit in relation to which that requirement applied by virtue of subsection (1)(a) or (b) above;

"specified" means prescribed by or determined in accordance with regulations;

"work-focused interview", in relation to a person, means an interview conducted for such purposes connected with employment or training in the case of that person as may be specified;

and the purposes which may be so specified include purposes connected with a person's existing or future employment or training prospects or needs, and (in particular) assisting or encouraging a person to enhance his employment prospects.

Supplementary provisions relating to work-focused interviews.

2B.—(1) Chapter II of Part I of the Social Security Act 1998 (social security decisions and appeals) shall have effect in relation to relevant decisions subject to and in accordance with subsections (3) to (8) below (and in those subsections "the 1998 Act" means that Act).

1998 c. 14.

(2) For the purposes of this section a "relevant decision" is a decision made under regulations under section 2A above that a person—

    (a) has failed to comply with a requirement to take part in an interview which applied to him by virtue of the regulations, or

    (b) has not shown, within the prescribed period mentioned in section 2A(3)(e)(ii) above, that he had good cause for such a failure.

(3) Section 8(1)(c) of the 1998 Act (decisions falling to be made under or by virtue of certain enactments are to be made by the Secretary of State) shall have effect subject to any provisions of regulations under section 2A above by virtue of which relevant decisions fall to be made otherwise than by the Secretary of State.

(4) For the purposes of each of sections 9 and 10 of the 1998 Act (revision and supersession of decisions of Secretary of State) any relevant decision made otherwise than by the Secretary of State shall be treated as if it were such a decision made by the Secretary of State (and accordingly may be revised by him under section 9 or superseded by a decision made by him under section 10).

(5) Subject to any provisions of regulations under either section 9 or 10 of the 1998 Act, any relevant decision made, or (by virtue of subsection (4) above) treated as made, by the Secretary of State may be—

    (a) revised under section 9 by a person or authority exercising functions under regulations under section 2A above other than the Secretary of State, or

    (b) superseded under section 10 by a decision made by such a person or authority,

as if that person or authority were the Secretary of State.

(6) Regulations shall make provision for conferring (except in any prescribed circumstances) a right of appeal under section 12 of the 1998 Act (appeal to appeal tribunal) against—

    (a) any relevant decision, and

    (b) any decision under section 10 of that Act superseding any such decision,

whether made by the Secretary of State or otherwise.

(7) Subsections (4) to (6) above apply whether—

    (a) the relevant decision, or

    (b) (in the case of subsection (6)(b)) the decision under section 10 of the 1998 Act,

is as originally made or has been revised (by the Secretary of State or otherwise) under section 9 of that Act; and regulations under subsection (6) above may make provision for treating, for the purposes of section 12 of that Act, any decision made or revised otherwise than by the Secretary of State as if it were a decision made or revised by him.

(8) Section 12 of the 1998 Act shall not apply to any decision falling within subsection (6) above except in accordance with regulations under that subsection.

(9) In the following provisions, namely—

(a) section 3(1) of the Social Security Act 1998 (use of information), and   1998 c. 14.

(b) section 72(6) of the Welfare Reform and Pensions Act 1999 (supply of information),

any reference to information relating to social security includes any information supplied by a person for the purposes of an interview which he is required to take part in by virtue of section 2A above.

(10) In this section "interview" means a work-focused interview within the meaning of section 2A above."

58. After section 2B of the Administration Act (inserted by section 57 above) there shall be inserted—   Optional work-focused interviews.

"Optional work-focused interviews.   2C.—(1) Regulations may make provision for conferring on local authorities functions in connection with conducting work-focused interviews in cases where such interviews are requested or consented to by persons to whom this section applies.

(2) This section applies to persons making claims for or entitled to—

(a) any of the benefits listed in section 2A(2) above, or

(b) any prescribed benefit;

and it so applies regardless of whether such persons have, in accordance with regulations under section 2A above, already taken part in interviews conducted under such regulations.

(3) The functions which may be conferred on a local authority by regulations under this section include functions relating to—

(a) the obtaining and receiving of information for the purposes of work-focused interviews conducted under the regulations;

(b) the recording and forwarding of information supplied at, or for the purposes of, such interviews;

(c) the taking of steps to identify potential employment or training opportunities for persons taking part in such interviews.

(4) Regulations under this section may make different provision for different areas or different authorities.

(5) In this section "work-focused interview", in relation to a person to whom this section applies, means an interview conducted for such purposes connected with employment or training in the case of such a person as may be prescribed; and the purposes which may be so prescribed include—

    (a) purposes connected with the existing or future employment or training prospects or needs of such a person, and

    (b) (in particular) assisting or encouraging such a person to enhance his employment prospects."

Jobseeker's allowance

Couples to make joint claim for allowance.

59. Schedule 7 (which makes provision in connection with requiring certain couples to make joint claims for an income-based jobseeker's allowance) shall have effect.

Special schemes for claimants for jobseeker's allowance.

60.—(1) The Secretary of State may by regulations make provision for or in connection with the participation of claimants for a jobseeker's allowance in schemes of any prescribed description, being schemes established for designated areas in Great Britain (or for the whole of Great Britain) and designed to assist such persons to obtain sustainable employment.

(2) Regulations under this section may, in particular, make provision—

    (a) for the imposition during any prescribed period, as additional conditions for entitlement to a jobseeker's allowance applying in the case of persons participating in schemes, of requirements to take steps determined in accordance with the regulations with a view to improving those persons' prospects of securing employment;

    (b) for the suspension, during any prescribed period, of any prescribed conditions that would otherwise apply to such persons.

1995 c. 18.

(3) Regulations under this section may make provision for any provisions of the Jobseekers Act 1995 to apply for the purposes of the regulations subject to prescribed modifications.

(4) The provisions of that Act which may be so applied include in particular any provisions of—

    (a) section 19 or 20A (circumstances in which jobseeker's allowance is not payable); or

    (b) section 20 or 20B (exemptions from section 19 or 20A).

(5) The Secretary of State may for the purposes of, or in connection with, any scheme—

    (a) make such arrangements (whether or not with other persons) for the provision of any facilities,

    (b) provide such support (by whatever means) for arrangements made by other persons for the provision of any facilities,

    (c) make such payments—

(i) by way of fees, grants, loans or otherwise, to persons undertaking the provision of facilities under arrangements within paragraph (a) or (b),

(ii) by way of grants, loans or otherwise, to persons participating in the scheme, or

(iii) in respect of any incidental expenses,

as he considers appropriate.

(6) For the purposes of, or in connection with, a scheme established for (or for an area which includes) Wales or a part of Wales, the National Assembly for Wales may, if it considers that facilities whose provision any person (including the Secretary of State) is undertaking under arrangements within subsection (5)(a) or (b) are capable of being supportive of the training of persons for employment, make such payments to that person as the Assembly considers appropriate; and any such payments—

(a) may be by way of fees, grants, loans or otherwise, and

(b) may, unless the Assembly otherwise specifies, be used by the person to whom they are made for the provision of any of the facilities provided under the arrangements.

(7) In subsections (5) and (6) "facilities" includes services, and any reference to the provision of facilities includes the making of payments to persons participating in the scheme.

(8) The power of the Secretary of State to make an order under section 26 of the Employment Act 1988 (status of trainees etc.) shall include power to make, in relation to—

1988 c. 19.

(a) persons participating in any scheme, and

(b) payments received by them by virtue of subsection (5) above,

provision corresponding to any provision which (by virtue of subsection (1) or (2) of that section) may be made in relation to persons using such facilities, and to such payments received by them, as are mentioned in subsection (1) of that section.

(9) In this section—

"designated" means designated by the Secretary of State;

"employment" has the meaning given by regulations under this section;

"prescribed" means specified in or determined in accordance with regulations under this section;

"scheme" means a scheme such as is mentioned in subsection (1).

Incapacity for work

61. For section 171C of the Contribution and Benefits Act there shall be substituted—

Incapacity for work: personal capability assessments.

"Personal capability assessments.

171C.—(1) Where the own occupation test is not applicable, or has ceased to apply, in the case of a person, the question whether the person is capable or incapable of work shall be determined in accordance with a personal capability assessment.

(2) Provision shall be made by regulations—

(a) defining a personal capability assessment by reference to the extent to which a person who has some specific disease or bodily or mental disablement is capable or incapable of performing such activities as may be prescribed;

(b) as to the manner of assessing whether a person is, in accordance with a personal capability assessment, incapable of work.

(3) Regulations may provide that, in any prescribed circumstances, a person to whom subsection (1) above applies shall, if the prescribed conditions are met, be treated as incapable of work in accordance with a personal capability assessment until such time as—

(a) such an assessment has been carried out in his case, or

(b) he falls to be treated as capable of work in accordance with regulations under section 171A(2) or (3) above or section 171E below.

The prescribed conditions may include the condition that it has not previously been determined, within such period as may be prescribed, that the person in question is or is to be treated as capable of work.

(4) Except in prescribed circumstances, a personal capability assessment carried out in the case of a person before the time when subsection (1) above applies to him shall be as effective for the purposes of that subsection as one carried out thereafter.

(5) The Secretary of State may, in the case of a person who for any purpose of this Act has been determined to be incapable of work in accordance with a personal capability assessment (including one carried out by virtue of this subsection), require the question whether the person is capable or incapable of work to be determined afresh in accordance with a further personal capability assessment."

Incapacity benefits

Incapacity benefit: restriction to recent contributors.

62.—(1) Paragraph 2 of Schedule 3 to the Contributions and Benefits Act (contribution conditions for short-term incapacity benefit) shall be amended as follows.

(2) In sub-paragraph (2) (the first condition), for paragraph (a) there shall be substituted—

"(a) the claimant must have actually paid contributions of a relevant class in respect of one of the last three complete years before the beginning of the relevant benefit year, and those contributions must have been paid before the relevant time; and".

(3) In sub-paragraph (7) (claim by person who does not satisfy second contribution condition to be disregarded in relation to subsequent claim), after "does not satisfy" there shall be inserted "the first contribution condition (specified in sub-paragraph (2) above) or, as the case may be,".

(4) After sub-paragraph (7) there shall be added—

"(8) Regulations may—

(a) provide for the first contribution condition (specified in sub-paragraph (2) above) to be taken to be satisfied in the case of persons who have been entitled to any prescribed description of benefit during any prescribed period or at any prescribed time;

(b) with a view to securing any relaxation of the requirements of that condition (as so specified) in relation to persons who have been so entitled, provide for that condition to apply in relation to them subject to prescribed modifications.

(9) In sub-paragraph (8)—

"benefit" includes (in addition to any benefit under Parts II to V of this Act)—

(a) any benefit under Parts VII to XII of this Act, and

(b) credits under regulations under section 22(5) above;

"modifications" includes additions, omissions and amendments."

63. After section 30D of the Contributions and Benefits Act there shall be inserted—

Incapacity benefit: reduction for pension payments.

"Incapacity benefit: reduction for pension payments.

30DD.—(1) Where—

(a) a person is entitled to incapacity benefit in respect of any period of a week or part of a week,

(b) a pension payment is payable to him in respect of that period (or a period which forms part of that period or includes that period or part of it), and

(c) the amount of that payment (or, as the case may be, the amount which in accordance with regulations is to be taken as payable to him by way of pension payments in respect of that period) exceeds the threshold,

the amount of that benefit shall be reduced by an amount equal to 50 per cent. of that excess.

(2) In subsection (1) above "the threshold" means—

(a) if the period in question is a week, £85 or such greater amount as may be prescribed; or

(b) if that period is not a week, such proportion of the amount mentioned in paragraph (a) as falls to be calculated in accordance with regulations on such basis as may be prescribed.

(3) Regulations may secure that a person of any prescribed description does not suffer any reduction under subsection (1) above in any amount of incapacity benefit to which he is entitled.

(4) Regulations may provide—

(a) for sums of any specified description to be disregarded for the purposes of this section;

(b) for sums of any specified description to be treated for those purposes as payable to persons as pension payments (including, in particular, sums in relation to which there is a deferred right of receipt);

(c) for the aggregation of sums of any specified description which are payable as pension payments (or treated as being so payable) in respect of the same or different periods;

(d) for such sums or aggregate sums to be apportioned between or otherwise allocated to periods in respect of which persons are entitled to incapacity benefit.

(5) In this section "pension payment" means—

(a) a periodical payment made in relation to a person under a personal pension scheme or, in connection with the coming to an end of an employment of his, under an occupational pension scheme or a public service pension scheme;

(b) a payment of any specified description, being a payment made under an insurance policy providing benefits in connection with physical or mental illness, disability, infirmity or defect; or

(c) a payment of any other specified description;

and "specified" means prescribed by or determined in accordance with regulations under this section.

(6) For the purposes of subsection (5) "occupational pension scheme", "personal pension scheme" and "public service pension scheme" each have the meaning given by section 1 of the Pension Schemes Act 1993, except that "personal pension scheme" includes a contract or trust scheme approved under Chapter III of Part XIV of the Income and Corporation Taxes Act 1988 (retirement annuities)."

1993 c. 48.

1988 c. 1.

Incapacity benefit: persons incapacitated in youth.

64.—(1) In subsection (1) of section 30A of the Contributions and Benefits Act (incapacity benefit: entitlement)—

(a) for "either of the following conditions" there shall be substituted—

"(a) either of the conditions mentioned in subsection (2) below; or

(b) if he satisfies neither of those conditions, each of the conditions mentioned in subsection (2A) below,"; and

(b) after "any day of incapacity for work" there shall be inserted "("the relevant day")".

(2) In subsection (2) of that section—

(a) after "conditions" there shall be inserted "mentioned in subsection (1)(a) above"; and

(b) in paragraph (a), for "the day in question" there shall be substituted "the relevant day".

(3) After that subsection there shall be inserted—

"(2A) The conditions mentioned in subsection (1)(b) above are that—

(a) he is aged 16 or over on the relevant day;

(b) he is under the age of 20 or, in prescribed cases, 25 on a day which forms part of the period of incapacity for work;

(c) he was incapable of work throughout a period of 196 consecutive days immediately preceding the relevant day, or an earlier day in the period of incapacity for work on which he was aged 16 or over;

(d) on the relevant day he satisfies the prescribed conditions as to residence in Great Britain, or as to presence there; and

(e) he is not, on that day, a person who is receiving full-time education."

(4) In subsection (3) of that section, after "benefit" there shall be inserted "under subsection (1)(a) above".

(5) After subsection (5) of that section there shall be inserted—

"(6) Regulations may provide that persons who have previously been entitled to incapacity benefit shall, in prescribed circumstances, be entitled to short-term incapacity benefit under subsection (1)(b) above notwithstanding that they do not satisfy the condition set out in paragraph (b) of subsection (2A) above.

(7) Regulations may prescribe the circumstances in which a person is or is not to be treated as receiving full-time education for the purposes of paragraph (e) of that subsection."

65. Sections 68 and 69 of the Contributions and Benefits Act (severe disablement allowance) shall cease to have effect.

Abolition of severe disablement allowance.

Disability benefits

66.—(1) After subsection (3) of section 64 of the Contributions and Benefits Act (entitlement to attendance allowance) there shall be added—

Attendance allowance.

"(4) Circumstances may be prescribed in which a person is to be taken to satisfy or not to satisfy such of the conditions mentioned in subsections (2) and (3) above as may be prescribed."

(2) In subsection (1) of section 66 of that Act (attendance allowance for the terminally ill)—

(a) in paragraph (a)(i), for the words from "for the remainder of his life" to "terminally ill" there shall be substituted "for so much of the period for which he is terminally ill as does not fall before the date of the claim";

(b) in paragraph (a)(ii), for "that date", in the first place where those words occur, there shall be substituted "the date of the claim or, if later, the first date on which he is terminally ill"; and

(c) in paragraph (b), for "the remainder of the person's life, beginning with that date" there shall be substituted "so much of the period for which he is terminally ill as does not fall before the date of the claim".

Disability living allowance.

67.—(1) In subsection (3) of section 71 of the Contributions and Benefits Act (disability living allowance), for "for life" there shall be substituted "for an indefinite period".

(2) In subsection (5)(b) of section 72 of that Act (the care component), for "for the remainder of his life beginning with that date" there shall be substituted "for so much of the period for which he is terminally ill as does not fall before the date of the claim".

(3) In subsection (1) of section 73 of that Act (the mobility component), for "the age of 5" there shall be substituted "the relevant age" and after that subsection there shall be inserted—

"(1A) In subsection (1) above "the relevant age" means—

(a) in relation to the conditions mentioned in paragraph (a), (b) or (c) of that subsection, the age of 3;

(b) in relation to the conditions mentioned in paragraph (d) of that subsection, the age of 5."

(4) Subsection (3) does not affect awards made before the day on which that subsection comes into force.

Miscellaneous

Certain overpayments of benefit not to be recoverable.

68.—(1) An overpayment to which this section applies shall not be recoverable from the payee, whether by the Secretary of State or a local authority, under any provision made by or under Part III of the Administration Act (overpayments and adjustments of benefit).

(2) This section applies to an overpayment if—

(a) it is in respect of a qualifying benefit;

(b) it is referable to a decision given on a review that there has been an alteration in the relevant person's condition, being a decision to which effect is required to be given as from a date earlier than that on which it was given;

(c) the decision was given before 1st June 1999; and

(d) the overpayment is not excluded by virtue of subsection (6).

(3) In subsection (2)(b) the reference to a decision on a review that there has been an alteration in the relevant person's condition is a reference to a decision so given that that person's physical or mental condition either was at the time when the original decision was given, or has subsequently become, different from that on which that decision was based, with the result—

(a) that he did not at that time, or (as the case may be) has subsequently ceased to, meet any of the conditions contained in the following provisions of the Contributions and Benefits Act, namely—

(i) section 64 (attendance allowance),

(ii) section 72(1) or (2) (care component of disability living allowance), and

(iii) section 73(1) or (2) (mobility component of that allowance); or

(b) that he was at that time, or (as the case may be) has subsequently become, capable of work in accordance with regulations made under section 171C(2) of that Act (the all work test).

(4) For the purposes of this section "qualifying benefit" means—

(a) attendance allowance;

(b) disability living allowance;

(c) any benefit awarded wholly or partly by reason of a person being (or being treated as being) in receipt of a component (at any rate) of disability living allowance or in receipt of attendance allowance;

(d) incapacity benefit;

(e) any benefit (other than incapacity benefit) awarded wholly or partly by reason of a person being (or being treated as being) incapable of work; or

(f) any benefit awarded wholly or partly by reason of a person being (or being treated as being) in receipt of any benefit falling within paragraph (c), (d) or (e).

(5) For the purposes of this section—

(a) "review" means a review taking place by virtue of section 25(1)(a) or (b), 30(2)(a) or (b) or 35(1)(a) or (b) of the Administration Act;

(b) "the relevant person", in relation to a review, means the person to whose entitlement to a qualifying benefit or to whose incapacity for work the review related; and

(c) "the original decision", in relation to a review, means the decision as to any such entitlement or incapacity to which the review related.

(6) An overpayment is excluded by virtue of this subsection if (before or after the passing of this Act)—

(a) the payee has agreed to pay a penalty in respect of the overpayment under section 115A of the Administration Act,

(b) the payee has been convicted of any offence (under section 111A or 112(1) or (1A) of that Act or otherwise) in connection with the overpayment, or

(c) proceedings have been instituted against the payee for such an offence and the proceedings have not been determined or abandoned.

(7) Nothing in this section applies to an overpayment to the extent that it was recovered from the payee (by any means) before 26th February 1999.

(8) In this section—

"benefit" includes any amount included in—

(a) the applicable amount in relation to an income-related benefit (as defined by section 135(1) of the Contributions and Benefits Act), or

1995 c. 18.

(b) the applicable amount in relation to a jobseeker's allowance (as defined by section 4(5) of the Jobseekers Act 1995);

"income-related benefit" has the meaning given by section 123(1) of the Contributions and Benefits Act;

"overpayment" means an amount of benefit paid in excess of entitlement;

"the payee", in relation to an overpayment, means the person to whom that amount was paid.

Child benefit: claimant to state national insurance number.

69. In section 13 of the Administration Act (entitlement to child benefit dependent on claim), after subsection (1) there shall be inserted—

"(1A) No person shall be entitled to child benefit unless subsection (1B) below is satisfied in relation to him.

(1B) This subsection is satisfied in relation to a person if—

(a) his claim for child benefit is accompanied by—

(i) a statement of his national insurance number and information or evidence establishing that that number has been allocated to him; or

(ii) information or evidence enabling the national insurance number that has been allocated to him to be ascertained; or

(b) he makes an application for a national insurance number to be allocated to him which is accompanied by information or evidence enabling such a number to be so allocated.

(1C) Regulations may make provision disapplying subsection (1A) above in the case of—

(a) prescribed descriptions of persons making claims, or

(b) prescribed descriptions of children in respect of whom child benefit is claimed,

or in other prescribed circumstances."

Welfare benefits: miscellaneous amendments.

70. Schedule 8 (which makes minor and consequential amendments of provisions relating to welfare benefits) shall have effect.

Supplementary

71. After section 7 of the Administration Act there shall be inserted—

"Sharing of functions as regards certain claims and information

Sharing of
functions as
regards certain
claims and
information.

7A.—(1) Regulations may, for the purpose of supplementing the persons or bodies to whom claims for relevant benefits may be made, make provision—

    (a) as regards housing benefit or council tax benefit, for claims for that benefit to be made to—

        (i) a Minister of the Crown, or

        (ii) a person providing services to a Minister of the Crown;

    (b) as regards any other relevant benefit, for claims for that benefit to be made to—

        (i) a local authority,

        (ii) a person providing services to a local authority, or

        (iii) a person authorised to exercise any function of a local authority relating to housing benefit or council tax benefit.

(2) Regulations may make provision for or in connection with—

    (a) the forwarding by a relevant authority of—

        (i) claims received by virtue of any provision authorised by subsection (1) above, and

        (ii) information or evidence supplied in connection with making such claims (whether supplied by persons making the claims or by other persons);

    (b) the receiving and forwarding by a relevant authority of information or evidence relating to social security matters supplied by, or the obtaining by a relevant authority of such information or evidence from—

        (i) persons making, or who have made, claims for a relevant benefit, or

        (ii) other persons in connection with such claims,

    including information or evidence not relating to the claims or benefit in question;

    (c) the recording by a relevant authority of information or evidence relating to social security matters supplied to, or obtained by, the authority and the holding by the authority of such information or evidence (whether as supplied or obtained or as recorded);

(d) the giving of information or advice with respect to social security matters by a relevant authority to persons making, or who have made, claims for a relevant benefit.

(3) In paragraphs (b) and (d) of subsection (2) above—

(a) references to claims for a relevant benefit are to such claims whether made as mentioned in subsection (1)(a) or (b) above or not; and

(b) references to persons who have made such claims include persons to whom awards of benefit have been made on the claims.

(4) Regulations under this section may make different provision for different areas.

(5) Regulations under any other enactment may make such different provision for different areas as appears to the Secretary of State expedient in connection with any exercise by regulations under this section of the power conferred by subsection (4) above.

(6) In this section—

(a) "benefit" includes child support or a war pension (any reference to a claim being read, in relation to child support, as a reference to an application under the Child Support Act 1991 for a maintenance assessment);

1991 c. 48.

(b) "local authority" means an authority administering housing benefit or council tax benefit;

(c) "relevant authority" means—

(i) a Minister of the Crown,

(ii) a person providing services to a Minister of the Crown,

(iii) a local authority,

(iv) a person providing services to a local authority, or

(v) a person authorised to exercise any function of a local authority relating to housing benefit or council tax benefit;

(d) "relevant benefit" means housing benefit, council tax benefit or any other benefit prescribed for the purposes of this section;

(e) "social security matters" means matters relating to social security, child support or war pensions;

1989 c. 24.

and in this subsection "war pension" means a war pension within the meaning of section 25 of the Social Security Act 1989 (establishment and functions of war pensions committees)."

72.—(1) The Secretary of State may by regulations make such
provision for or in connection with any of the following matters, namely—

    (a) the use by a person within subsection (2) of social security information held by that person,

    (b) the supply (whether to a person within subsection (2) or otherwise) of social security information held by a person within that subsection,

    (c) the relevant purposes for which a person to whom such information is supplied under the regulations may use it, and

    (d) the circumstances and extent (if any) in and to which a person to whom such information is supplied under the regulations may supply it to any other person (whether within subsection (2) or not),

as the Secretary of State considers appropriate in connection with any provision to which subsection (3) applies or in connection with any scheme or arrangements to which subsection (4) applies.

(2) The persons within this subsection are—

    (a) a Minister of the Crown;

    (b) a person providing services to, or designated for the purposes of this section by an order of, a Minister of the Crown;

    (c) a local authority (within the meaning of the Administration Act); and

    (d) a person providing services to, or authorised to exercise any function of, any such authority.

(3) This subsection applies to any provision made by or under—

    (a) any of the sections of the Administration Act inserted by section 57, 58 or 71 of this Act,

    (b) section 60 of this Act, or

    (c) the Jobseekers Act 1995.

(4) This subsection applies to—

    (a) any scheme designated by regulations under subsection (1), being a scheme operated by the Secretary of State (whether under arrangements with any other person or not) for any purposes connected with employment or training in the case of persons of a particular category or description;

    (b) any arrangements of a description specified in such regulations, being arrangements made by the Secretary of State for any such purposes.

(5) Regulations under subsection (1) may, in particular, authorise information supplied to a person under the regulations—

    (a) to be used for the purpose of amending or supplementing other information held by that person; and

    (b) if it is so used, to be supplied to any other person, and used for any purpose, to whom or for which that other information could be supplied or used.

(6) In this section—

"relevant purposes" means purposes connected with—

> (a) social security, child support or war pensions, or

> (b) employment or training;

"social security information" means information relating to social security, child support or war pensions;

1989 c. 24.

and in this subsection "war pensions" means war pensions within the meaning of section 25 of the Social Security Act 1989 (establishment and functions of war pensions committees).

(7) Any reference in this section to purposes connected with employment or training includes purposes connected with the existing or future employment or training prospects or needs of persons, and (in particular) assisting or encouraging persons to enhance their employment prospects.

CHAPTER II

NATIONAL INSURANCE CONTRIBUTIONS

New threshold for primary Class 1 contributions.
1993 c. 48.

73. Schedule 9 (which amends the Contributions and Benefits Act, the Administration Act and the Pension Schemes Act 1993 so as to make provision for and in connection with the introduction of a new primary threshold for primary Class 1 contributions) shall have effect.

New threshold for primary Class 1 contributions: Northern Ireland.
1992 c. 7.
1992 c. 8.
1993 c. 49.

74. Schedule 10 (which amends the Social Security Contributions and Benefits (Northern Ireland) Act 1992, the Social Security Administration (Northern Ireland) Act 1992 and the Pension Schemes (Northern Ireland) Act 1993 so as to make provision for and in connection with the introduction for Northern Ireland of a new primary threshold for primary Class 1 contributions) shall have effect.

Earnings of workers supplied by service companies etc.

75. After section 4 of the Contributions and Benefits Act there shall be inserted—

"Earnings of workers supplied by service companies etc.

4A.—(1) Regulations may make provision for securing that where—

> (a) an individual ("the worker") personally performs, or is under an obligation personally to perform, services for the purposes of a business carried on by another person ("the client"),

> (b) the performance of those services by the worker is (within the meaning of the regulations) referable to arrangements involving a third person (and not referable to any contract between the client and the worker), and

> (c) the circumstances are such that, were the services to be performed by the worker under a contract between him and the client, he would be

regarded for the purposes of the applicable provisions of this Act as employed in employed earner's employment by the client,

relevant payments or benefits are, to the specified extent, to be treated for those purposes as earnings paid to the worker in respect of an employed earner's employment of his.

(2) For the purposes of this section—

(a) "the intermediary" means—

(i) where the third person mentioned in subsection (1)(b) above has such a contractual or other relationship with the worker as may be specified, that third person, or

(ii) where that third person does not have such a relationship with the worker, any other person who has both such a relationship with the worker and such a direct or indirect contractual or other relationship with the third person as may be specified; and

(b) a person may be the intermediary despite being—

(i) a person with whom the worker holds any office or employment, or

(ii) a body corporate, unincorporated body or partnership of which the worker is a member;

and subsection (1) above applies whether or not the client is a person with whom the worker holds any office or employment.

(3) Regulations under this section may, in particular, make provision—

(a) for the worker to be treated for the purposes of the applicable provisions of this Act, in relation to the specified amount of relevant payments or benefits (the worker's "attributable earnings"), as employed in employed earner's employment by the intermediary;

(b) for the intermediary (whether or not he fulfils the conditions prescribed under section 1(6)(a) above for secondary contributors) to be treated for those purposes as the secondary contributor in respect of the worker's attributable earnings;

(c) for determining—

(i) any deductions to be made, and

(ii) in other respects the manner and basis in and on which the amount of the worker's attributable earnings for any specified period is to be calculated or estimated,

in connection with relevant payments or benefits;

(d) for aggregating any such amount, for purposes relating to contributions, with other earnings of the worker during any such period;

(e) for determining the date by which contributions payable in respect of the worker's attributable earnings are to be paid and accounted for;

(f) for apportioning payments or benefits of any specified description, in such manner or on such basis as may be specified, for the purpose of determining the part of any such payment or benefit which is to be treated as a relevant payment or benefit for the purposes of the regulations;

(g) for disregarding for the purposes of the applicable provisions of this Act, in relation to relevant payments or benefits, an employed earner's employment in which the worker is employed (whether by the intermediary or otherwise) to perform the services in question;

(h) for otherwise securing that a double liability to pay any amount by way of a contribution of any description does not arise in relation to a particular payment or benefit or (as the case may be) a particular part of a payment or benefit;

(i) for securing that, to the specified extent, two or more persons, whether—

1988 c. 1.

(i) connected persons (within the meaning of section 839 of the Income and Corporation Taxes Act 1988), or

(ii) persons of any other specified description,

are treated as a single person for any purposes of the regulations;

(j) (without prejudice to paragraph (i) above) for securing that a contract made with a person other than the client is to be treated for any such purposes as made with the client;

(k) for excluding or modifying the application of the regulations in relation to such cases, or payments or benefits of such description, as may be specified.

(4) Regulations made in pursuance of subsection (3)(c) above may, in particular, make provision—

(a) for the making of a deduction of a specified amount in respect of general expenses of the intermediary as well as deductions in respect of particular expenses incurred by him;

(b) for securing reductions in the amount of the worker's attributable earnings on account of—

   (i) any secondary Class 1 contributions already paid by the intermediary in respect of actual earnings of the worker, and

   (ii) any such contributions that will be payable by him in respect of the worker's attributable earnings.

(5) Regulations under this section may make provision for securing that, in applying any provisions of the regulations, any term of a contract or other arrangement which appears to be of a description specified in the regulations is to be disregarded.

(6) In this section—

   "the applicable provisions of this Act" means this Part of this Act and Parts II to V below;

   "business" includes any activity carried on—

      (a) by a government department or public or local authority (in the United Kingdom or elsewhere), or

      (b) by a body corporate, unincorporated body or partnership;

   "relevant payments or benefits" means payments or benefits of any specified description made or provided (whether to the intermediary or the worker or otherwise) in connection with the performance by the worker of the services in question;

   "specified" means prescribed by or determined in accordance with regulations under this section.

(7) Any reference in this section to the performance by the worker of any services includes a reference to any such obligation of his to perform them as is mentioned in subsection (1)(a) above.

(8) Regulations under this section shall be made by the Treasury with the concurrence of the Secretary of State.

(9) If, on any modification of the statutory provisions relating to income tax, it appears to the Treasury to be expedient to modify any of the preceding provisions of this section for the purpose of assimilating the law relating to income tax and the law relating to contributions under this Part of this Act, the Treasury may with the concurrence of the Secretary of State by order make such modifications of the preceding provisions of this section as the Treasury think appropriate for that purpose."

Earnings of
workers supplied
by service
companies etc:
Northern Ireland.

1992 c. 7.

76. After section 4 of the Social Security Contributions and Benefits (Northern Ireland) Act 1992 there shall be inserted—

"Earnings of workers supplied by service companies etc.

4A.—(1) Regulations may make provision for securing that where—

(a) an individual ("the worker") personally performs, or is under an obligation personally to perform, services for the purposes of a business carried on by another person ("the client"),

(b) the performance of those services by the worker is (within the meaning of the regulations) referable to arrangements involving a third person (and not referable to any contract between the client and the worker), and

(c) the circumstances are such that, were the services to be performed by the worker under a contract between him and the client, he would be regarded for the purposes of the applicable provisions of this Act as employed in employed earner's employment by the client,

relevant payments or benefits are, to the specified extent, to be treated for those purposes as earnings paid to the worker in respect of an employed earner's employment of his.

(2) For the purposes of this section—

(a) "the intermediary" means—

(i) where the third person mentioned in subsection (1)(b) above has such a contractual or other relationship with the worker as may be specified, that third person, or

(ii) where that third person does not have such a relationship with the worker, any other person who has both such a relationship with the worker and such a direct or indirect contractual or other relationship with the third person as may be specified; and

(b) a person may be the intermediary despite being—

(i) a person with whom the worker holds any office or employment, or

(ii) a body corporate, unincorporated body or partnership of which the worker is a member;

and subsection (1) above applies whether or not the client is a person with whom the worker holds any office or employment.

(3) Regulations under this section may, in particular, make provision—

(a) for the worker to be treated for the purposes of the applicable provisions of this Act, in relation to the specified amount of relevant payments or benefits (the worker's "attributable earnings"), as employed in employed earner's employment by the intermediary;

(b) for the intermediary (whether or not he fulfils the conditions prescribed under section 1(6)(a) above for secondary contributors) to be treated for those purposes as the secondary contributor in respect of the worker's attributable earnings;

(c) for determining—

(i) any deductions to be made, and

(ii) in other respects the manner and basis in and on which the amount of the worker's attributable earnings for any specified period is to be calculated or estimated,

in connection with relevant payments or benefits;

(d) for aggregating any such amount, for purposes relating to contributions, with other earnings of the worker during any such period;

(e) for determining the date by which contributions payable in respect of the worker's attributable earnings are to be paid and accounted for;

(f) for apportioning payments or benefits of any specified description, in such manner or on such basis as may be specified, for the purpose of determining the part of any such payment or benefit which is to be treated as a relevant payment or benefit for the purposes of the regulations;

(g) for disregarding for the purposes of the applicable provisions of this Act, in relation to relevant payments or benefits, an employed earner's employment in which the worker is employed (whether by the intermediary or otherwise) to perform the services in question;

(h) for otherwise securing that a double liability to pay any amount by way of a contribution of any description does not arise in relation to a particular payment or benefit or (as the case may be) a particular part of a payment or benefit;

(i) for securing that, to the specified extent, two or more persons, whether—

(i) connected persons (within the meaning of section 839 of the Income and Corporation Taxes Act 1988), or   1988 c. 1.

(ii) persons of any other specified description,

are treated as a single person for any purposes of the regulations;

(j) (without prejudice to paragraph (i) above) for securing that a contract made with a person other than the client is to be treated for any such purposes as made with the client;

(k) for excluding or modifying the application of the regulations in relation to such cases, or payments or benefits of such description, as may be specified.

(4) Regulations made in pursuance of subsection (3)(c) above may, in particular, make provision—

(a) for the making of a deduction of a specified amount in respect of general expenses of the intermediary as well as deductions in respect of particular expenses incurred by him;

(b) for securing reductions in the amount of the worker's attributable earnings on account of—

(i) any secondary Class 1 contributions already paid by the intermediary in respect of actual earnings of the worker, and

(ii) any such contributions that will be payable by him in respect of the worker's attributable earnings.

(5) Regulations under this section may make provision for securing that, in applying any provisions of the regulations, any term of a contract or other arrangement which appears to be of a description specified in the regulations is to be disregarded.

(6) In this section—

"the applicable provisions of this Act" means this Part of this Act and Parts II to V below;

"business" includes any activity carried on—

(a) by a government department or public or local authority (in the United Kingdom or elsewhere), or

(b) by a body corporate, unincorporated body or partnership;

"relevant payments or benefits" means payments or benefits of any specified description made or provided (whether to the intermediary or the worker or otherwise) in connection with the performance by the worker of the services in question;

"specified" means prescribed by or determined in accordance with regulations under this section.

(7) Any reference in this section to the performance by the worker of any services includes a reference to any such obligation of his to perform them as is mentioned in subsection (1)(a) above.

(8) Regulations under this section shall be made by the Treasury with the concurrence of the Department.

(9) If, on any modification of the statutory provisions relating to income tax, it appears to the Treasury to be expedient to modify any of the preceding provisions of this section for the purpose of assimilating the law relating to income tax and the law relating to contributions under this Part of this Act, the Treasury may with the concurrence of the Department by order make such modifications of the preceding provisions of this section as the Treasury think appropriate for that purpose."

77. In section 10A of the Contributions and Benefits Act (Class 1B contributions), for subsection (6) (level of Class 1B percentage) there shall be substituted—

> "(6) In subsection (3) above "the Class 1B percentage" means a percentage rate equal to that specified as the secondary percentage in section 9(2) above for the tax year in question."

Class 1B contributions.

78. In section 10A of the Social Security Contributions and Benefits (Northern Ireland) Act 1992 (Class 1B contributions), for subsection (6) (level of Class 1B percentage) there shall be substituted—

> "(6) In subsection (3) above "the Class 1B percentage" means a percentage rate equal to that specified as the secondary percentage in section 9(2) above for the tax year in question."

Class 1B contributions: Northern Ireland.
1992 c. 7.

CHAPTER III

OTHER WELFARE PROVISIONS

79.—(1) The Secretary of State may by regulations make a scheme providing for a housing benefit claimant, where he moves from an under-occupied dwelling in the public or social rented sector to a qualifying dwelling, to be entitled to be paid an amount calculated by reference to the difference between—

Measures to reduce under-occupation by housing benefit claimants.

(a) the prescribed payments he was liable to make in respect of his former dwelling, and

(b) those he is liable to make in respect of his new dwelling.

(2) In subsection (1) the reference to a qualifying dwelling is to a dwelling (whether in the public or social rented sector or not) which, in relation to the claimant, either—

(a) is not under-occupied, or

(b) is under-occupied to a lesser extent than the claimant's former dwelling.

(3) Regulations under this section may, in particular, make provision—

(a) as to the circumstances in which, in relation to a housing benefit claimant, a dwelling is or is not to be regarded for the purposes of the scheme as under-occupied or under-occupied to a lesser extent than another dwelling;

(b) as to the manner in which an amount payable to such a claimant under the scheme is to be calculated;

(c) for any such amount to be payable (subject to subsection (7))—

(i) in a case where the claimant's former and new dwellings are situated in the area of the same local authority, by that authority, or

(ii) in a case where they are situated in the areas of different local authorities, by whichever of those authorities is prescribed.

(4) Regulations made in pursuance of subsection (3)(b) may provide for the amount payable to a housing benefit claimant under the scheme ("the relevant amount") to be reduced on account of—

(a) any arrears of rent payable by him, or

(b) any amount paid to him by way of housing benefit which constitutes an overpayment for housing benefit purposes;

but regulations under this section shall not otherwise provide for the making of any reduction in the relevant amount on account of any sum due to or recoverable by any public or local authority.

(5) A person aggrieved by a determination of any prescribed description made under regulations under this section may appeal to such court or tribunal as may be prescribed; and the regulations may make provision as to the procedure to be followed in connection with appeals under this subsection.

(6) Regulations under this section may provide that the scheme is to apply only in relation to one or more prescribed areas; and, if they do so, they may also—

(a) provide that (unless continued in force by subsequent regulations under this section) the scheme is to remain in force there only for a prescribed period;

(b) include such transitional, consequential or saving provisions as the Secretary of State considers appropriate in connection with the scheme ceasing to be in force in relation to the area or areas at the end of that period.

(7) Despite the fact that the scheme is in force in relation to the area of a local authority (whether by virtue of subsection (6) or otherwise), it shall not have effect in relation to the authority unless it has been adopted by resolution of the authority.

(8) Where a local authority makes any payment under the scheme the authority shall be reimbursed by the Secretary of State in respect of that payment in such manner and subject to such conditions as to claims, records, certificates or other information or evidence as may be prescribed (any reduction made by virtue of subsection (4) being disregarded for the purposes of this subsection).

(9) Subject to any prescribed exceptions or modifications, the provisions of the Administration Act shall have effect in relation to payments under the scheme as they have effect in relation to housing benefit.

(10) For the purposes of this section a dwelling occupied by a housing benefit claimant is in the public or social rented sector if the payments which the claimant is liable to make in respect of the dwelling (and on account of which he is entitled to housing benefit) are to be made to—

(a) a local authority,

(b) a body eligible for registration as a social landlord under Part I of the Housing Act 1996 (whether so registered or not), or

(c) in Scotland, a registered housing association within the meaning of the Housing Associations Act 1985.

1996 c. 52.

1985 c. 69.

(11) In this section—

"dwelling" has the same meaning as in Part VII of the Contributions and Benefits Act (income-related benefits);

"housing benefit claimant", in relation to a dwelling, means a person entitled to housing benefit by virtue of being liable to make payments in respect of the dwelling;

"local authority" has the same meaning as in the Administration Act;

"prescribed" means specified in or determined in accordance with regulations under this section.

80. After paragraph 1 of Schedule 2 to the Child Support Act 1991 there shall be inserted—

Supply of information for child support purposes.
1991 c. 48.

"1A.—(1) This paragraph applies to any information which—

(a) relates to any earnings or other income of an absent parent in respect of a tax year in which he is or was a self-employed earner, and

(b) is required by the Secretary of State or the Department of Health and Social Services for Northern Ireland for any purposes of this Act.

(2) No obligation as to secrecy imposed by statute or otherwise on a person employed in relation to the Inland Revenue shall prevent any such information obtained or held in connection with the assessment or collection of income tax from being disclosed to—

(a) the Secretary of State;

(b) the Department of Health and Social Services for Northern Ireland; or

(c) an officer of either of them authorised to receive such information in connection with the operation of this Act.

(3) This paragraph extends only to disclosure by or under the authority of the Commissioners of Inland Revenue.

(4) Information which is the subject of disclosure to any person by virtue of this paragraph shall not be further disclosed to any person except where the further disclosure is made—

(a) to a person to whom disclosure could be made by virtue of sub-paragraph (2); or

(b) for the purposes of any proceedings (civil or criminal) in connection with the operation of this Act.

(5) For the purposes of this paragraph "self-employed earner" and "tax year" have the same meaning as in Parts I to VI of the Social Security Contributions and Benefits Act 1992."

1992 c. 4.

PART VI

GENERAL

Miscellaneous

Contributions and pensions administration.

81. Schedule 11 (which contains amendments dealing with administrative matters relating to contributions and pensions) shall have effect.

Authorisation of certain expenditure.

82.—(1) Where—

(a) a Minister of the Crown is proposing that or considering whether an Act should change the law as from a specified date, or a date to be determined, and

(b) the Secretary of State is of the opinion that the change is such that, unless expenditure for preparing for the change is incurred during the period before the passing of that Act, it will not be possible for a service for which he has or will have responsibility to be effectively provided as from that date,

the Secretary of State may, subject to subsections (2) and (3), incur such expenditure during that period.

(2) Expenditure is not authorised by virtue of subsection (1) unless—

(a) the Secretary of State has with the consent of the Treasury laid before the House of Commons a report which states—

(i) the change in the law which the Minister of the Crown is proposing or considering, and

(ii) the amount of the expenditure which the Secretary of State proposes to incur and the purposes for which he proposes to incur it; and

(b) the report has been approved by a resolution of the House of Commons.

(3) Expenditure is not authorised by virtue of subsection (1) at any time after the end of the period of two years beginning with the day on which the resolution under subsection (2)(b) is passed.

(4) Subsection (1) is without prejudice to any power of the Secretary of State to incur expenditure otherwise than by virtue of that subsection.

(5) There shall be made out of the National Insurance Fund into the Consolidated Fund such payments as the Secretary of State determines (in accordance with any directions of the Treasury) to be appropriate in consequence of the operation of this section.

(6) Any payments falling to be made by virtue of subsection (5) shall be made at such times and in such manner as may be determined by the Treasury.

(7) In this section "the Secretary of State" means the Secretary of State having responsibility for social security.

Supplementary

83.—(1) Any power under this Act to make regulations or orders (other than orders under section 72(2)) shall be exercisable by statutory instrument.

(2) A statutory instrument—

    (a) which contains (whether alone or with other provisions) regulations made under this Act, and

    (b) which is not subject to any requirement that a draft of the instrument be laid before and approved by a resolution of each House of Parliament,

shall be subject to annulment in pursuance of a resolution of either House of Parliament.

(3) A statutory instrument containing an order under section 27(3) shall be subject to annulment in pursuance of a resolution of either House of Parliament.

(4) Any power under this Act to make regulations or orders may be exercised—

    (a) either in relation to all cases to which the power extends, or in relation to those cases subject to specified exceptions, or in relation to any specified cases or classes of case;

    (b) so as to make, as respects the cases in relation to which it is exercised—

        (i) the full provision to which the power extends or any less provision (whether by way of exception or otherwise);

        (ii) the same provision for all cases in relation to which the power is exercised, or different provision for different cases or different classes of case or different provision as respects the same case or class of case for different purposes of this Act;

        (iii) any such provision either unconditionally or subject to any specified condition.

(5) Where any such power is expressed to be exercisable for alternative purposes it may be exercised in relation to the same case for any or all of those purposes.

(6) Any such power includes power—

    (a) to make such incidental, supplementary, consequential, saving or transitional provision (including provision amending, repealing or revoking enactments) as appears to the authority making the regulations or order to be expedient; and

    (b) to provide for a person to exercise a discretion in dealing with any matter.

(7) Any power to make regulations or an order for the purposes of any provision of this Act is without prejudice to any power to make regulations or an order for the purposes of any other provision of this or any other Act.

(8) Any power conferred by this Act to make regulations or an order relating to—

(a) housing benefit, or

(b) council tax benefit,

includes power to make different provision for different areas or different authorities; and regulations under section 60 or 79 may make different provision for different areas.

(9) Without prejudice to the generality of any of the preceding provisions of this section, regulations under section 60 or 72 may provide for all or any of the provisions of the regulations to apply only in relation to any area or areas specified in the regulations.

(10) Any power to make regulations under Part IV, except sections 28 and 48, shall, if the Treasury so direct, be exercisable only in conjunction with them.

(11) Before exercising any power to make regulations under Part IV, the authority on whom the power is conferred, or, if the power is the subject of a direction under subsection (10), that authority and the Treasury acting jointly, shall consult such persons as the authority, or the authority and the Treasury, may consider appropriate.

Consequential amendments etc.

84.—(1) The consequential amendments specified in Schedule 12 shall have effect.

(2) The Secretary of State may by regulations make such amendments or revocations of any instrument made under an Act as he thinks necessary or expedient in consequence of the coming into force of any of the provisions specified in subsection (4).

(3) The Secretary of State may, for the purposes of or in connection with the coming into force of any of the provisions specified in subsection (4), make by regulations any provision which could be made by an order bringing the provision into force.

(4) The provisions mentioned in subsections (2) and (3) are—

(a) Part IV;

(b) subsection (1) above so far as relating to paragraphs 14 to 63 of Schedule 12; and

(c) section 88 so far as relating to Part III of Schedule 13.

Transitional provisions.

85.—(1) The Secretary of State may, for the purposes of or in connection with the coming into force of any provisions of Parts I and II, by regulations make such transitional adaptations or modifications—

(a) of those provisions, or

(b) in connection with those provisions, of any provisions of—

(i) this Act,

1993 c. 48.   (ii) the Pension Schemes Act 1993, or

1995 c. 26.   (iii) the Pensions Act 1995,

then in force,

as he considers necessary or expedient.

(2) For the purposes of subsection (1), section 88 so far as relating to Part I of Schedule 13, together with that Part of that Schedule, shall be taken to be comprised in Part II of this Act.

(3) No pension sharing order may be made—

(a) under section 24B of the Matrimonial Causes Act 1973 if the proceedings in which the decree is granted were begun before the day on which section 19 comes into force, or

(b) under section 31(7B) of that Act if the marriage was dissolved by a decree granted in proceedings so begun.

(4) Paragraph 3 of Schedule 3 does not have effect if the proceedings in which the decree is granted were begun before the day on which section 19 comes into force.

(5) Where an action of divorce or an action for declarator of nullity has been brought before the day on which section 20 comes into force—

(a) no pension-sharing order may be made under section 8(1) of the Family Law (Scotland) Act 1985, and

1985 c. 37.

(b) neither paragraph (f) of section 28(1) nor paragraph (f) of section 48(1) shall apply,

in relation to that divorce or declarator.

(6) The Secretary of State may by regulations make such transitional or consequential provision, or such savings, as he considers necessary or expedient for the purposes of or in connection with—

(a) the coming into force of any provision of Part V, or

(b) the operation of any enactment repealed or amended by a provision of Part V during any period when the repeal or amendment is not wholly in force.

(7) For the purposes of subsection (6), section 88 so far as relating to Parts IV to VII of Schedule 13, together with those Parts of that Schedule, shall be taken to be comprised in Part V of this Act.

86.—(1) There shall be paid out of money provided by Parliament—

General financial provisions.

(a) any expenditure incurred by a Minister of the Crown or government department under this Act; and

(b) any increase attributable to this Act in the sums which under any other Act are payable out of money so provided.

(2) There shall be paid into the Consolidated Fund any increase attributable to this Act in the sums which under any other Act are payable into that Fund.

87. An Order in Council under paragraph 1(1)(b) of Schedule 1 to the Northern Ireland Act 1974 (legislation for Northern Ireland in the interim period) which contains a statement that it is made only for purposes corresponding to those of this Act—

Corresponding provisions for Northern Ireland.
1974 c. 28.

(a) shall not be subject to paragraph 1(4) and (5) of that Schedule (affirmative resolution of both Houses of Parliament), but

(b) shall be subject to annulment in pursuance of a resolution of either House of Parliament.

88. The enactments specified in Schedule 13 (which include certain enactments no longer of practical utility) are hereby repealed to the extent specified in the third column of that Schedule.

Repeals.

89.—(1) Subject to the provisions of this section, the provisions of this Act shall not come into force until such day as the Secretary of State may by order appoint.

(2) The following provisions shall not come into force until such day as the Lord Chancellor may by order appoint—

(a) sections 19, 21 and 22;

(b) section 84(1) so far as relating to paragraphs 1 to 4 and 64 to 66 of Schedule 12;

(c) section 85(3) and (4); and

1973 c. 18.
1984 c. 42.
1996 c. 27.

(d) section 88 so far as relating to the entries in Part II of Schedule 13 in respect of the Matrimonial Causes Act 1973, the Matrimonial and Family Proceedings Act 1984 and sections 9(8) and 16 of the Family Law Act 1996.

(3) The following provisions shall not come into force until such day as the Treasury may by order appoint—

(a) sections 73 to 78;

(b) section 84(1) so far as relating to paragraphs 74, 76 to 78 and 84 to 86 of Schedule 12; and

(c) section 88 so far as relating to Parts VI and VII of Schedule 13.

(4) The following provisions come into force on the day on which this Act is passed—

(a) sections 52, 57, 58, 60, 68 and 71;

(b) section 70 so far as relating to Part V of Schedule 8;

(c) section 72;

(d) sections 79 to 83;

(e) section 84(1) so far as relating to paragraphs 13, 79 to 83 and 87 of Schedule 12;

(f) section 84(2) to (4);

(g) section 85(1), (2), (6) and (7); and

(h) sections 86 and 87, this section and sections 90 and 91.

(5) The following provisions come into force on the day on which this Act is passed, but for the purpose only of the exercise of any power to make regulations—

(a) Parts I to IV;

(b) sections 59 and 61; and

(c) section 70 so far as relating to paragraph 23 of Schedule 8.

(6) Without prejudice to section 83, an order under this section may appoint different days for different purposes or different areas.

Extent.

90.—(1) The following provisions extend to England and Wales only—

(a) section 15;

(b) paragraph 2 of Schedule 2, and section 18 so far as relating thereto;

(c) sections 19, 21 and 22 and Schedules 3 and 4;

(d) paragraphs 1 to 4, 64 to 66 and 70 to 72 of Schedule 12, and section 84(1) so far as relating thereto; and

(e) section 85(3) and (4).

(2) The following provisions extend to Scotland only—

    (a) sections 13 and 16;

    (b) paragraph 1 of Schedule 2, and section 18 so far as relating thereto;

    (c) section 20;

    (d) paragraphs 5 to 12 and 67 to 69 of Schedule 12, and section 84(1) so far as relating thereto; and

    (e) section 85(5).

(3) The following provisions extend to England and Wales and Scotland only—

    (a) Part I;

    (b) sections 9 to 12, 14 and 17;

    (c) Schedule 2 (except for paragraphs 1, 2, 3(1), 7(2) and 16), and section 18 so far as relating thereto;

    (d) sections 23, 24 and 26;

    (e) Part IV except sections 42 to 44;

    (f) Chapter I of Part V (except paragraph 1 of Schedule 8, and section 70 so far as relating thereto);

    (g) sections 73, 75 and 77 and Schedule 9;

    (h) section 79;

    (i) paragraphs 1 to 8, 20 to 23, 32(b), 33, 35 and 37 of Schedule 11, and section 81 so far as relating thereto;

    (j) paragraphs 14 to 63, 66(17), 76 to 80, 82, 83 and 87 of Schedule 12, and section 84(1) so far as relating thereto; and

    (k) section 84(2) to (4).

(4) The following provisions extend to England and Wales, Scotland and Northern Ireland—

    (a) paragraphs 3(1) and 16 of Schedule 2, and section 18 so far as relating thereto;

    (b) sections 42 to 44;

    (c) paragraph 1 of Schedule 8, and section 70 so far as relating thereto;

    (d) section 80;

    (e) paragraphs 29 to 31 and 32(a) of Schedule 11, and section 81 so far as relating thereto;

    (f) sections 82 and 83;

    (g) paragraphs 13, 73 to 75 and 81 of Schedule 12, and section 84(1) so far as relating thereto;

    (h) sections 85(1), (2), (6) and (7) and 86; and

    (i) section 89, this section and section 91.

(5) The following provisions extend to Northern Ireland only—

    (a) paragraph 7(2) of Schedule 2, and section 18 so far as relating thereto;

    (b) sections 74, 76 and 78 and Schedule 10;

(c) paragraphs 9 to 19, 24 to 28, 34, 36 and 38 of Schedule 11, and section 81 so far as relating thereto;

(d) paragraphs 84 to 86 of Schedule 12, and section 84(1) so far as relating thereto; and

(e) section 87.

(6) Nothing in the preceding provisions of this section applies to any repeal made by this Act; and the extent of any such repeal is the same as that of the enactment repealed.

Short title, general interpretation and Scottish devolution.

91.—(1) This Act may be cited as the Welfare Reform and Pensions Act 1999.

(2) In this Act—

1992 c. 5.

"the Administration Act" means the Social Security Administration Act 1992;

1992 c. 4.

"the Contributions and Benefits Act" means the Social Security Contributions and Benefits Act 1992.

(3) In this Act, except sections 84(2) and (3), 85(1) and (6) and 89, and in any Act amended by this Act, references to the coming into force of any provision of this Act are to its coming into force otherwise than for the purpose of authorising the making of regulations.

1998 c. 46.

(4) For the purposes of the Scotland Act 1998, the following provisions shall be taken to be pre-commencement enactments within the meaning of that Act—

(a) paragraphs 8(3) and (4) and 10 of Schedule 12; and

(b) so far as relating to those provisions, sections 83, 84(1) and 89(1) and (5).

SCHEDULES

SCHEDULE 1   Section 6.

APPLICATION OF 1993 AND 1995 ACTS TO REGISTERED SCHEMES

1.—(1) The provisions specified in sub-paragraph (2) shall apply as if any pension scheme established under a trust which—

(a) is not an occupational pension scheme, but

(b) is or has been registered under section 2,

were an occupational pension scheme.

(2) The provisions are—

(a) subsections (4) to (9) of section 175 of the 1993 Act (levies towards certain expenditure); and

(b) the following provisions of Part I of the 1995 Act—

(i) sections 3 to 11, 13 and 15 (supervision by the Authority) except sections 8(1) and (2), 11(3)(c) and 15(1);

(ii) sections 27 to 31 (trustees: general);

(iii) sections 32 to 36 and 39 (functions of trustees) except the reference to sections 16(3)(b) and 25(2) in section 32(4), the reference to section 56 in section 35(2) and section 35(5)(b);

(iv) section 41 (functions of trustees or managers);

(v) sections 47 and 48 (advisers);

(vi) section 49 (receipts, payment and records) except subsections (5) and (8) to (13);

(vii) section 50 (resolution of disputes);

(viii) section 68 (power of trustees to modify scheme by resolution) except subsection (3);

(ix) sections 81 to 86 (the compensation payments) except section 81(1)(b);

(x) sections 91, 92 and 94 (assignment and forfeiture etc.) except section 91(5)(d);

(xi) section 96(2)(c) (review of decisions of the Authority);

(xii) section 108 (other permitted disclosures);

(xiii) section 110 (provision of information to Compensation Board);

(xiv) section 117 (overriding requirements); and

(xv) sections 124 and 125 (interpretation).

(3) Section 47(9) of the 1995 Act (as applied by sub-paragraph (1)) shall have effect as if the reference to any person who is or has been the employer were a reference to any person who, in pursuance of section 3(5), is or has been required—

(a) to deduct an employee's contributions to the scheme from his remuneration; and

(b) to pay them to the trustees or managers of the scheme or to a prescribed person.

(4) Section 68 of the 1995 Act (as so applied) shall have effect as if the purposes specified in subsection (2) included enabling the conditions set out in section 1 to be fulfilled in relation to the scheme.

(5) Section 124(1) of the 1995 Act (as so applied) shall have effect as if the definition of "member" were omitted.

2.—(1) Sections 98 to 100 of the 1995 Act (gathering information: the Authority) shall apply as if any pension scheme which—

(a) is not an occupational pension scheme, but

(b) is or has been registered under section 2,

were an occupational pension scheme.

(2) Section 99 of the 1995 Act (as applied by sub-paragraph (1)) shall have effect as if the regulatory provisions, for the purposes of subsection (1) of that section, were—

(a) provisions made by or under the provisions specified in paragraph 1(2), other than section 110 of the 1995 Act;

(b) sections 111, 115 and 116 of that Act;

(c) any provisions in force in Northern Ireland corresponding to the provisions mentioned in paragraphs (a) and (b); and

(d) sections 1 and 2(4) to (6).

(3) Section 100 of the 1995 Act (as so applied) shall have effect as if the references in subsections (1)(c)(i) and (4)(b) to that Act included references to section 2(5).

(4) Any reference in this paragraph or paragraph 3 which is or includes a reference to, or to any subsection of, section 1 or 2 includes a reference to any provision in force in Northern Ireland corresponding to that section or (as the case may be) that subsection; and the reference in sub-paragraph (1) to any pension scheme includes a personal pension scheme (as well as an occupational scheme) within the meaning of the Pension Schemes (Northern Ireland) Act 1993.

1993 c. 49.

3.—(1) Section 99 of the 1995 Act shall have effect in relation to any occupational pension scheme which is or has been registered under section 2 as if the regulatory provisions for the purposes of subsection (1) of section 99 included sections 1 and 2(4) to (6).

(2) Section 100 of the 1995 Act shall have effect in relation to any occupational pension scheme which is or has been registered under section 2 as if the references in subsections (1)(c)(i) and (4)(b) to that Act included references to section 2(5).

Section 18.

SCHEDULE 2

PENSIONS: MISCELLANEOUS AMENDMENTS

Income payments orders against pension payments

1985 c. 66.

1. In section 32(2) of the Bankruptcy (Scotland) Act 1985 (vesting of estate, and dealings of debtor, after sequestration), at the beginning insert "Notwithstanding anything in section 11 or 12 of the Welfare Reform and Pensions Act 1999,".

1986 c. 45.

2. In section 310(7) of the Insolvency Act 1986 (bankrupt's income against which income payments orders may be made includes certain payments under pension schemes), after "employment and" insert "(despite anything in section 11 or 12 of the Welfare Reform and Pensions Act 1999)".

Extended meaning of "personal pension scheme"

3.—(1) In the Pension Schemes Act 1993—

1993 c. 48.

    (a) in section 1 (categories of pension schemes), in the definition of "personal pension scheme", for "employed earners" substitute "earners (whether employed or self-employed)"; and

    (b) in section 181(1) (general interpretation), for the definition of "employed earner" substitute—

        ""employed earner" and "self-employed earner" have the meanings given by section 2 of the Social Security Contributions and Benefits Act 1992;".

1992 c. 4.

(2) In consequence of sub-paragraph (1), the following provisions of that Act shall cease to have effect, namely—

    (a) in subsection (2)(a)(ii) of section 73 (short service benefit), the words "or a self-employed pension arrangement" and "or arrangement";

    (b) in subsection (2)(a) of section 96 (exercise of option under section 95), sub-paragraph (iii) and the word "or" immediately preceding that sub-paragraph; and

    (c) in subsection (1) of section 181 (general interpretation), the definition of "self-employed pension arrangement".

Revaluation of earnings factors: meaning of "relevant year"

4. In section 16(5) of the Pension Schemes Act 1993 (revaluation of earnings factors for purposes of section 14: early leavers etc.), for the definition of "relevant year" substitute—

    ""relevant year" means any tax year in the earner's working life,".

Interim arrangements

5.—(1) Section 28 of the Pension Schemes Act 1993 (ways of giving effect to protected rights) is amended as follows.

(2) In subsection (1)—

    (a) omit paragraph (aa) (but not the final "and"); and

    (b) in paragraph (b), for "permitted" substitute "provided for".

(3) For subsection (1A) substitute—

    "(1A) Where the scheme is a personal pension scheme which provides for the member to elect to receive payments in accordance with this subsection, and the member so elects, effect shall be given to his protected rights during the interim period by the making of payments under an interim arrangement which—

        (a) complies with section 28A, and

        (b) satisfies such conditions as may be prescribed;

    and in such a case subsections (2) to (4) accordingly apply as regards giving effect to his protected rights as from the end of that period."

(4) In subsection (3) for "(1A)(a) or" substitute "(1A) or".

Effect of certain orders on guaranteed minimum pensions

6. In section 47 of the Pension Schemes Act 1993 (entitlement to guaranteed minimum pension for the purposes of the relationship with social security benefits), after subsection (6) (which is inserted by section 32(4) of this Act) add—

1986 c. 45.
1985 c. 66.

"(7) For the purposes of section 46, a person shall be treated as entitled to any guaranteed minimum pension to which he would have been entitled but for any order under section 342A of the Insolvency Act 1986 (recovery of excessive pension contributions) or under section 36A of the Bankruptcy (Scotland) Act 1985."

Mandatory payment of contributions equivalent premiums

1993 c. 48.

7.—(1) In section 55 of the Pension Schemes Act 1993 (contributions equivalent premiums)—

(a) in subsection (2), after "the prescribed person" insert "shall, if subsection (2B) applies, pay and otherwise";

(b) in subsection (2A), omit the words following paragraph (e); and

(c) after that subsection insert—

"(2B) Except in prescribed circumstances, this subsection applies in any case where the earner has no accrued right to any benefit under the scheme.

(2C) Where a contributions equivalent premium is required to be paid in respect of an earner by virtue of subsection (2), the prescribed person must notify the Inland Revenue of that fact within the prescribed period and in the prescribed manner."

1993 c. 49.

(2) In section 51 of the Pension Schemes (Northern Ireland) Act 1993 (contributions equivalent premiums)—

(a) in subsection (2), after "the prescribed person" insert "shall, if subsection (2B) applies, pay and otherwise";

(b) in subsection (2A), omit the words following paragraph (e); and

(c) after that subsection insert—

"(2B) Except in prescribed circumstances, this subsection applies in any case where the earner has no accrued right to any benefit under the scheme.

(2C) Where a contributions equivalent premium is required to be paid in respect of an earner by virtue of subsection (2), the prescribed person must notify the Inland Revenue of that fact within the prescribed period and in the prescribed manner."

Payment by Secretary of State of unpaid pension contributions

8.—(1) Paragraph 2 of Schedule 4 to the Pension Schemes Act 1993 (priority in bankruptcy for amounts paid by Secretary of State in respect of unpaid pension contributions) is amended as follows.

(2) For sub-paragraphs (1) to (3) substitute—

"(1) This Schedule applies to any sum owed on account of an employer's contributions to a salary related contracted-out scheme which were payable in the period of 12 months immediately preceding the relevant date.

(1A) The amount of the debt having priority by virtue of sub-paragraph (1) shall be taken to be an amount equal to the appropriate amount.

(2) This Schedule applies to any sum owed on account of an employer's minimum payments to a money purchase contracted-out scheme falling to be made in the period of 12 months immediately preceding the relevant date.

(3) In so far as payments cannot from the terms of the scheme be identified as falling within sub-paragraph (2), the amount of the debt having priority by virtue of that sub-paragraph shall be taken to be an amount equal to the appropriate amount.

SCH. 2

(3A) In sub-paragraph (1A) or (3) "the appropriate amount" means the aggregate of—

(a) the percentage for non-contributing earners of the total reckonable earnings paid or payable, in the period of 12 months referred to in sub-paragraph (1) or (2) (as the case may be), to or for the benefit of non-contributing earners; and

(b) the percentage for contributing earners of the total reckonable earnings paid or payable, in that period, to or for the benefit of contributing earners."

(3) In sub-paragraph (4), for "sub-paragraph (3)" substitute "sub-paragraph (3A)".

Supervision by the Occupational Pensions Regulatory Authority

9. In section 3(2)(b) of the Pensions Act 1995 (power of Authority to remove pension scheme trustee to whom section 3 applies by virtue of any other provision of Part I of the Act), for "this Part" substitute "this or any other Act".

1995 c. 26.

10. In section 8(4) of the Pensions Act 1995 (provision which may be contained in orders made by the Authority appointing pension scheme trustees), omit the word "or" at the end of paragraph (a).

11. In section 10 of the Pensions Act 1995 (imposition of civil penalties by the Authority), after subsection (8) insert—

"(8A) Any penalty recoverable under this section—

(a) shall, if a county court so orders, be recoverable by execution issued from the county court or otherwise as if it were payable under an order of that court; and

(b) may be enforced as if it were an extract registered decree arbitral bearing a warrant for execution issued by the sheriff court of any sheriffdom in Scotland."

Occupational pension schemes: institutions who may hold money deposited by trustees etc.

12.—(1) Section 49 of the Pensions Act 1995 (other responsibilities of trustees, employers, etc.) is amended as follows.

(2) In each of subsections (1) and (5) (money to be kept by trustees or employers in accounts with institutions authorised under the Banking Act 1987), for "an institution authorised under the Banking Act 1987" substitute "a relevant institution".

1987 c. 22.

(3) After subsection (1) insert—

"(1A) In this section "relevant institution" means—

(a) an institution authorised under the Banking Act 1987;

(b) an institution within any of paragraphs 1 to 6 of Schedule 2 to that Act (institutions not requiring authorisation); or

(c) a European authorised institution within the meaning of the Banking Coordination (Second Council Directive) Regulations 1992 which may lawfully accept deposits in the United Kingdom in accordance with those regulations."

S.I. 1992/3218.

Annual increase in rate of pension

1995 c. 26.

13. In section 54(3) of the Pensions Act 1995 (supplementary provisions about annual increases in pensions), in the definition of "appropriate percentage", for the words from "the revaluation period" onwards substitute "the latest revaluation period specified in the order under paragraph 2 of Schedule 3 to the

1993 c. 48.

Pension Schemes Act 1993 (revaluation of accrued pension benefits) which is in force at the time of the increase (expressions used in this definition having the same meaning as in that paragraph),".

Occupational pension schemes: certificates etc. relating to minimum funding requirement

14.—(1) In section 58 of the Pensions Act 1995 (schedules of contributions), in subsection (6)(a) (certification by actuary of adequacy of rates of contributions to meet minimum funding requirement)—

(a) for the words from "on the date" to "is met," substitute "it appears to him that the minimum funding requirement was met on the prescribed date,"; and

(b) omit the words "continue to".

(2) In section 59 of that Act (determination of contributions: supplementary), in subsection (3) (duty of trustees etc. to prepare report of failure to meet minimum funding requirement), after "they must" insert ", within such further period as may be prescribed,".

Excess assets of wound-up schemes

15. In section 77(5) of the Pensions Act 1995 (penalties for trustees who deal improperly with excess assets of wound-up occupational pension schemes), for "section 3 applies" substitute "sections 3 and 10 apply".

Pensions Compensation Board

16.—(1) In section 79(1) of the Pensions Act 1995 (annual reports of Pensions Compensation Board)—

(a) for "the first twelve months of their existence, and a report for each succeeding period of twelve months," substitute "each financial year of the Board"; and

(b) at the end insert—

"Sub-paragraph (4) of paragraph 17 of Schedule 2 (meaning of "financial year") applies for the purposes of this subsection as for those of that paragraph."

(2) The amendments made by sub-paragraph (1) have effect in relation to the financial year beginning on the first 6th April falling after that sub-paragraph comes into force and to each subsequent financial year; and the period which begins with the last 1st August before, and ends with the 5th April immediately preceding, that 6th April shall be taken to be the last period in respect of which the Board are required to prepare a report under section 79(1) as originally enacted.

Diligence against pensions: Scotland

1995 c. 26.

17. In section 94(3) of the Pensions Act 1995 (application of sections 91 and 92 to Scotland), at the end insert—

"(f) after subsection 91(4) there is inserted—

1987 c. 18.

"(4A) Subject to section 73(3)(d) of the Debtors (Scotland) Act 1987, nothing in this section prevents any diligence mentioned in section 46 of that Act being done against a pension under an occupational pension scheme.""

Welfare Reform and Pensions Act 1999   c. **30**   107

SCH. 2

Pensionable service

18. In section 124(3) of the Pensions Act 1995 (matters to be disregarded in determining "pensionable service"), at the end insert—

> "but, in its application for the purposes of section 51, paragraph (b) does not affect the operation of any rules of the scheme by virtue of which a period of service is to be rounded up or down by a period of less than a month."

1995 c. 26.

Occupational pension schemes: rights of employee who is director of corporate trustee

19.—(1) The Employment Rights Act 1996 is amended as follows.

1996 c. 18.

(2) In section 46 (employee who is a trustee of a pension scheme not to be subject to detriment referable to his carrying out his functions as such a trustee), after subsection (2) insert—

> "(2A) This section applies to an employee who is a director of a company which is a trustee of a relevant occupational pension scheme as it applies to an employee who is a trustee of such a scheme (references to such a trustee being read for this purpose as references to such a director)."

(3) In section 58 (right to time off for pension scheme trustees), after subsection (2) insert—

> "(2A) This section applies to an employee who is a director of a company which is a trustee of a relevant occupational pension scheme as it applies to an employee who is a trustee of such a scheme (references to such a trustee being read for this purpose as references to such a director)."

(4) In section 102 (unfair dismissal of pension scheme trustees), after subsection (1) insert—

> "(1A) This section applies to an employee who is a director of a company which is a trustee of a relevant occupational pension scheme as it applies to an employee who is a trustee of such a scheme (references to such a trustee being read for this purpose as references to such a director)."

SCHEDULE 3

Section 19.

PENSION SHARING ORDERS: ENGLAND AND WALES

1. The Matrimonial Causes Act 1973 is amended as follows.

1973 c. 18.

2. After section 21 there is inserted—

"Pension sharing orders.

21A.—(1) For the purposes of this Act, a pension sharing order is an order which—

> (a) provides that one party's—
>> (i) shareable rights under a specified pension arrangement, or
>> (ii) shareable state scheme rights,
>> be subject to pension sharing for the benefit of the other party, and
> (b) specifies the percentage value to be transferred.

(2) In subsection (1) above—

    (a) the reference to shareable rights under a pension arrangement is to rights in relation to which pension sharing is available under Chapter I of Part IV of the Welfare Reform and Pensions Act 1999, or under corresponding Northern Ireland legislation,

    (b) the reference to shareable state scheme rights is to rights in relation to which pension sharing is available under Chapter II of Part IV of the Welfare Reform and Pensions Act 1999, or under corresponding Northern Ireland legislation, and

    (c) "party" means a party to a marriage."

    3. In section 24 (property adjustment orders in connection with divorce proceedings, etc), in paragraphs (c) and (d) of subsection (1), there is inserted at the end ", other than one in the form of a pension arrangement (within the meaning of section 25D below)".

    4. After section 24A there is inserted—

"Pension sharing orders in connection with divorce proceedings etc.

    24B.—(1) On granting a decree of divorce or a decree of nullity of marriage or at any time thereafter (whether before or after the decree is made absolute), the court may, on an application made under this section, make one or more pension sharing orders in relation to the marriage.

    (2) A pension sharing order under this section is not to take effect unless the decree on or after which it is made has been made absolute.

    (3) A pension sharing order under this section may not be made in relation to a pension arrangement which—

    (a) is the subject of a pension sharing order in relation to the marriage, or

    (b) has been the subject of pension sharing between the parties to the marriage.

    (4) A pension sharing order under this section may not be made in relation to shareable state scheme rights if—

    (a) such rights are the subject of a pension sharing order in relation to the marriage, or

    (b) such rights have been the subject of pension sharing between the parties to the marriage.

    (5) A pension sharing order under this section may not be made in relation to the rights of a person under a pension arrangement if there is in force a requirement imposed by virtue of section 25B or 25C below which relates to benefits or future benefits to which he is entitled under the pension arrangement.

Pension sharing orders: duty to stay.

    24C.—(1) No pension sharing order may be made so as to take effect before the end of such period after the making of the order as may be prescribed by regulations made by the Lord Chancellor.

    (2) The power to make regulations under this section shall be exercisable by statutory instrument which shall be subject to annulment in pursuance of a resolution of either House of Parliament.

Pension sharing orders: apportionment of charges.

    24D. If a pension sharing order relates to rights under a pension arrangement, the court may include in the order provision about the apportionment between the parties of any charge under section 41 of the Welfare Reform and Pensions

Act 1999 (charges in respect of pension sharing costs), or under corresponding Northern Ireland legislation."

5. In section 25 (matters to which the court is to have regard in deciding how to exercise its powers with respect to financial relief)—

(a) in subsection (1), for "or 24A" there is substituted ", 24A or 24B", and

(b) in subsection (2), for "or 24A" there is substituted ", 24A or 24B".

6. In section 25A(1) (court's duty to consider desirability of exercising power to achieve clean break), for "or 24A" there is substituted ", 24A or 24B".

7.—(1) Section 31 (variation, discharge etc. of certain orders for financial relief) is amended as follows.

(2) In subsection (2), at the end there is inserted—

"(g) a pension sharing order under section 24B above which is made at a time before the decree has been made absolute."

(3) After subsection (4) there is inserted—

"(4A) In relation to an order which falls within paragraph (g) of subsection (2) above ("the subsection (2) order")—

(a) the powers conferred by this section may be exercised—

(i) only on an application made before the subsection (2) order has or, but for paragraph (b) below, would have taken effect; and

(ii) only if, at the time when the application is made, the decree has not been made absolute; and

(b) an application made in accordance with paragraph (a) above prevents the subsection (2) order from taking effect before the application has been dealt with.

(4B) No variation of a pension sharing order shall be made so as to take effect before the decree is made absolute.

(4C) The variation of a pension sharing order prevents the order taking effect before the end of such period after the making of the variation as may be prescribed by regulations made by the Lord Chancellor."

(4) In subsection (5)—

(a) for "(7F)" there is substituted "(7G)",

(b) for "or (e)" there is substituted ", (e) or (g)", and

(c) after "property adjustment order" there is inserted "or pension sharing order".

(5) In subsection (7B), after paragraph (b) there is inserted—

"(ba) one or more pension sharing orders;".

(6) After subsection (7F) there is inserted—

"(7G) Subsections (3) to (5) of section 24B above apply in relation to a pension sharing order under subsection (7B) above as they apply in relation to a pension sharing order under that section."

(7) After subsection (14) there is inserted—

"(15) The power to make regulations under subsection (4C) above shall be exercisable by statutory instrument which shall be subject to annulment in pursuance of a resolution of either House of Parliament."

8. In section 33A (consent orders), in subsection (3), in the definition of "order for financial relief", after "24A" there is inserted ", 24B".

9. In section 37 (avoidance of transactions intended to prevent or reduce financial relief), in subsection (1), after "24," there is inserted "24B,".

10. After section 40 there is inserted—

"Appeals relating to pension sharing orders which have taken effect.

40A.—(1) Subsections (2) and (3) below apply where an appeal against a pension sharing order is begun on or after the day on which the order takes effect.

(2) If the pension sharing order relates to a person's rights under a pension arrangement, the appeal court may not set aside or vary the order if the person responsible for the pension arrangement has acted to his detriment in reliance on the taking effect of the order.

(3) If the pension sharing order relates to a person's shareable state scheme rights, the appeal court may not set aside or vary the order if the Secretary of State has acted to his detriment in reliance on the taking effect of the order.

(4) In determining for the purposes of subsection (2) or (3) above whether a person has acted to his detriment in reliance on the taking effect of the order, the appeal court may disregard any detriment which in its opinion is insignificant.

(5) Where subsection (2) or (3) above applies, the appeal court may make such further orders (including one or more pension sharing orders) as it thinks fit for the purpose of putting the parties in the position it considers appropriate.

(6) Section 24C above only applies to a pension sharing order under this section if the decision of the appeal court can itself be the subject of an appeal.

(7) In subsection (2) above, the reference to the person responsible for the pension arrangement is to be read in accordance with section 25D(4) above."

11. In section 52 (interpretation), in subsection (2), for "and" at the end of paragraph (a) there is substituted—

"(aa) references to pension sharing orders shall be construed in accordance with section 21A above; and".

Section 21.

SCHEDULE 4

AMENDMENTS OF SECTIONS 25B TO 25D OF THE MATRIMONIAL CAUSES ACT 1973

1973 c. 18.

1.—(1) Section 25B of the Matrimonial Causes Act 1973 is amended as follows.

(2) In subsection (1), for "scheme", wherever occurring, there is substituted "arrangement".

(3) Subsection (2) ceases to have effect.

(4) In subsection (3), for "scheme" there is substituted "arrangement".

(5) In subsection (4)—

(a) for "scheme", wherever occurring, there is substituted "arrangement", and

(b) for "trustees or managers of" there is substituted "person responsible for".

(6) For subsection (5) there is substituted—

"(5) The order must express the amount of any payment required to be made by virtue of subsection (4) above as a percentage of the payment which becomes due to the party with pension rights."

(7) In subsection (6)—

(a) for "trustees or managers", in the first place, there is substituted "person responsible for the arrangement", and

(b) for "the trustees or managers", in the second place, there is substituted "his".

(8) In subsection (7)—

(a) for the words from "may require any" to "those benefits" there is substituted "has a right of commutation under the arrangement, the order may require him to exercise it to any extent",

(b) for "the payment of any amount commuted" there is substituted "any payment due in consequence of commutation", and

(c) for "scheme" there is substituted "arrangement".

(9) After that subsection there is inserted—

"(7A) The power conferred by subsection (7) above may not be exercised for the purpose of commuting a benefit payable to the party with pension rights to a benefit payable to the other party.

(7B) The power conferred by subsection (4) or (7) above may not be exercised in relation to a pension arrangement which—

(a) is the subject of a pension sharing order in relation to the marriage, or

(b) has been the subject of pension sharing between the parties to the marriage.

(7C) In subsection (1) above, references to benefits under a pension arrangement include any benefits by way of pension, whether under a pension arrangement or not."

2.—(1) Section 25C of that Act is amended as follows.

(2) In subsection (1), for "scheme" there is substituted "arrangement".

(3) In subsection (2)—

(a) in paragraph (a)—

(i) for the words from "trustees" to "have" there is substituted "person responsible for the pension arrangement in question has", and

(ii) for "them" there is substituted "him", and

(b) in paragraph (c), for "trustees or managers of the pension scheme" there is substituted "person responsible for the pension arrangement".

(4) In subsection (3)—

(a) for "trustees or managers" there is substituted "person responsible for the arrangement", and

(b) for "the trustees, or managers," there is substituted "his".

(5) At the end there is inserted—

"(4) The powers conferred by this section may not be exercised in relation to a pension arrangement which—

(a) is the subject of a pension sharing order in relation to the marriage, or

(b) has been the subject of pension sharing between the parties to the marriage."

3.—(1) Section 25D of that Act is amended as follows.

(2) For subsection (1) there is substituted—

"(1) Where—

(a) an order made under section 23 above by virtue of section 25B or 25C above imposes any requirement on the person responsible for a pension arrangement ("the first arrangement") and the party with pension rights acquires rights under another pension arrangement ("the new arrangement") which are derived (directly or indirectly) from the whole of his rights under the first arrangement, and

(b) the person responsible for the new arrangement has been given notice in accordance with regulations made by the Lord Chancellor,

the order shall have effect as if it had been made instead in respect of the person responsible for the new arrangement."

(3) In subsection (2)—

(a) for "Regulations may" there is substituted "The Lord Chancellor may by regulations",

(b) in paragraph (a), for "trustees or managers of a pension scheme" there is substituted "person responsible for a pension arrangement",

(c) after that paragraph there is inserted—

"(ab) make, in relation to payment under a mistaken belief as to the continuation in force of a provision included by virtue of section 25B or 25C above in an order under section 23 above, provision about the rights or liabilities of the payer, the payee or the person to whom the payment was due,"

(d) after paragraph (b) there is inserted—

"(ba) make provision for the person responsible for a pension arrangement to be discharged in prescribed circumstances from a requirement imposed by virtue of section 25B or 25C above,"

(e) paragraphs (c) and (d) are omitted,

(f) for paragraph (e) there is substituted—

"(e) make provision about calculation and verification in relation to the valuation of—

(i) benefits under a pension arrangement, or

(ii) shareable state scheme rights,

for the purposes of the court's functions in connection with the exercise of any of its powers under this Part of this Act.", and

(g) the words after paragraph (e) are omitted.

(4) After that subsection there is inserted—

"(2A) Regulations under subsection (2)(e) above may include—

(a) provision for calculation or verification in accordance with guidance from time to time prepared by a prescribed person, and

(b) provision by reference to regulations under section 30 or 49(4) of the Welfare Reform and Pensions Act 1999.

(2B) Regulations under subsection (2) above may make different provision for different cases.

(2C) Power to make regulations under this section shall be exercisable by statutory instrument which shall be subject to annulment in pursuance of a resolution of either House of Parliament."

(5) For subsections (3) and (4) there is substituted—

"(3) In this section and sections 25B and 25C above—

"occupational pension scheme" has the same meaning as in the Pension Schemes Act 1993;

1993 c. 48.

"the party with pension rights" means the party to the marriage who has or is likely to have benefits under a pension arrangement and "the other party" means the other party to the marriage;

"pension arrangement" means—

(a) an occupational pension scheme,

(b) a personal pension scheme,

(c) a retirement annuity contract,

(d) an annuity or insurance policy purchased, or transferred, for the purpose of giving effect to rights under an occupational pension scheme or a personal pension scheme, and

(e) an annuity purchased, or entered into, for the purpose of discharging liability in respect of a pension credit under section 29(1)(b) of the Welfare Reform and Pensions Act 1999 or under corresponding Northern Ireland legislation;

"personal pension scheme" has the same meaning as in the Pension Schemes Act 1993;

"prescribed" means prescribed by regulations;

"retirement annuity contract" means a contract or scheme approved under Chapter III of Part XIV of the Income and Corporation Taxes Act 1988;

1988 c. 1.

"shareable state scheme rights" has the same meaning as in section 21A(1) above; and

"trustees or managers", in relation to an occupational pension scheme or a personal pension scheme, means—

(a) in the case of a scheme established under a trust, the trustees of the scheme, and

(b) in any other case, the managers of the scheme.

(4) In this section and sections 25B and 25C above, references to the person responsible for a pension arrangement are—

(a) in the case of an occupational pension scheme or a personal pension scheme, to the trustees or managers of the scheme,

(b) in the case of a retirement annuity contract or an annuity falling within paragraph (d) or (e) of the definition of "pension arrangement" above, the provider of the annuity, and

(c) in the case of an insurance policy falling within paragraph (d) of the definition of that expression, the insurer."

Section 35.

SCHEDULE 5

PENSION CREDITS: MODE OF DISCHARGE

Funded pension schemes

1.—(1) This paragraph applies to a pension credit which derives from—

(a) a funded occupational pension scheme, or

(b) a personal pension scheme.

(2) The trustees or managers of the scheme from which a pension credit to which this paragraph applies derives may discharge their liability in respect of the credit by conferring appropriate rights under that scheme on the person entitled to the credit—

(a) with his consent, or

(b) in accordance with regulations made by the Secretary of State.

(3) The trustees or managers of the scheme from which a pension credit to which this paragraph applies derives may discharge their liability in respect of the credit by paying the amount of the credit to the person responsible for a qualifying arrangement with a view to acquiring rights under that arrangement for the person entitled to the credit if—

(a) the qualifying arrangement is not disqualified as a destination for the credit,

(b) the person responsible for that arrangement is able and willing to accept payment in respect of the credit, and

(c) payment is made with the consent of the person entitled to the credit, or in accordance with regulations made by the Secretary of State.

(4) For the purposes of sub-paragraph (2), no account is to be taken of consent of the person entitled to the pension credit unless—

(a) it is given after receipt of notice in writing of an offer to discharge liability in respect of the credit by making a payment under sub-paragraph (3), or

(b) it is not withdrawn within 7 days of receipt of such notice.

Unfunded public service pension schemes

2.—(1) This paragraph applies to a pension credit which derives from an occupational pension scheme which is—

(a) not funded, and

(b) a public service pension scheme.

(2) The trustees or managers of the scheme from which a pension credit to which this paragraph applies derives may discharge their liability in respect of the credit by conferring appropriate rights under that scheme on the person entitled to the credit.

(3) If such a scheme as is mentioned in sub-paragraph (1) is closed to new members, the appropriate authority in relation to that scheme may by regulations specify another public service pension scheme as an alternative to it for the purposes of this paragraph.

(4) Where the trustees or managers of a scheme in relation to which an alternative is specified under sub-paragraph (3) are subject to liability in respect of a pension credit, they may—

(a) discharge their liability in respect of the credit by securing that appropriate rights are conferred on the person entitled to the credit by the trustees or managers of the alternative scheme, and

    (b) for the purpose of so discharging their liability, require the trustees or managers of the alternative scheme to take such steps as may be required.

    (5) In sub-paragraph (3), "the appropriate authority", in relation to a public service pension scheme, means such Minister of the Crown or government department as may be designated by the Treasury as having responsibility for the scheme.

Other unfunded occupational pension schemes

    3.—(1) This paragraph applies to a pension credit which derives from an occupational pension scheme which is—

    (a) not funded, and

    (b) not a public service pension scheme.

    (2) The trustees or managers of the scheme from which a pension credit to which this paragraph applies derives may discharge their liability in respect of the credit by conferring appropriate rights under that scheme on the person entitled to the credit.

    (3) The trustees or managers of the scheme from which a pension credit to which this paragraph applies derives may discharge their liability in respect of the credit by paying the amount of the credit to the person responsible for a qualifying arrangement with a view to acquiring rights under that arrangement for the person entitled to the credit if—

    (a) the qualifying arrangement is not disqualified as a destination for the credit,

    (b) the person responsible for that arrangement is able and willing to accept payment in respect of the credit, and

    (c) payment is made with the consent of the person entitled to the credit, or in accordance with regulations made by the Secretary of State.

Other pension arrangements

    4.—(1) This paragraph applies to a pension credit which derives from—

    (a) a retirement annuity contract,

    (b) an annuity or insurance policy purchased or transferred for the purpose of giving effect to rights under an occupational pension scheme or a personal pension scheme, or

    (c) an annuity purchased, or entered into, for the purpose of discharging liability in respect of a pension credit.

    (2) The person responsible for the pension arrangement from which a pension credit to which this paragraph applies derives may discharge his liability in respect of the credit by paying the amount of the credit to the person responsible for a qualifying arrangement with a view to acquiring rights under that arrangement for the person entitled to the credit if—

    (a) the qualifying arrangement is not disqualified as a destination for the credit,

    (b) the person responsible for that arrangement is able and willing to accept payment in respect of the credit, and

    (c) payment is made with the consent of the person entitled to the credit, or in accordance with regulations made by the Secretary of State.

    (3) The person responsible for the pension arrangement from which a pension credit to which this paragraph applies derives may discharge his liability in respect of the credit by entering into an annuity contract with the person entitled to the credit if the contract is not disqualified as a destination for the credit.

(4) The person responsible for the pension arrangement from which a pension credit to which this paragraph applies derives may, in such circumstances as the Secretary of State may prescribe by regulations, discharge his liability in respect of the credit by assuming an obligation to provide an annuity for the person entitled to the credit.

(5) In sub-paragraph (1)(c), "pension credit" includes a credit under Northern Ireland legislation corresponding to section 29(1)(b).

Appropriate rights

5. For the purposes of this Schedule, rights conferred on the person entitled to a pension credit are appropriate if—

    (a) they are conferred with effect from, and including, the day on which the order, or provision, under which the credit arises takes effect, and

    (b) their value, when calculated in accordance with regulations made by the Secretary of State, equals the amount of the credit.

Qualifying arrangements

6.—(1) The following are qualifying arrangements for the purposes of this Schedule—

    (a) an occupational pension scheme,

    (b) a personal pension scheme,

    (c) an appropriate annuity contract,

    (d) an appropriate policy of insurance, and

S.I. 1996/1462.   (e) an overseas arrangement within the meaning of the Contracting-out (Transfer and Transfer Payment) Regulations 1996.

(2) An annuity contract or policy of insurance is appropriate for the purposes of sub-paragraph (1) if, at the time it is entered into or taken out, the insurance company with which it is entered into or taken out—

    (a) is carrying on ordinary long-term insurance business in the United Kingdom or any other member State, and

    (b) satisfies such requirements as the Secretary of State may prescribe by regulations.

1982 c. 50.   (3) In this paragraph, "ordinary long-term insurance business" has the same meaning as in the Insurance Companies Act 1982.

Disqualification as destination for pension credit

1988 c. 1.   7.—(1) If a pension credit derives from a pension arrangement which is approved for the purposes of Part XIV of the Income and Corporation Taxes Act 1988, an arrangement is disqualified as a destination for the credit unless—

    (a) it is also approved for those purposes, or

    (b) it satisfies such requirements as the Secretary of State may prescribe by regulations.

(2) If the rights by reference to which the amount of a pension credit is determined are or include contracted-out rights or safeguarded rights, an arrangement is disqualified as a destination for the credit unless—

    (a) it is of a description prescribed by the Secretary of State by regulations, and

    (b) it satisfies such requirements as he may so prescribe.

(3) An occupational pension scheme is disqualified as a destination for a pension credit unless the rights to be acquired under the arrangement by the person entitled to the credit are rights whose value, when calculated in accordance with regulations made by the Secretary of State, equals the credit.

(4) An annuity contract or insurance policy is disqualified as a destination for a pension credit in such circumstances as the Secretary of State may prescribe by regulations.

(5) The requirements which may be prescribed under sub-paragraph (1)(b) include, in particular, requirements of the Inland Revenue.

(6) In sub-paragraph (2)—

"contracted-out rights" means such rights under, or derived from—

(a) an occupational pension scheme contracted-out by virtue of section 9(2) or (3) of the Pension Schemes Act 1993, or   1993 c. 48.

(b) a personal pension scheme which is an appropriate scheme for the purposes of that Act,

as the Secretary of State may prescribe by regulations;

"safeguarded rights" has the meaning given by section 68A of the Pension Schemes Act 1993.

Adjustments to amount of pension credit

8.—(1) If—

(a) a pension credit derives from an occupational pension scheme,

(b) the scheme is one to which section 56 of the Pensions Act 1995 (minimum funding requirement for funded salary related schemes) applies,   1995 c. 26.

(c) the scheme is underfunded on the valuation day, and

(d) such circumstances as the Secretary of State may prescribe by regulations apply,

paragraph 1(3) shall have effect in relation to the credit as if the reference to the amount of the credit were to such lesser amount as may be determined in accordance with regulations made by the Secretary of State.

(2) Whether a scheme is underfunded for the purposes of sub-paragraph (1)(c) shall be determined in accordance with regulations made by the Secretary of State.

(3) For the purposes of that provision, the valuation day is the day by reference to which the cash equivalent on which the amount of the pension credit depends falls to be calculated.

9. If—

(a) a person's shareable rights under a pension arrangement have become subject to a pension debit, and

(b) the person responsible for the arrangement makes a payment which is referable to those rights without knowing of the pension debit,

this Schedule shall have effect as if the amount of the corresponding pension credit were such lesser amount as may be determined in accordance with regulations made by the Secretary of State.

10. The Secretary of State may by regulations make provision for paragraph 1(3), 3(3) or 4(2) to have effect, where payment is made after the end of the implementation period for the pension credit, as if the reference to the amount of the credit were to such larger amount as may be determined in accordance with the regulations.

General

11. Liability in respect of a pension credit shall be treated as discharged if the effect of paragraph 8(1) or 9 is to reduce it to zero.

12. Liability in respect of a pension credit may not be discharged otherwise than in accordance with this Schedule.

13. Regulations under paragraph 5(b) or 7(3) may provide for calculation of the value of rights in accordance with guidance from time to time prepared by a person specified in the regulations.

14. In this Schedule—

"funded", in relation to an occupational pension scheme, means that the scheme meets its liabilities out of a fund accumulated for the purpose during the life of the scheme;

1993 c. 48.   "public service pension scheme" has the same meaning as in the Pension Schemes Act 1993.

Section 50.

SCHEDULE 6

Effect of State Scheme Pension Debits and Credits

1. The Contributions and Benefits Act is amended as follows.

2. After section 45A there is inserted—

"Reduction of additional pension in Category A retirement pension: pension sharing.

45B.—(1) The weekly rate of the additional pension in a Category A retirement pension shall be reduced as follows in any case where—

(a) the pensioner has become subject to a state scheme pension debit, and

(b) the debit is to any extent referable to the additional pension.

(2) If the pensioner became subject to the debit in or after the final relevant year, the weekly rate of the additional pension shall be reduced by the appropriate weekly amount.

(3) If the pensioner became subject to the debit before the final relevant year, the weekly rate of the additional pension shall be reduced by the appropriate weekly amount multiplied by the relevant revaluation percentage.

(4) The appropriate weekly amount for the purposes of subsections (2) and (3) above is the weekly rate, expressed in terms of the valuation day, at which the cash equivalent, on that day, of the pension mentioned in subsection (5) below is equal to so much of the debit as is referable to the additional pension.

(5) The pension referred to above is a notional pension for the pensioner by virtue of section 44(3)(b) above which becomes payable on the later of—

(a) his attaining pensionable age, and

(b) the valuation day.

(6) For the purposes of subsection (3) above, the relevant revaluation percentage is the percentage specified, in relation to earnings factors for the tax year in which the pensioner became

subject to the debit, by the last order under section 148 of the Administration Act to come into force before the end of the final relevant year.

(7) Cash equivalents for the purposes of this section shall be calculated in accordance with regulations.

(8) In this section—

"final relevant year" means the tax year immediately preceding that in which the pensioner attains pensionable age;

"state scheme pension debit" means a debit under section 49(1)(a) of the Welfare Reform and Pensions Act 1999 (debit for the purposes of this Part of this Act);

"valuation day" means the day on which the pensioner became subject to the state scheme pension debit."

3. After section 55 there is inserted—

"Shared additional pension

Shared additional pension.

55A.—(1) A person shall be entitled to a shared additional pension if he is—

(a) over pensionable age, and

(b) entitled to a state scheme pension credit.

(2) A person's entitlement to a shared additional pension shall continue throughout his life.

(3) The weekly rate of a shared additional pension shall be the appropriate weekly amount, unless the pensioner's entitlement to the state scheme pension credit arose before the final relevant year, in which case it shall be that amount multiplied by the relevant revaluation percentage.

(4) The appropriate weekly amount for the purposes of subsection (3) above is the weekly rate, expressed in terms of the valuation day, at which the cash equivalent, on that day, of the pensioner's entitlement, or prospective entitlement, to the shared additional pension is equal to the state scheme pension credit.

(5) The relevant revaluation percentage for the purposes of that subsection is the percentage specified, in relation to earnings factors for the tax year in which the entitlement to the state scheme pension credit arose, by the last order under section 148 of the Administration Act to come into force before the end of the final relevant year.

(6) Cash equivalents for the purposes of this section shall be calculated in accordance with regulations.

(7) In this section—

"final relevant year" means the tax year immediately preceding that in which the pensioner attains pensionable age;

"state scheme pension credit" means a credit under section 49(1)(b) of the Welfare Reform and Pensions Act 1999 (credit for the purposes of this Part of this Act);

"valuation day" means the day on which the pensioner becomes entitled to the state scheme pension credit.

Reduction of
shared additional
pension: pension
sharing.

55B.—(1) The weekly rate of a shared additional pension shall be reduced as follows in any case where—

(a) the pensioner has become subject to a state scheme pension debit, and

(b) the debit is to any extent referable to the pension.

(2) If the pensioner became subject to the debit in or after the final relevant year, the weekly rate of the pension shall be reduced by the appropriate weekly amount.

(3) If the pensioner became subject to the debit before the final relevant year, the weekly rate of the additional pension shall be reduced by the appropriate weekly amount multiplied by the relevant revaluation percentage.

(4) The appropriate weekly amount for the purposes of subsections (2) and (3) above is the weekly rate, expressed in terms of the valuation day, at which the cash equivalent, on that day, of the pension mentioned in subsection (5) below is equal to so much of the debit as is referable to the shared additional pension.

(5) The pension referred to above is a notional pension for the pensioner by virtue of section 55A above which becomes payable on the later of—

(a) his attaining pensionable age, and

(b) the valuation day.

(6) For the purposes of subsection (3) above, the relevant revaluation percentage is the percentage specified, in relation to earnings factors for the tax year in which the pensioner became subject to the debit, by the last order under section 148 of the Administration Act to come into force before the end of the final relevant year.

(7) Cash equivalents for the purposes of this section shall be calculated in accordance with regulations.

(8) In this section—

"final relevant year" means the tax year immediately preceding that in which the pensioner attains pensionable age;

"state scheme pension debit", means a debit under section 49(1)(a) of the Welfare Reform and Pensions Act 1999 (debit for the purposes of this Part of this Act);

"valuation day" means the day on which the pensioner became subject to the state scheme pension debit.

Increase of shared
additional
pension where
entitlement is
deferred.

55C.—(1) For the purposes of this section, a person's entitlement to a shared additional pension is deferred—

(a) where he would be entitled to a Category A or Category B retirement pension but for the fact that his entitlement to such a pension is deferred, if and so long as his entitlement to such a pension is deferred, and

(b) otherwise, if and so long as he does not become entitled to the shared additional pension by reason only of not satisfying the conditions of section 1 of the Administration Act (entitlement to benefit dependent on claim),

and, in relation to a shared additional pension, "period of deferment" shall be construed accordingly.

(2) Where a person's entitlement to a shared additional pension is deferred, the rate of his shared additional pension shall be increased by an amount equal to the aggregate of the increments to which he is entitled under subsection (3) below, but only if that amount is enough to increase the rate of the pension by at least 1 per cent.

(3) A person is entitled to an increment under this subsection for each complete incremental period in his period of enhancement.

(4) The amount of the increment for an incremental period shall be 1/7th per cent. of the weekly rate of the shared additional pension to which the person would have been entitled for the period if his entitlement had not been deferred.

(5) Amounts under subsection (4) above shall be rounded to the nearest penny, taking any 1/2p as nearest to the next whole penny.

(6) Where an amount under subsection (4) above would, apart from this subsection, be a sum less than 1/2p, the amount shall be taken to be zero, notwithstanding any other provision of this Act, the Pensions Act 1995 or the Administration Act.   1995 c. 26.

(7) Where one or more orders have come into force under section 150 of the Administration Act during the period of enhancement, the rate for any incremental period shall be determined as if the order or orders had come into force before the beginning of the period of enhancement.

(8) The sums which are the increases in the rates of shared additional pensions under this section are subject to alteration by order made by the Secretary of State under section 150 of the Administration Act.

(9) In this section—

"incremental period" means any period of six days which are treated by regulations as days of increment for the purposes of this section in relation to the person and pension in question; and

"period of enhancement", in relation to that person and that pension, means the period which—

(a) begins on the same day as the period of deferment in question, and

(b) ends on the same day as that period or, if earlier, on the day before the 5th anniversary of the beginning of that period."

Section 59.

SCHEDULE 7

Jᴏɪɴᴛ ᴄʟᴀɪᴍꜱ ꜰᴏʀ ᴊᴏʙꜱᴇᴇᴋᴇʀ'ꜱ ᴀʟʟᴏᴡᴀɴᴄᴇ

Jobseekers Act 1995 (c.18)

1. The Jobseekers Act 1995 has effect subject to the following amendments.

2.—(1) Section 1 (entitlement to jobseeker's allowance) is amended as follows.

(2) In subsection (2) (conditions of entitlement), for paragraph (d) (claimant must satisfy conditions set out in section 2 or 3) substitute—

"(d) satisfies the conditions set out in section 2;".

(3) After subsection (2) insert—

"(2A) Subject to the provisions of this Act, a claimant who is not a member of a joint-claim couple is entitled to a jobseeker's allowance if he satisfies—

(a) the conditions set out in paragraphs (a) to (c) and (e) to (i) of subsection (2); and

(b) the conditions set out in section 3.

(2B) Subject to the provisions of this Act, a joint-claim couple are entitled to a jobseeker's allowance if—

(a) a claim for the allowance is made jointly by the couple;

(b) each member of the couple satisfies the conditions set out in paragraphs (a) to (c) and (e) to (i) of subsection (2); and

(c) the conditions set out in section 3A are satisfied in relation to the couple.

(2C) Regulations may prescribe circumstances in which subsection (2A) is to apply to a claimant who is a member of a joint-claim couple.

(2D) Regulations may, in respect of cases where a person would (but for the regulations) be a member of two or more joint-claim couples, make provision for only one of those couples to be a joint-claim couple; and the provision which may be so made includes provision for the couple which is to be the joint-claim couple to be nominated—

(a) by the persons who are the members of the couples, or

(b) in default of one of the couples being so nominated, by the Secretary of State."

(4) In subsection (4)—

(a) in the definition of "an income-based jobseeker's allowance", at the end insert "or a joint-claim jobseeker's allowance;" and

(b) after that definition insert—

""a joint-claim couple" means a married or unmarried couple who—

(a) are not members of any family whose members include a person in respect of whom a member of the couple is entitled to child benefit, and

(b) are of a prescribed description;

"a joint-claim jobseeker's allowance" means a jobseeker's allowance entitlement to which arises by virtue of subsection (2B)."

3. In section 2(1) (the contribution-based conditions), for "section 1(2)(d)(i)" substitute "section 1(2)(d)".

4.—(1) In subsection (1) of section 3 (the income-based conditions), for "section 1(2)(d)(ii)" substitute "section 1(2A)(b)".

(2) After that section insert—

"The conditions for claims by joint-claim couples.

3A.—(1) The conditions referred to in section 1(2B)(c) are—

(a) that the income of the joint-claim couple does not exceed the applicable amount (determined in accordance with regulations under section 4) or the couple have no income;

(b) that no member of a family of which the couple are members is entitled to income support;

(c) that no member of any such family (other than the couple) is entitled to an income-based jobseeker's allowance;

(d) that at least one member of the couple has reached the age of 18; and

(e) that if only one member of the couple has reached the age of 18, the other member of the couple is a person—

(i) in respect of whom a direction under section 16 is in force; or

(ii) who has, in prescribed circumstances to be taken into account for a prescribed period, reached the age of 16.

(2) Subsections (2) and (4) of section 3 shall apply in relation to a member of the couple to whom subsection (1)(e)(i) or (ii) above applies as they apply in relation to a claimant to whom subsection (1)(f)(ii) or (iii) of that section applies.

(3) In subsection (1)(e)(ii) above "period" shall be construed in accordance with section 3(3).

Joint-claim couples: the nominated member.

3B.—(1) Where a joint-claim couple make a claim for a joint-claim jobseeker's allowance, they may nominate one of them as the member of the couple to whom the allowance is to be payable.

(2) In default of one of them being so nominated, the allowance shall be payable to whichever of them is nominated by the Secretary of State.

(3) Subsections (1) and (2) have effect subject to section 4A(4) and (7).

(4) In this Act references to the nominated member of a joint-claim couple are, except where section 20A(7) applies, to the member of the couple nominated under subsection (1) or (2) above; and where section 20A(7) applies, references to the nominated member of such a couple are to the member of the couple to whom section 20A(7) provides for the allowance to be payable.

(5) Nothing in this section or section 20A(7) affects the operation of any statutory provision by virtue of which any amount of the allowance is required or authorised to be paid to someone other than the nominated member of the couple."

5.—(1) Section 4 (amount of jobseeker's allowance) is amended as follows.

(2) In subsection (3) (amount payable in respect of an income-based jobseeker's allowance), after "allowance" insert "(other than a joint-claim jobseeker's allowance)".

(3) After subsection (3) insert—

"(3A) In the case of a joint-claim jobseeker's allowance, the amount payable in respect of a joint-claim couple shall be—

(a) if the couple have no income, the applicable amount;

(b) if the couple have an income, the amount by which the applicable amount exceeds the couple's income."

(4) After subsection (11) insert—

"(11A) In subsections (6) to (11) "claimant" does not include—

(a) a joint-claim couple, or

(b) a member of such a couple (other than a person to whom regulations under section 1(2C) apply);

but section 4A, which contains corresponding provisions relating to joint-claim couples, applies instead."

6. After section 4 insert—

"Amount payable in respect of joint-claim couple.

4A.—(1) This section applies where—

(a) a joint-claim couple are entitled to a joint-claim jobseeker's allowance, and

(b) one or each of the members of the couple is in addition entitled to a contribution-based jobseeker's allowance;

and in such a case the provisions of this section have effect in relation to the couple in place of section 4(3A).

(2) If a joint-claim couple falling within subsection (1) have no income, the amount payable in respect of the couple by way of a jobseeker's allowance shall be—

(a) the applicable amount, if that is greater than the couple's personal rate; and

(b) the couple's personal rate, if it is not.

(3) Where the amount payable in accordance with subsection (2) is the applicable amount, the amount payable in respect of the couple by way of a jobseeker's allowance shall be taken to consist of two elements—

(a) one being an amount equal to the couple's personal rate; and

(b) the other being an amount equal to the excess of the applicable amount over the couple's personal rate.

(4) Where the amount payable in accordance with subsection (2) is the couple's personal rate, then—

(a) if each member of the couple is entitled to a contribution-based jobseeker's allowance, an amount equal to the member's own personal rate shall be payable in respect of the member by way of such an allowance;

(b) if only one of them is so entitled, an amount equal to that member's personal rate shall be payable in respect of the member by way of such an allowance;

and in either case nothing shall be payable in respect of the couple by way of a joint-claim jobseeker's allowance.

(5) If a joint-claim couple falling within subsection (1) have an income, the amount payable in respect of the couple by way of a jobseeker's allowance shall be—

(a) the amount by which the applicable amount exceeds the couple's income, if the amount of that excess is greater than the couple's personal rate; and

(b) the couple's personal rate, if it is not.

(6) Where the amount payable in accordance with subsection (5) is the amount by which the applicable amount exceeds the couple's income, the amount payable in respect of the couple by way of a jobseeker's allowance shall be taken to consist of two elements—

(a) one being an amount equal to the couple's personal rate; and

(b) the other being an amount equal to the amount by which the difference between the applicable amount and the couple's income exceeds the couple's personal rate.

(7) Where the amount payable in accordance with subsection (5) is the couple's personal rate, subsection (4) shall apply as it applies in a case where the amount payable in accordance with subsection (2) is that rate.

(8) The element of a jobseeker's allowance mentioned in subsection (3)(a) and that mentioned in subsection (6)(a) shall be treated, for the purpose of identifying the source of the allowance, as attributable—

(a) in a case where only one member of the joint-claim couple is entitled to a contribution-based jobseeker's allowance, to that member's entitlement to such an allowance; and

(b) in a case where each member of the couple is entitled to a contribution-based jobseeker's allowance, rateably according to their individual entitlements to such an allowance.

(9) The element of a jobseeker's allowance mentioned in subsection (3)(b) and that mentioned in subsection (6)(b) shall be treated, for the purpose of identifying the source of the allowance, as attributable to the couple's entitlement to a joint-claim jobseeker's allowance.

(10) In this section "the couple's personal rate", in relation to a joint-claim couple, means—

(a) where only one member of the couple is entitled to a contribution-based jobseeker's allowance, that member's personal rate;

(b) where each member of the couple is entitled to such an allowance, the aggregate of their personal rates."

7.—(1) Section 8 (power to make regulations requiring attendance etc.) is amended as follows.

(2) In subsection (1), after "claimant" insert "(other than a joint-claim couple claiming a joint-claim jobseeker's allowance)".

(3) After subsection (1) insert—

"(1A) Regulations may make provision—

    (a) for requiring each member of a joint-claim couple claiming a joint-claim jobseeker's allowance to attend at such place and such time as the Secretary of State may specify;

    (b) for requiring a member of such a couple to provide information and such evidence as may be prescribed as to his circumstances, his availability for employment and the extent to which he is actively seeking employment;

    (c) for requiring such a couple to jointly provide information and such evidence as may be prescribed as to the circumstances of each or either member of the couple, the availability for employment of each or either member of the couple and the extent to which each or either member of the couple is actively seeking employment;

    (d) where any requirement to provide information or evidence is imposed on such a couple by virtue of paragraph (c), for the joint obligation of the couple to be capable of being discharged by the provision of the information or evidence by one member of the couple."

(4) In subsection (2), after "Regulations under subsection (1)" insert "or (1A)".

(5) In subsection (2)(a) (cases where entitlement to allowance may cease on account of non-compliance), after "in the case of a claimant who" insert ", or (as the case may be) a joint-claim couple claiming a joint-claim jobseeker's allowance a member of which,".

(6) In subsection (2)(b) (cases where entitlement to allowance may cease by reference to the time expired since the claimant's last attendance)—

    (a) after "he" insert "or, as the case may be, a member of the joint-claim couple"; and

    (b) after "subsection (1)(a)" insert "or (1A)(a)".

(7) For paragraph (c) of subsection (2) (provision for entitlement not to cease where good cause shown) substitute—

"(c) provide for entitlement not to cease if the claimant or (as the case may be) either member of the joint-claim couple shows, within a prescribed period of the failure to comply on the part of the claimant or (as the case may be) a member of the couple, that the claimant or (as the case may be) the defaulting member of the couple had good cause for that failure; and".

8. In section 9(12) (jobseeker's agreement ends when allowance ends), at the end insert "or to a joint-claim couple of which he is a member."

9.—(1) Section 13 (income and capital for the purposes of an income-based allowance) is amended as follows.

(2) After subsection (2) insert—

"(2A) Subsections (1) and (2) do not apply as regards a joint-claim jobseeker's allowance; but a joint-claim couple shall not be entitled to a joint-claim jobseeker's allowance if the couple's capital, or a prescribed part of it, exceeds the prescribed amount.

(2B) Where a joint-claim couple claim a joint-claim jobseeker's allowance—

    (a) the couple's income and capital includes the separate income and capital of each of them; and

    (b) the income and capital of any other person who is a member of any family of which the couple are members shall, except in prescribed circumstances, be treated as income and capital of the couple."

(3) In subsection (3) (treating capital as income), after "subsection (1)" insert "or (2A)".

10. After section 15 (effect on family of one member being involved in a trade dispute) insert—

"Trade disputes: joint-claim couples.

    15A.—(1) Sections 14 and 15 shall, in relation to a joint-claim couple claiming a joint-claim jobseeker's allowance, apply in accordance with this section.

    (2) Where each member of the couple is prevented by section 14 from being entitled to a jobseeker's allowance, the couple are not entitled to a joint-claim jobseeker's allowance.

    (3) But where only one member of the couple is prevented by that section from being entitled to a jobseeker's allowance, the couple are not for that reason alone prevented from being entitled to a joint-claim jobseeker's allowance.

    (4) Section 15(1) does not have effect in relation to the couple but, except in prescribed circumstances, section 15(2) applies for the purposes of calculating the couple's entitlement to a joint-claim jobseeker's allowance where—

        (a) a member of the couple, or

        (b) any other person who is a member of any family of which the couple are members,

is, or would be, prevented by section 14 from being entitled to a jobseeker's allowance.

    (5) Where section 15(2) applies in relation to the couple by virtue of subsection (4) above, that provision and section 15(4) apply with the following modifications—

        (a) references to the claimant are to be taken as references to the couple;

        (b) references to "A" are to the person mentioned in subsection (4)(a) or (b) above;

        (c) section 15(2)(b) has effect as if for "where the claimant and A are a married or unmarried couple," there were substituted "where A is a member of the couple,"; and

        (d) section 15(2)(c)(ii) has effect as if for "of his family" there were substituted "of any family of which the couple are members"."

11. In section 17 (reduction of allowance payable to young persons), after subsection (1) insert—

"(1A) Regulations may provide for the amount of a joint-claim jobseeker's allowance payable in respect of any joint-claim couple where a member of the couple is a young person to whom this section applies to be reduced—

    (a) in such circumstances,

(b) by such a percentage, and

(c) for such a period,

as may be prescribed."

12. In section 19 (allowance not payable though conditions for entitlement are satisfied), after subsection (1) insert—

"(1A) Subject to section 20A(9), this section does not apply as regards a joint-claim jobseeker's allowance (but sections 20A and 20B make, in relation to such an allowance, provision corresponding to that made by this section and section 20)."

13. After section 20 insert—

"Denial or reduction of joint-claim jobseeker's allowance.

20A.—(1) Where this section applies to a member of a joint-claim couple, that member of the couple shall be subject to sanctions for the purposes of this section.

(2) This section applies to a member of a joint-claim couple if that member of the couple—

(a) has, without good cause, refused or failed to carry out any jobseeker's direction which was reasonable, having regard to his circumstances;

(b) has, without good cause—

(i) neglected to avail himself of a reasonable opportunity of a place on a training scheme or employment programme;

(ii) after a place on such a scheme or programme has been notified to him by an employment officer as vacant or about to become vacant, refused or failed to apply for it or to accept it when offered to him;

(iii) given up a place on such a scheme or programme; or

(iv) failed to attend such a scheme or programme on which he has been given a place;

(c) has lost his place on such a scheme or programme through misconduct;

(d) has lost his employment as an employed earner through misconduct;

(e) has voluntarily left such employment without just cause;

(f) has, without good cause, after a situation in any employment has been notified to him by an employment officer as vacant or about to become vacant, refused or failed to apply for it or to accept it when offered to him; or

(g) has, without good cause, neglected to avail himself of a reasonable opportunity of employment.

(3) Where this section applies to a member of a joint-claim couple by virtue of any of paragraphs (a) to (c) of subsection (2), the period for which he is to be subject to sanctions shall be such period (of at least one week but not more than 26 weeks) as may be prescribed.

(4) Where this section applies to a member of a joint-claim couple by virtue only of any of paragraphs (d) to (g) of

subsection (2), the period for which he is to be subject to sanctions shall be such period (of at least one week but not more than 26 weeks) as may be determined by the Secretary of State.

(5) Even though the conditions for entitlement to a joint-claim jobseeker's allowance are satisfied in relation to a joint-claim couple—

    (a) the allowance shall not be payable for any period during which both members of the couple are subject to sanctions; and

    (b) the amount of the allowance payable in respect of the couple for any period during which only one member of the couple is subject to sanctions shall be reduced to an amount calculated by the prescribed method ("the reduced amount").

(6) The method prescribed for calculating the reduced amount may, in particular, involve—

    (a) deducting amounts from, or making percentage reductions of, the amount which would be the amount of the allowance if neither member of the couple were subject to sanctions;

    (b) disregarding portions of the applicable amount;

    (c) treating amounts as being income or capital of the couple.

(7) During any period for which the amount of a joint-claim jobseeker's allowance payable in respect of a joint-claim couple is the reduced amount, the allowance shall be payable to the member of the couple who is not subject to sanctions.

(8) Regulations may prescribe—

    (a) circumstances which the Secretary of State is to take into account, and

    (b) circumstances which he is not to take into account,

in determining a period under subsection (4).

(9) Subsections (7) to (10) of section 19 apply for the purposes of this section as for those of that section but as if references in subsection (10)(b) of that section to the claimant were to the member of the joint-claim couple to whom subsection (2)(a) above applies.

20B.—(1) Section 20A shall not be taken to apply to a member of a joint-claim couple merely because he has refused to seek or accept employment in a situation which is vacant in consequence of a stoppage of work due to a trade dispute.

(2) Section 20A does not apply to a member of a joint-claim couple by virtue of any of paragraphs (a) to (c) of subsection (2) of that section if—

    (a) a direction is in force under section 16 with respect to that member of the couple; and

    (b) he has acted in such a way as to risk—

        (i) having that direction revoked under subsection (3)(b) of section 16; or

        (ii) having the amount of the couple's entitlement to a joint-claim jobseeker's allowance reduced by virtue of section 17 because the condition in section 17(3)(b) or (c) is established.

(3) Regulations shall make provision for the purpose of enabling any person of a prescribed description to accept any employed earner's employment without section 20A applying to him by virtue of paragraph (e) or (g) of subsection (2) of that section should he leave that employment voluntarily and without just cause at any time during a trial period.

(4) In such circumstances as may be prescribed, a joint-claim jobseeker's allowance shall be payable in respect of a joint-claim couple even though section 20A(5)(a) prevents payment of such a jobseeker's allowance to the couple.

(5) A jobseeker's allowance shall be payable by virtue of subsection (4) only if the couple have complied with such requirements as to the provision of information as may be prescribed for the purposes of this subsection.

(6) Regulations under subsection (4) may, in particular, provide for a jobseeker's allowance payable by virtue of that subsection to be—

    (a) payable at a prescribed rate;

    (b) payable for a prescribed period (which may differ from the period during which both members of the couple are subject to sanctions for the purposes of section 20A).

(7) In subsection (3), "trial period" has such meaning as may be prescribed.

(8) Regulations may make provision for determining, for the purposes of this section, the day on which a person's employment is to be regarded as commencing."

14.—(1) Section 31 (termination of awards where another entitlement exists) is amended as follows.

(2) In subsection (1) (termination of award of income support where there will be an entitlement to a jobseeker's allowance), after "or where he is a member of a married or unmarried couple his partner" insert "or the couple".

(3) In subsection (2) (termination of award of a jobseeker's allowance where there will be an entitlement to income support), after "or where he is a member of a married or unmarried couple his partner," insert "or where the award was made to a couple a member of the couple,".

15.—(1) Section 35 (interpretation) is amended as follows.

(2) In the definition of "claimant", at the end insert "except that in relation to a joint-claim couple claiming a joint-claim jobseeker's allowance it means the couple, or each member of the couple, as the context requires;".

(3) After the definition of "job-seeking period" insert—

    ""joint-claim couple" and "joint-claim jobseeker's allowance" have the meanings given by section 1(4);".

(4) After the definition of "married couple" insert—

    ""the nominated member", in relation to a joint-claim couple, shall be construed in accordance with section 3B(4);".

16.—(1) Schedule 1 (jobseeker's allowance: supplementary provisions) is amended as follows.

(2) After paragraph 8 (entitlement without satisfying conditions) insert—

"8A.—(1) Regulations may prescribe circumstances in which a joint-claim couple may be entitled to a joint-claim jobseeker's allowance without each member of the couple satisfying all the conditions referred to in section 1(2B)(b).

(2) Regulations may prescribe circumstances in which, and a period for which, a transitional case couple may be entitled to a joint-claim jobseeker's allowance without having jointly made a claim for it.

(3) In sub-paragraph (2)—

    (a) "a transitional case couple" means a joint-claim couple a member of which is entitled to an income-based jobseeker's allowance on the coming into force of Schedule 7 to the Welfare Reform and Pensions Act 1999; and

    (b) "period" shall be construed in accordance with section 3(3)."

(3) In paragraph 9(a) (rate of allowance payable under paragraph 8), after "paragraph 8" insert "or 8A".

(4) After paragraph 9 insert—

"Continuity of claims and awards: persons ceasing to be a joint-claim couple

9A.—(1) Regulations may make provision about the entitlement to a jobseeker's allowance of persons ("ex-members") who cease to be members of a joint-claim couple.

(2) Regulations under this paragraph may, in particular, provide—

    (a) for treating each or either of the ex-members as having made any claim made by the couple or, alternatively, for any such claim to lapse;

    (b) for any award made in respect of the couple to be replaced by an award (a "replacement award") in respect of each or either of the ex-members of the couple or, alternatively, for any such award to lapse.

Continuity of claims and awards: persons again becoming a joint-claim couple

9B.—(1) Regulations may make provision about the entitlement to a jobseeker's allowance of persons ("ex-members") who, having ceased to be members of a joint-claim couple, again become the members of a joint-claim couple.

(2) Regulations under this paragraph may, in particular, provide—

    (a) for any claim made by the ex-members when they were previously a joint-claim couple to be revived or otherwise given effect as a claim made by the couple;

    (b) for any award made in respect of the ex-members when they were previously a joint-claim couple to be restored;

    (c) for any such award, or any replacement award (within the meaning of paragraph 9A) made in respect of either of them, to be replaced by an award (a "new award") in respect of the couple.

Continuity of claims and awards: couple becoming a joint-claim couple

9C.—(1) Regulations may make provision about the entitlement to a jobseeker's allowance of persons who become members of a joint-claim couple as a result of the married or unmarried couple of which they are members becoming a joint-claim couple.

(2) Regulations under this paragraph may, in particular, provide—

    (a) for any claim made by either member of the couple before the couple became a joint-claim couple to be given effect as a claim made by the couple;

    (b) for any award, or any replacement award (within the meaning of paragraph 9A), made in respect of either member of the couple before the couple became a joint-claim couple to be replaced by an award (a "new award") in respect of the couple.

Paragraphs 9A to 9C: supplementary

9D.—(1) Regulations may provide, in relation to any replacement award (within the meaning of paragraph 9A) or new award (within the meaning of paragraph 9B or 9C)—

    (a) for the award to be of an amount determined in a prescribed manner;

    (b) for entitlement to the award to be subject to compliance with prescribed requirements as to the provision of information and evidence.

(2) In paragraphs 9A to 9C and this paragraph—

"award" means an award of a jobseeker's allowance;

"claim" means a claim for a jobseeker's allowance."

(5) For paragraph 10(1) (entitlement before claim determined) substitute—

"(1) In such circumstances as may be prescribed—

    (a) a claimant for a jobseeker's allowance other than a joint-claim jobseeker's allowance,

    (b) a joint-claim couple claiming a joint-claim jobseeker's allowance, or

    (c) a member of such a couple,

may be treated as being entitled to an income-based jobseeker's allowance before his or (as the case may be) the couple's claim for the allowance has been determined."

(6) In paragraph 10(2) (allowance where payment suspended), for "to a claimant even though payment to him" substitute "to—

    (a) a claimant for a jobseeker's allowance other than a joint-claim jobseeker's allowance,

    (b) a joint-claim couple claiming a joint-claim jobseeker's allowance, or

    (c) a member of such a couple,

even though payment to him or (as the case may be) the couple".

(7) In paragraph 10(3) (information to be supplied to obtain payments under sub-paragraph (1) or (2)), after "the claimant" insert "or (as the case may be) the couple or the member of the couple".

Social Security Act 1998 (c.14)

17. In section 39(1) of the Social Security Act 1998 (interpretation of Chapter II of Part I), after the definition of "appeal tribunal" insert—

1995 c. 18.

""claimant", in relation to a joint-claim couple claiming a joint-claim jobseeker's allowance (within the meaning of the Jobseekers Act 1995), means the couple or either member of the couple;".

SCHEDULE 8   Section 70.

WELFARE BENEFITS: MINOR AND CONSEQUENTIAL AMENDMENTS

PART I

BEREAVEMENT BENEFITS

Income and Corporation Taxes Act 1988 (c.1)

1.—(1) Section 617 of the Income and Corporation Taxes Act 1988 (social security benefits and contributions) is amended as follows.

(2) In subsection (1)(a)—

  (a) after "maternity allowance," insert "bereavement payments,"; and

  (b) omit "widow's payments,".

(3) Omit subsection (6).

Social Security Contributions and Benefits Act 1992 (c.4)

2. The Contributions and Benefits Act has effect subject to the following amendments.

3.—(1) Section 20 (descriptions of contributory benefits) is amended as follows.

(2) In subsection (1)—

  (a) in paragraph (e), omit sub-paragraph (i); and

  (b) after that paragraph insert—

    "(ea) bereavement benefits, comprising—

      (i) bereavement payment;

      (ii) widowed parent's allowance (with increase for child dependants);

      (iii) bereavement allowance;".

(3) In subsection (2), in the definition of "long-term benefit", after paragraph (b) insert—

    "(ba) a widowed parent's allowance;

    (bb) a bereavement allowance;".

4.—(1) Section 21 (contribution conditions) is amended as follows.

(2) In subsection (2)—

  (a) for "Widow's payment" substitute "Bereavement payment"; and

  (b) after the entry relating to widowed mother's allowance insert—

| "Widowed parent's allowance | Class 1, 2 or 3 |
| Bereavement allowance | Class 1, 2 or 3". |

(3) In subsection (4), for "widow's payment" substitute "bereavement payment".

5. In section 46(2) (modifications of s. 45 for calculating additional pension in certain benefits)—

  (a) after "section 39(1)" insert "or 39C(1)"; and

  (b) for "or 48B(2)" substitute ", 48B(2) or 48BB(5)".

6. In section 48B (Category B retirement pension for widows and widowers), at the end add—

"(8) Nothing in subsections (4) to (7) above applies in a case where the spouse dies on or after the appointed day (as defined by section 36A(3))."

7. In section 48C(4) (category B retirement pension: general), for "or 48B(2)" substitute ", 48B(2) or 48BB(5)".

8.—(1) Section 60 (complete or partial failure to satisfy contribution conditions) is amended as follows.

(2) In subsection (1), after paragraph (a) insert—

"(aa) a widowed parent's allowance,

(ab) a bereavement allowance".

(3) In subsection (3)—

(a) for paragraph (a) substitute—

"(a) a bereavement payment;"; and

(b) after paragraph (b) insert—

"(ba) a widowed parent's allowance;

(bb) a bereavement allowance;"; and

(c) in paragraph (d), after "48B" insert "or 48BB".

9. In section 61(1) (exclusion of increase of benefit for failure to satisfy contribution condition), after "widowed mother's allowance" insert "or widowed parent's allowance".

10. In section 61A(3) (contributions paid in error)—

(a) at the end of paragraph (b) insert "(payable by virtue of section 48B or 48BB above)"; and

(b) after "widow's pension," insert—

"(ca) widowed parent's allowance,".

11. In section 80(5) (beneficiary's dependent children)—

(a) for "payable by virtue of subsection (1)(a) of section 37" substitute "or a widowed parent's allowance payable by virtue of section 37(1)(a) or (as the case may be) section 39A(2)(a)"; and

(b) for "subsection (2)(a), (b) or (c) of that section" substitute "section 37(2)(a), (b) or (c) or (as the case may be) section 39A(3)(a), (b) or (c)".

12. In section 150 (interpretation of provisions relating to Christmas bonus), in subsection (1)(c), after "allowance" insert ", widowed parent's allowance".

13.—(1) Schedule 3 (contribution conditions for entitlement to benefit) is amended as follows.

(2) In paragraph 4(1) (contribution condition for widow's payment) and in the cross-heading preceding paragraph 4, for "widow's payment" and "Widow's payment" substitute "bereavement payment" and "Bereavement payment" respectively.

(3) In paragraph 5(1) (contribution conditions for widowed mother's allowance, widow's pension etc.), after "allowance," insert " a widowed parent's

allowance, a bereavement allowance,"; and in the cross-heading preceding paragraph 5, after "allowance" insert ", widowed parent's allowance, bereavement allowance".

(4) In paragraph 7(1) and (3) (satisfaction of conditions in early years of contribution), for "widow's payment" substitute "bereavement payment".

(5) In paragraph 9 (satisfaction of condition where condition for short-term benefit satisfied)—

    (a) for "a woman claims a widow's payment" substitute "a claim is made for a bereavement payment"; and

    (b) for "widow's payment" (in the second place where it occurs) substitute "bereavement payment".

14. In Part IV of Schedule 4 (increases for dependants), after the entry relating to widowed mother's allowance insert—

"4A. Widowed parent's allowance   11.35   —".

Social Security Administration Act 1992 (c.5)

15. The Administration Act is amended as follows.

16. In section 1(2)(a) (entitlement to benefit dependent on claim), for "widow's payment, she" substitute "bereavement payment, the person".

17. For section 3 (and the cross-heading preceding it) substitute—

"Bereavement benefits

Late claims for bereavement benefit where death is difficult to establish.

3.—(1) This section applies where a person's spouse has died or may be presumed to have died on or after the appointed day and the circumstances are such that—

    (a) more than 12 months have elapsed since the date of death; and

    (b) either—

        (i) the spouse's body has not been discovered or identified or, if it has been discovered and identified, the surviving spouse does not know that fact; or

        (ii) less than 12 months have elapsed since the surviving spouse first knew of the discovery and identification of the body.

(2) Where this section applies, notwithstanding that any time prescribed for making a claim for a bereavement benefit in respect of the death has elapsed, then—

    (a) in any case falling within paragraph (b)(i) of subsection (1) above where it has been decided under section 8 of the Social Security Act 1998 that the spouse has died or is presumed to have died; or

1998 c. 14.

    (b) in any case falling within paragraph (b)(ii) of subsection (1) above where the identification was made not more than 12 months before the surviving spouse first knew of the discovery and identification of the body,

such a claim may be made or treated as made at any time before the expiration of the period of 12 months beginning with the date on which that decision was made or, as the case may be, the date on which the surviving spouse first knew of the discovery and identification.

(3) If, in a case where a claim for a bereavement benefit is made or treated as made by virtue of this section, the claimant would, apart from subsection (2) of section 1 above, be entitled to—

(a) a bereavement payment in respect of the spouse's death more than 12 months before the date on which the claim is made or treated as made; or

(b) any other bereavement benefit in respect of his or her death for a period more than 12 months before that date,

then, notwithstanding anything in that section, the surviving spouse shall be entitled to that payment or, as the case may be, to that other benefit (together with any increase under section 80(5) of the Contributions and Benefits Act).

(4) In subsection (1) above "the appointed day" means the day appointed for the coming into force of sections 54 to 56 of the Welfare Reform and Pensions Act 1999."

Pension Schemes Act 1993 (c.48)

18.—(1) Section 46 of the Pension Schemes Act 1993 (effect of entitlement to guaranteed minimum pensions on payment of social security benefit) is amended as follows.

(2) In subsection (1), after "widowed mother's allowance" insert ", a widowed parent's allowance".

(3) In subsection (6)(b)(iii), for "or 48B" substitute ", 48B or 48BB".

Pensions Act 1995 (c.26)

19.—(1) Section 128 of the Pensions Act 1995 (additional pension: calculation of surpluses) is amended as follows.

(2) In subsection (4), after "subsections (5)" insert ", (5A)".

(3) After subsection (5) insert—

"(5A) This section has effect in the case of additional pension falling to be calculated under sections 44 and 45 of the Social Security Contributions and Benefits Act 1992 by virtue of section 39C(1) of that Act (widowed parent's allowance), including Category B retirement pension payable under section 48BB(2), if the pensioner's spouse—

(a) dies after 5th April 2000, and

(b) has not attained pensionable age on or before that date."

(4) In subsection (6), for "or 48B(2)" substitute ", 48B(2) or 48BB(5)".

PART II

INCAPACITY

Social Security Contributions and Benefits Act 1992 (c.4)

20. The Contributions and Benefits Act has effect subject to the following amendments.

21. In section 21 (contribution conditions)—

(a) in subsection (1), after "other than" insert "short-term incapacity benefit under subsection (1)(b) of section 30A below," and for "30A below" substitute "subsection (5) of that section"; and

(b) in subsection (2), for "30A" substitute "30A(1)(a)".

22. In section 30B (incapacity benefit: rate), at the end add—

"(8) This section has effect subject to sections 30DD (reduction for pension payments) and section 30E (reduction for councillor's allowance) below."

23.—(1) Section 171A (test of incapacity for work) is amended as follows.

(2) After subsection (2) insert—

"(2A) In subsection (2)(a) above the reference to such information or evidence as is there mentioned includes information or evidence capable of being used for assisting or encouraging the person in question to obtain work or enhance his prospects of obtaining it."

(3) In subsection (3) (requirement to have medical examination), for "a question arises as to" substitute "it falls to be determined".

(4) After subsection (4) add—

"(5) All information supplied in pursuance of this section shall be taken for all purposes to be information relating to social security."

24. In section 171B(1) (the "own occupation test"), for "the test applicable is the own occupation test" substitute "the own occupation test is applicable in his case."

25. In section 176 (parliamentary control), in subsection (1)(a) (regulations subject to affirmative resolution procedure), after "section 28(3);" insert—

"section 30DD(5)(b) or (c);".

PART III

ABOLITION OF SEVERE DISABLEMENT ALLOWANCE

Social Security Contributions and Benefits Act 1992 (c.4)

26. In section 90 of the Contributions and Benefits Act (beneficiaries under sections 68 and 70)—

(a) for the words from "rates" to "allowance, and" substitute "rate"; and

(b) for "the allowance in question" substitute "the allowance".

Criminal Justice Act 1991 (c.53)

27. In section 24(4) of the Criminal Justice Act 1991 (recovery of fines etc. by deductions from income support), in the definition of "income support", for ", retirement pension or severe disablement allowance" substitute "or retirement pension".

PART IV

INCOME SUPPORT

Social Security Contributions and Benefits Act 1992 (c.4)

28. In section 124(1)(f) of the Contributions and Benefits Act (entitlement to income support conditional on claimant and any partner not being entitled to an income-based jobseeker's allowance), after "the other member of the couple is not" insert ", and the couple are not,".

Part V

Jobseeker's Allowance

Jobseekers Act 1995 (c.18)

29.—(1) The Jobseekers Act 1995 is amended as follows.

(2) In section 4 (amount payable by way of a jobseeker's allowance), in each of subsections (6) and (8) (amount payable where claimant satisfies the contribution-based, and the income-based, conditions)—

(a) for "satisfies both the contribution-based conditions and the income-based conditions" substitute "is entitled to both a contribution-based jobseeker's allowance and an income-based jobseeker's allowance"; and

(b) after "the amount payable" insert "by way of a jobseeker's allowance".

(3) In section 8 (attendance, information and evidence)—

(a) in subsection (1)(a) (power of Secretary of State to specify place and time for claimant to attend), for "the Secretary of State" substitute "an employment officer"; and

(b) at the end add—

"(3) In subsection (1) "employment officer" means an officer of the Secretary of State or such other person as may be designated for the purposes of that subsection by an order made by the Secretary of State."

(4) In section 17(1) (reduction of allowance payable to young persons), for "payable to" substitute "payable in respect of".

(5) In section 20(4) (allowance payable to claimant even though section 19 prevents payment to him), for "payable to" there shall be substituted "payable in respect of".

(6) In section 36(1) (orders to be made by statutory instrument unless made under specified provision), after "section" insert "8(3),".

(7) In paragraph 10(2) of Schedule 1 (allowance payable to claimant even though payment to him has been suspended), for "payable to" there shall be substituted "payable in respect of".

Part VI

Maternity Allowance

Social Security Contributions and Benefits Act 1992 (c.4)

30. The Contributions and Benefits Act has effect subject to the following amendments.

31.—(1) Section 21 (contribution conditions) is amended as follows.

(2) In subsection (1), after "30A below" insert ", maternity allowance under section 35 below".

(3) In subsection (2), omit the entry relating to maternity allowance.

(4) In subsection (4), omit ", other than maternity allowance,".

32. In section 176(1)(c) (parliamentary control), after "section 28(2)" insert—
      "section 35A(7);".

PART VII

RETIREMENT PENSIONS

Social Security Contributions and Benefits Act 1992 (c.4)

33. In section 48A of the Contributions and Benefits Act (category B retirement pension for married person), after subsection (4) insert—

"(4A) Subsection (4) above shall have effect with the omission of the words from "plus" to the end if the pensioner is not the widow or widower of the person by virtue of whose contributions the pension is payable."

PART VIII

ADMINISTRATION OF BENEFITS

34.—(1) In each of the provisions of the Administration Act to which this paragraph applies—

(a) any reference to a person authorised to exercise any function of a relevant authority relating to housing benefit or council tax benefit shall include a reference to a person providing services to a relevant authority which relate to such a benefit; and

(b) any reference to the exercise of any function relating to such a benefit shall include a reference to the provision of any services so relating.

(2) This paragraph applies to the following provisions of the Administration Act—

(a) section 110A (appointment of inspectors by authorities administering housing benefit or council tax benefit);

(b) sections 122C, 122D and 122E (supply of information in connection with administration of housing benefit or council tax benefit);

(c) section 126A (power to require information from landlords etc. in connection with claims for housing benefit);

(d) section 182B (information about redirection of post); and

(e) Schedule 4 (persons covered by offence relating to unauthorised disclosures).

(3) In this paragraph "relevant authority" means an authority administering housing benefit or council tax benefit.

SCHEDULE 9

NEW THRESHOLD FOR PRIMARY CLASS 1 CONTRIBUTIONS

PART I

NEW PRIMARY THRESHOLD

Earnings limits and thresholds for Class 1 contributions

1. For section 5 of the Contributions and Benefits Act substitute—

"Earnings limits and thresholds for Class 1 contributions.

5.—(1) For the purposes of this Act there shall for every tax year be—

(a) the following for primary Class 1 contributions—

(i) a lower earnings limit,

(ii) a primary threshold, and

(iii) an upper earnings limit; and

(b) a secondary threshold for secondary Class 1 contributions.

Those limits and thresholds shall be the amounts specified for that year by regulations which, in the case of those limits, shall be made in accordance with subsections (2) and (3) below.

(2) The amount specified as the lower earnings limit for any tax year shall be an amount equal to or not more than 99p less than—

(a) the sum which at the beginning of that year is specified in section 44(4) below as the weekly rate of the basic pension in a Category A retirement pension; or

(b) that sum as increased by any Act or order passed or made before the beginning of that year and taking effect before 6th May in that year.

(3) The amount specified as the upper earnings limit for any tax year shall be an amount which either—

(a) is equal to 7 times the sum which is the primary threshold for that year; or

(b) exceeds or falls short of 7 times that sum by an amount not exceeding half that sum.

(4) Regulations may, in the case of each of the limits or thresholds mentioned in subsection (1) above, prescribe an equivalent of that limit or threshold in relation to earners paid otherwise than weekly (and references in this or any other Act to "the prescribed equivalent", in the context of any of those limits or thresholds, are accordingly references to the equivalent prescribed under this subsection in relation to such earners).

(5) The power conferred by subsection (4) above to prescribe an equivalent of any of those limits or thresholds includes power to prescribe an amount which exceeds, by not more than £1.00, the amount which is the arithmetical equivalent of that limit or threshold.

(6) Regulations under this section shall be made by the Treasury."

Liability for Class 1 contributions

2. For section 6 of the Contributions and Benefits Act substitute—

"Liability for Class 1 contributions.

6.—(1) Where in any tax week earnings are paid to or for the benefit of an earner over the age of 16 in respect of any one employment of his which is employed earner's employment—

(a) a primary Class 1 contribution shall be payable in accordance with this section and section 8 below if the amount paid exceeds the current primary threshold (or the prescribed equivalent); and

(b) a secondary Class 1 contribution shall be payable in accordance with this section and section 9 below if the amount paid exceeds the current secondary threshold (or the prescribed equivalent).

(2) No primary or secondary Class 1 contribution shall be payable in respect of earnings if a Class 1B contribution is payable in respect of them.

(3) Except as may be prescribed, no primary Class 1 contribution shall be payable in respect of earnings paid to or

for the benefit of an employed earner after he attains pensionable age, but without prejudice to any liability to pay secondary Class 1 contributions in respect of any such earnings.

(4) The primary and secondary Class 1 contributions referred to in subsection (1) above are payable as follows—

    (a) the primary contribution shall be the liability of the earner; and

    (b) the secondary contribution shall be the liability of the secondary contributor;

but nothing in this subsection shall prejudice the provisions of paragraph 3 of Schedule 1 to this Act relating to the manner in which the earner's liability falls to be discharged.

(5) Except as provided by this Act, the primary and secondary Class 1 contributions in respect of earnings paid to or for the benefit of an earner in respect of any one employment of his shall be payable without regard to any other such payment of earnings in respect of any other employment of his.

(6) Regulations may provide for reducing primary or secondary Class 1 contributions which are payable in respect of persons to whom Part XI of the Employment Rights Act 1996 (redundancy payments) does not apply by virtue of section 199(2) or 209 of that Act.

(7) Regulations under this section shall be made by the Treasury."

Notional payment of primary Class 1 contribution where earnings not less than lower earnings limit

3. After section 6 of the Contributions and Benefits Act insert—

"Notional payment of primary Class 1 contribution where earnings not less than lower earnings limit.

6A.—(1) This section applies where in any tax week earnings are paid to or for the benefit of an earner over the age of 16 in respect of any one employment of his which is employed earner's employment and the amount paid—

    (a) is not less than the current lower earnings limit (or the prescribed equivalent), but

    (b) does not exceed the current primary threshold (or the prescribed equivalent).

(2) Subject to any prescribed exceptions or modifications—

    (a) the earner shall be treated as having actually paid a primary Class 1 contribution in respect of that week, and

    (b) those earnings shall be treated as earnings upon which such a contribution has been paid,

for any of the purposes mentioned in subsection (3) below.

(3) The purposes are—

    (a) the purposes of section 14(1)(a) below;

    (b) the purposes of the provisions mentioned in section 21(5A)(a) to (c) below;

    (c) any other purposes relating to contributory benefits; and

    (d) any purposes relating to jobseeker's allowance.

(4) Regulations may provide for any provision of this Act which, in whatever terms, refers—

SCH. 9

(a) to primary Class 1 contributions being payable by a person, or

(b) otherwise to a person's liability to pay such contributions,

to have effect for the purposes of this section with any prescribed modifications.

(5) Except as may be prescribed, nothing in this section applies in relation to earnings paid to or for the benefit of an employed earner after he attains pensionable age.

(6) Except as provided by this Act, this section applies in relation to earnings paid to or for the benefit of an earner in respect of any one employment of his irrespective of any other such payment of earnings in respect of any other employment of his.

(7) Regulations under this section shall be made by the Treasury."

Calculation of primary Class 1 contributions

4. For section 8 of the Contributions and Benefits Act substitute—

"Calculation of primary Class 1 contributions.

8.—(1) Where a primary Class 1 contribution is payable as mentioned in section 6(1)(a) above, the amount of that contribution shall be the primary percentage of so much of the earner's earnings paid in the tax week, in respect of the employment in question, as—

(a) exceeds the current primary threshold (or the prescribed equivalent); and

(b) does not exceed the current upper earnings limit (or the prescribed equivalent);

but this subsection is subject to regulations under section 6(6) above and sections 116 to 120 below and to section 41 of the Pensions Act (reduced rates of Class 1 contributions for earners in contracted-out employment).

(2) For the purposes of this Act the primary percentage shall be 10 per cent; but the percentage is subject to alteration under sections 143 and 145 of the Administration Act."

Calculation of secondary Class 1 contributions

5. For section 9 of the Contributions and Benefits Act substitute—

"Calculation of secondary Class 1 contributions.

9.—(1) Where a secondary Class 1 contribution is payable as mentioned in section 6(1)(b) above, the amount of that contribution shall be the secondary percentage of so much of the earnings paid in the tax week, in respect of the employment in question, as exceeds the current secondary threshold (or the prescribed equivalent).

(2) For the purposes of subsection (1) above, the secondary percentage shall be 12.2 per cent; but the percentage is subject to alteration under sections 143 and 145 of the Administration Act.

(3) Subsection (1) above is subject to regulations under section 6(6) above and sections 116 to 120 below and to section 41 of the Pensions Act."

Pᴀʀᴛ II

Rᴇᴅᴜᴄᴇᴅ ᴄᴏɴᴛʀɪʙᴜᴛɪᴏɴs ɪɴ ʀᴇsᴘᴇᴄᴛ ᴏғ ᴍᴇᴍʙᴇʀs ᴏғ ᴄᴏɴᴛʀᴀᴄᴛᴇᴅ-ᴏᴜᴛ sᴄʜᴇᴍᴇs

Reduced rates for members of salary related contracted-out schemes

6.—(1) Section 41 of the Pension Schemes Act 1993 is amended as follows.   1993 c. 48.

(2) In subsection (1), for "(1C)" substitute "(1E)".

(3) For subsections (1A) to (1C) substitute—

"(1A) The amount of any primary Class 1 contribution in respect of the earnings shall be reduced by an amount equal to 1.6 per cent of the relevant part of the earnings ("Amount R1").

(1B) The amount of any secondary Class 1 contribution in respect of the earnings shall be reduced by an amount equal to 3 per cent of the relevant part of the earnings ("Amount R2").

(1C) The aggregate of Amounts R1 and R2 shall be set off—

(a) first against the aggregate amount which the secondary contributor is liable to pay in respect of the contributions mentioned in subsections (1A) and (1B); and

(b) then (as to any balance) against any amount which the secondary contributor is liable to pay in respect of any primary or secondary Class 1 contribution in respect of earnings—

(i) paid to or for the benefit of any other employed earner (whether in contracted-out employment or not), and

(ii) in relation to which the secondary contributor is such a contributor;

and in this subsection any reference to a liability to pay an amount in respect of a primary Class 1 contribution is a reference to such a liability under paragraph 3 of Schedule 1 to the Social Security Contributions and Benefits Act 1992.

(1D) If—

(a) any balance remains, and

(b) the secondary contributor makes an application for the purpose to the Inland Revenue,

the Inland Revenue shall, in such manner and at such time (or within such period) as may be prescribed, pay to the secondary contributor an amount equal to the remaining balance.

But regulations may make provision for the adjustment of an amount that would otherwise be payable under this subsection so as to avoid the payment of trivial or fractional amounts.

(1E) If the Inland Revenue pay any amount under subsection (1D) which they are not required to pay, they may recover that amount from the secondary contributor in such manner and at such time (or within such period) as may be prescribed."

Reduced rates for members of money purchase contracted-out schemes

7.—(1) Section 42A of the Pension Schemes Act 1993 is amended as follows.

(2) In subsection (1), for "(3)" substitute "(2D) and (3)".

(3) For subsections (2) to (2B) substitute—

"(2) The amount of any primary Class 1 contribution in respect of the earnings shall be reduced by an amount equal to the appropriate flat-rate percentage of the relevant part of the earnings ("Amount R1").

Sch. 9

(2A) The amount of any secondary Class 1 contribution in respect of the earnings shall be reduced by an amount equal to the appropriate flat-rate percentage of the relevant part of the earnings ("Amount R2").

(2B) The aggregate of Amounts R1 and R2 shall be set off—

(a) first against the aggregate amount which the secondary contributor is liable to pay in respect of the contributions mentioned in subsections (2) and (2A); and

(b) then (as to any balance) against any amount which the secondary contributor is liable to pay in respect of a primary or secondary Class 1 contribution in respect of earnings—

(i) paid to or for the benefit of any other employed earner (whether in contracted-out employment or not), and

(ii) in relation to which the secondary contributor is such a contributor;

and in this subsection any reference to a liability to pay an amount in respect of a primary Class 1 contribution is a reference to such a liability under paragraph 3 of Schedule 1 to the Social Security Contributions and Benefits Act 1992.

(2C) If—

(a) any balance remains, and

(b) the secondary contributor makes an application for the purpose to the Inland Revenue,

the Inland Revenue shall, in such manner and at such time (or within such period) as may be prescribed, pay to the secondary contributor an amount equal to the remaining balance.

But regulations may make provision for the adjustment of an amount that would otherwise be payable under this subsection so as to avoid the payment of trivial or fractional amounts.

(2D) If the Inland Revenue pay any amount under subsection (2C) which they are not required to pay, they may recover that amount from the secondary contributor in such manner and at such time (or within such period) as may be prescribed."

Payments by Inland Revenue out of and into National Insurance Fund

1993 c. 48.

8.—(1) Section 177 of the Pension Schemes Act 1993 is amended as follows.

(2) In subsection (2)(za), for "section 42A(3)" substitute "section 41(1D) or section 42A(2C) or (3)".

(3) In subsection (7)(a), for "42A(5) or" substitute "41(1E), 42A(2D) or (5) or".

PART III

NATIONAL HEALTH SERVICE ALLOCATION

9.—(1) Section 162 of the Administration Act is amended as follows.

(2) In subsection (5)—

(a) in paragraph (a), for "the lower earnings limit" substitute "the primary threshold"; and

(b) in paragraph (b), before "earnings" insert "total".

(3) In subsection (6A)—

   (a) for "the lower or upper earnings limit" substitute "the primary threshold or the upper earnings limit"; and

   (b) for "that limit prescribed under section 8(3)" substitute "that threshold or limit prescribed under section 5(4)".

SCHEDULE 10

NEW THRESHOLD FOR PRIMARY CLASS 1 CONTRIBUTIONS: NORTHERN IRELAND

PART I

NEW PRIMARY THRESHOLD

Earnings limits and thresholds for Class 1 contributions

Section 74.

1. For section 5 of the Social Security Contributions and Benefits (Northern Ireland) Act 1992 substitute—

1992 c. 7.

"Earnings limits and thresholds for Class 1 contributions.

   5.—(1) For the purposes of this Act there shall for every tax year be—

     (a) the following for primary Class 1 contributions—

        (i) a lower earnings limit,

        (ii) a primary threshold, and

        (iii) an upper earnings limit; and

     (b) a secondary threshold for secondary Class 1 contributions.

Those limits and thresholds shall be the amounts specified for that year by regulations which, in the case of those limits, shall be made in accordance with subsections (2) and (3) below.

   (2) The amount specified as the lower earnings limit for any tax year shall be an amount equal to or not more than 99p less than—

     (a) the sum which at the beginning of that year is specified in section 44(4) below as the weekly rate of the basic pension in a Category A retirement pension; or

     (b) that sum as increased by any Act, Measure or order passed or made before the beginning of that year and taking effect before 6th May in that year.

   (3) The amount specified as the upper earnings limit for any tax year shall be an amount which either—

     (a) is equal to 7 times the sum which is the primary threshold for that year; or

     (b) exceeds or falls short of 7 times that sum by an amount not exceeding half that sum.

   (4) Regulations may, in the case of each of the limits or thresholds mentioned in subsection (1) above, prescribe an equivalent of that limit or threshold in relation to earners paid otherwise than weekly (and references in this Act or any other statutory provision to "the prescribed equivalent", in the context of any of those limits or thresholds, are accordingly references to the equivalent prescribed under this subsection in relation to such earners).

   (5) The power conferred by subsection (4) above to prescribe an equivalent of any of those limits or thresholds includes

SCH. 10

power to prescribe an amount which exceeds, by not more than £1.00, the amount which is the arithmetical equivalent of that limit or threshold.

(6) Regulations under this section shall be made by the Treasury."

Liability for Class 1 contributions

1992 c. 7.

2. For section 6 of the Social Security Contributions and Benefits (Northern Ireland) Act 1992 substitute—

"Liability for Class 1 contributions.

6.—(1) Where in any tax week earnings are paid to or for the benefit of an earner over the age of 16 in respect of any one employment of his which is employed earner's employment—

(a) a primary Class 1 contribution shall be payable in accordance with this section and section 8 below if the amount paid exceeds the current primary threshold (or the prescribed equivalent); and

(b) a secondary Class 1 contribution shall be payable in accordance with this section and section 9 below if the amount paid exceeds the current secondary threshold (or the prescribed equivalent).

(2) No primary or secondary Class 1 contribution shall be payable in respect of earnings if a Class 1B contribution is payable in respect of them.

(3) Except as may be prescribed, no primary Class 1 contribution shall be payable in respect of earnings paid to or for the benefit of an employed earner after he attains pensionable age, but without prejudice to any liability to pay secondary Class 1 contributions in respect of any such earnings.

(4) The primary and secondary Class 1 contributions referred to in subsection (1) above are payable as follows—

(a) the primary contribution shall be the liability of the earner; and

(b) the secondary contribution shall be the liability of the secondary contributor;

but nothing in this subsection shall prejudice the provisions of paragraph 3 of Schedule 1 to this Act relating to the manner in which the earner's liability falls to be discharged.

(5) Except as provided by this Act, the primary and secondary Class 1 contributions in respect of earnings paid to or for the benefit of an earner in respect of any one employment of his shall be payable without regard to any other such payment of earnings in respect of any other employment of his.

(6) Regulations may provide for reducing primary or secondary Class 1 contributions which are payable in respect of persons to whom Part XII of the Employment Rights (Northern Ireland) Order 1996 (redundancy payments) does not apply by virtue of Article 242(2) or 250 of that Order.

S.I. 1996/1919 (N.I. 16).

(7) Regulations under this section shall be made by the Treasury."

Notional payment of primary Class 1 contribution where earnings not less than lower earnings limit

3. After section 6 of the Social Security Contributions and Benefits (Northern Ireland) Act 1992 insert— 1992 c. 7.

"Notional payment of primary Class 1 contribution where earnings not less than lower earnings limit.

6A.—(1) This section applies where in any tax week earnings are paid to or for the benefit of an earner over the age of 16 in respect of any one employment of his which is employed earner's employment and the amount paid—

(a) is not less than the current lower earnings limit (or the prescribed equivalent), but

(b) does not exceed the current primary threshold (or the prescribed equivalent).

(2) Subject to any prescribed exceptions or modifications—

(a) the earner shall be treated as having actually paid a primary Class 1 contribution in respect of that week, and

(b) those earnings shall be treated as earnings upon which such a contribution has been paid,

for any of the purposes mentioned in subsection (3) below.

(3) The purposes are—

(a) the purposes of section 14(1)(a) below;

(b) the purposes of the provisions mentioned in section 21(5A)(a) to (c) below;

(c) any other purposes relating to contributory benefits; and

(d) any purposes relating to jobseeker's allowance.

(4) Regulations may provide for any provision of this Act which, in whatever terms, refers—

(a) to primary Class 1 contributions being payable by a person, or

(b) otherwise to a person's liability to pay such contributions,

to have effect for the purposes of this section with any prescribed modifications.

(5) Except as may be prescribed, nothing in this section applies in relation to earnings paid to or for the benefit of an employed earner after he attains pensionable age.

(6) Except as provided by this Act, this section applies in relation to earnings paid to or for the benefit of an earner in respect of any one employment of his irrespective of any other such payment of earnings in respect of any other employment of his.

(7) Regulations under this section shall be made by the Treasury."

Calculation of primary Class 1 contributions

4. For section 8 of the Social Security Contributions and Benefits (Northern Ireland) Act 1992 substitute—

"Calculation of primary Class 1 contributions.

8.—(1) Where a primary Class 1 contribution is payable as mentioned in section 6(1)(a) above, the amount of that contribution shall be the primary percentage of so much of the earner's earnings paid in the tax week, in respect of the employment in question, as—

    (a) exceeds the current primary threshold (or the prescribed equivalent); and

    (b) does not exceed the current upper earnings limit (or the prescribed equivalent);

but this subsection is subject to regulations under section 6(6) above and sections 116 to 119 below and to section 37 of the Pensions Act (reduced rates of Class 1 contributions for earners in contracted-out employment).

(2) For the purposes of this Act the primary percentage shall be 10 per cent; but the percentage is subject to alteration under section 129 of the Administration Act."

Calculation of secondary Class 1 contributions

1992 c. 7.

5. For section 9 of the Social Security Contributions and Benefits (Northern Ireland) Act 1992 substitute—

"Calculation of secondary Class 1 contributions.

    9.—(1) Where a secondary Class 1 contribution is payable as mentioned in section 6(1)(b) above, the amount of that contribution shall be the secondary percentage of so much of the earnings paid in the tax week, in respect of the employment in question, as exceeds the current secondary threshold (or the prescribed equivalent).

(2) For the purposes of subsection (1) above, the secondary percentage shall be 12.2 per cent; but the percentage is subject to alteration under section 129 of the Administration Act.

(3) Subsection (1) above is subject to regulations under section 6(6) above and sections 116 to 119 below and to section 37 of the Pensions Act."

Part II

Reduced contributions in respect of members of contracted-out schemes

Reduced rates for members of salary related contracted-out schemes

1993 c. 49.

6.—(1) Section 37 of the Pension Schemes (Northern Ireland) Act 1993 is amended as follows.

(2) In subsection (1), for "(1C)" substitute "(1E)".

(3) For subsections (1A) to (1C) substitute—

"(1A) The amount of any primary Class 1 contribution in respect of the earnings shall be reduced by an amount equal to 1.6 per cent of the relevant part of the earnings ("Amount R1").

(1B) The amount of any secondary Class 1 contribution in respect of the earnings shall be reduced by an amount equal to 3 per cent of the relevant part of the earnings ("Amount R2").

(1C) The aggregate of Amounts R1 and R2 shall be set off—

    (a) first against the aggregate amount which the secondary contributor is liable to pay in respect of the contributions mentioned in subsections (1A) and (1B); and

    (b) then (as to any balance) against any amount which the secondary contributor is liable to pay in respect of any primary or secondary Class 1 contribution in respect of earnings—

        (i) paid to or for the benefit of any other employed earner (whether in contracted-out employment or not), and

(ii) in relation to which the secondary contributor is such a contributor;

and in this subsection any reference to a liability to pay an amount in respect of a primary Class 1 contribution is a reference to such a liability under paragraph 3 of Schedule 1 to the Social Security Contributions and Benefits (Northern Ireland) Act 1992.

1992 c. 7.

(1D) If—

(a) any balance remains, and

(b) the secondary contributor makes an application for the purpose to the Inland Revenue,

the Inland Revenue shall, in such manner and at such time (or within such period) as may be prescribed by regulations made by the Secretary of State, pay to the secondary contributor an amount equal to the remaining balance.

But such regulations may make provision for the adjustment of an amount that would otherwise be payable under this subsection so as to avoid the payment of trivial or fractional amounts.

(1E) If the Inland Revenue pay any amount under subsection (1D) which they are not required to pay, they may recover that amount from the secondary contributor in such manner and at such time (or within such period) as may be prescribed by such regulations."

Reduced rates for members of money purchase contracted-out schemes

7.—(1) Section 38A of the Pension Schemes (Northern Ireland) Act 1993 is amended as follows.

1993 c. 49.

(2) In subsection (1), for "(3)" substitute "(2D) and (3)".

(3) For subsections (2) to (2B) substitute—

"(2) The amount of any primary Class 1 contribution in respect of the earnings shall be reduced by an amount equal to the appropriate flat-rate percentage of the relevant part of the earnings ("Amount R1").

(2A) The amount of any secondary Class 1 contribution in respect of the earnings shall be reduced by an amount equal to the appropriate flat-rate percentage of the relevant part of the earnings ("Amount R2").

(2B) The aggregate of Amounts R1 and R2 shall be set off—

(a) first against the aggregate amount which the secondary contributor is liable to pay in respect of the contributions mentioned in subsections (2) and (2A); and

(b) then (as to any balance) against any amount which the secondary contributor is liable to pay in respect of a primary or secondary Class 1 contribution in respect of earnings—

(i) paid to or for the benefit of any other employed earner (whether in contracted-out employment or not), and

(ii) in relation to which the secondary contributor is such a contributor;

and in this subsection any reference to a liability to pay an amount in respect of a primary Class 1 contribution is a reference to such a liability under paragraph 3 of Schedule 1 to the Social Security Contributions and Benefits (Northern Ireland) Act 1992.

(2C) If—

(a) any balance remains, and

(b) the secondary contributor makes an application for the purpose to the Inland Revenue,

the Inland Revenue shall, in such manner and at such time (or within such period) as may be prescribed by regulations made by the Secretary of State, pay to the secondary contributor an amount equal to the remaining balance.

But such regulations may make provision for the adjustment of an amount that would otherwise be payable under this subsection so as to avoid the payment of trivial or fractional amounts.

(2D) If the Inland Revenue pay any amount under subsection (2C) which they are not required to pay, they may recover that amount from the secondary contributor in such manner and at such time (or within such period) as may be prescribed by such regulations."

Payments by Inland Revenue out of and into National Insurance Fund

1993 c. 49.   8.—(1) Section 172 of the Pension Schemes (Northern Ireland) Act 1993 is amended as follows.

(2) In subsection (1)(za), for "section 38A(3)" substitute "section 37(1D) or section 38A(2C) or (3)".

(3) In subsection (7), for "section 38A(5) or" substitute "section 37(1E), 38A(2D) or (5) or".

PART III

HEALTH SERVICE ALLOCATION

1992 c. 8.   9.—(1) Section 142 of the Social Security Administration (Northern Ireland) Act 1992 is amended as follows.

(2) In subsection (5)—

(a) in paragraph (a), for "the lower earnings limit" substitute "the primary threshold"; and

(b) in paragraph (b), before "earnings" insert "total".

(3) In subsection (6A)—

(a) for "the lower or upper earnings limit" substitute "the primary threshold or the upper earnings limit"; and

(b) for "that limit prescribed under section 8(3)" substitute "that threshold or limit prescribed under section 5(4)".

Section 81.   ## SCHEDULE 11

CONTRIBUTIONS AND PENSIONS ADMINISTRATION

Social Security Contributions and Benefits Act 1992 (c.4)

1. The Contributions and Benefits Act is amended as follows.

2. In section 2 (categories of earners), for subsection (2A) there is substituted—

"(2A) Regulations under subsection (2) above shall be made by the Treasury and, in the case of regulations under paragraph (b) of that subsection, with the concurrence of the Secretary of State."

3. In paragraph 8 of Schedule 1 (general regulation-making powers), at the end of sub-paragraph (1A) there is inserted "acting with the concurrence of the Inland Revenue".

Social Security Administration Act 1992 (c.5)

4. The Administration Act is amended as follows.

5. In section 116 (legal proceedings), in subsection (5A) for the words from the beginning to "that section" there is substituted "In relation to proceedings for an offence under section 114 above".

6. In section 121A (recovery of contributions etc. in England and Wales), in subsection (8) for "Regulations may" there is substituted "The Inland Revenue may by regulations".

7. In section 121E (supply of contributions etc. information held by Inland Revenue), in subsection (1) after "statutory maternity pay" there is inserted "or functions under Part III of the Pensions Act".

8. In section 121F (supply to Inland Revenue for purposes of contributions etc. of information held by Secretary of State), at the end of subsection (2) there is inserted "or functions under Part III of the Pensions Act".

Social Security Contributions and Benefits (Northern Ireland) Act 1992 (c. 7)

9. The Social Security Contributions and Benefits (Northern Ireland) Act 1992 is amended as follows.

10. In section 2 (categories of earners), for subsection (2A) there is substituted—

"(2A) Regulations under subsection (2) above shall be made by the Treasury and, in the case of regulations under paragraph (b) of that subsection, with the concurrence of the Department."

11. In section 172 (Assembly, etc. control of regulations and orders), in subsection (2)(c) for ", 153(2) or" there is substituted "or 153(2)".

12. In paragraph 8 of Schedule 1 (general regulation-making powers), at the end of sub-paragraph (1A) there is inserted "acting with the concurrence of the Inland Revenue".

Social Security Administration (Northern Ireland) Act 1992 (c.8)

13. The Social Security Administration (Northern Ireland) Act 1992 is amended as follows.

14. In section 110 (legal proceedings), for subsection (5A) there is substituted—

"(5A) In relation to proceedings for an offence under section 108 above—

(a) the reference in subsection (2)(a) above to the Department, and

(b) the reference in subsection (3)(a) above to the Head or a secretary, under secretary or assistant secretary of the Department,

shall have effect as references to the Inland Revenue."

15. In section 115D (supply of contributions, etc. information held by Inland Revenue), in subsection (1) after "statutory maternity pay" there is inserted "or functions under Part III of the Pensions Act".

16. In section 115E (supply to Inland Revenue for purposes of contributions etc. of information held by Department or Secretary of State), at the end of subsection (2) there is inserted "or functions under Part III of the Pensions Act".

17.—(1) In section 116 (supply of information held by tax authorities for fraud prevention and verification), for subsection (1) there is substituted—

"(1) This section applies—

(a) to information which is held—

(i) by the Inland Revenue, or

(ii) by a person providing services to the Inland Revenue, in connection with the provision of those services,

but is not information to which section 115D above applies, and

(b) to information which is held—

(i) by the Commissioners of Customs and Excise, or

(ii) by a person providing services to the Commissioners of Customs and Excise, in connection with the provision of those services."

(2) This amendment shall be deemed to have come into force on 1st April 1999 in place of that made by paragraph 2(2) of Schedule 5 to the Social Security Contributions (Transfer of Functions, etc.) (Northern Ireland) Order 1999.

S.I. 1999/671.

18.—(1) In section 145 (adjustments between the Northern Ireland National Insurance Fund and the Consolidated Fund of Northern Ireland)—

(a) in subsection (1)(a), sub-paragraphs (i) and (ii) are omitted; and

(b) in subsection (3)(a), for "subsection (1)(a) and (b)" there is substituted "subsection (1)(b)".

(2) These amendments shall be deemed to have come into force on 5th October 1999 in place of those made by paragraph 34 of Schedule 2 to the Tax Credits Act 1999.

1999 c. 10.

19.—(1) In section 165 (regulations and orders - general), in subsection (9)(c), for "142(7), 145(4)" there is substituted "145(4)(a)".

(2) This amendment shall be deemed to have come into force on 1st April 1999 in place of that made by paragraph 49(3) of Schedule 3 to the Social Security Contributions (Transfer of Functions, etc.) (Northern Ireland) Order 1999.

Pension Schemes Act 1993 (c.48)

20. The Pension Schemes Act 1993 is amended as follows.

21. In section 40 (scope of Chapter II of Part III), in paragraph (b) for "Secretary of State" there is substituted "Inland Revenue".

22. In section 170 (decisions and appeals), as amended by section 16(2) of the Social Security Contributions (Transfer of Functions, etc.) Act 1999, in subsection (5)—

1999 c. 2.

(a) for paragraphs (a) and (b) there is substituted—

"(a) generally with respect to the making of relevant decisions;

(b) with respect to the procedure to be adopted on any application made under section 9 or 10 of the 1998 Act by virtue of subsection (4); and

(c) generally with respect to such applications, revisions under section 9 and decisions under section 10;", and

(b) for "such a revision or decision" there is substituted "a revision under section 9 or decision under section 10".

23. In section 185 (consultation about regulations), in subsection (8) for "section 170(8)" there is substituted "section 170(5)".

Pension Schemes (Northern Ireland) Act 1993 (c.49)

24. The Pension Schemes (Northern Ireland) Act 1993 is amended as follows.

25.—(1) In section 154 (disclosure of information between government departments, etc.), in subsection (5) after "Subsections (1) and (1A)" there is inserted "extend".

(2) This amendment shall be deemed to have come into force on 1st April 1999.

26. In section 165 (decisions and appeals), as amended by Article 15(2) of the Social Security Contributions (Transfer of Functions, etc.) (Northern Ireland) Order 1999, in subsection (5)— S.I. 1999/671.

(a) for paragraphs (a) and (b) there is substituted—

"(a) generally with respect to the making of relevant decisions;

(b) with respect to the procedure to be adopted on any application made under Article 10 or 11 of the 1998 Order by virtue of subsection (4); and

(c) generally with respect to such applications, revisions under Article 10 and decisions under Article 11;", and

(b) for "such a revision or decision" there is substituted "a revision under Article 10 or decision under Article 11".

27.—(1) In section 177 (orders and regulations - general provisions), for subsection (7) there is substituted—

"(7) Any power conferred on the Secretary of State to make regulations or orders (other than an order under section 162) is exercisable by statutory instrument, and subsections (2) to (4) and section 178(1) apply to regulations or orders made in exercise of any such power of the Secretary of State as they apply to regulations made by the Department."

(2) This amendment shall be deemed to have come into force on 1st April 1999 in place of those made by paragraph 75(3) of Schedule 1 to the Social Security Contributions (Transfer of Functions, etc.) (Northern Ireland) Order 1999.

28. In section 180(2) (consultation about regulations)—

(a) for "the appropriate government department" there is substituted "the Department or, as the case may be, the Secretary of State", and

(b) after "it" there is inserted "or him".

Social Security Contributions (Transfer of Functions, etc.) Act 1999 (c.2)

29. The Social Security Contributions (Transfer of Functions, etc.) Act 1999 is amended as follows.

1890 c. 21.

30. In section 3 (general functions of Inland Revenue), subsection (3)(c) (which excludes the application of section 27 of the Inland Revenue Regulation Act 1890 but has not come into force) is omitted.

31. In section 4 (recovery of contributions where income tax recovery provisions not applicable)—

1992 c. 7.

    (a) in paragraph (a), after "1992" there is inserted "or paragraph 6 of Schedule 1 to the Social Security Contributions and Benefits (Northern Ireland) Act 1992",

1992 c. 4.

    (b) in paragraph (b), for "that Act" there is substituted "the Social Security Contributions and Benefits Act 1992 or section 18 of the Social Security Contributions and Benefits (Northern Ireland) Act 1992", and

    (c) in paragraph (c), for "that Act" there is substituted "the Social Security Contributions and Benefits Act 1992 or paragraph 7A or 7B of Schedule 1 to the Social Security Contributions and Benefits (Northern Ireland) Act 1992".

32. In Schedule 1 (transfer of Contributions Agency functions and associated functions), the following provisions are omitted, namely—

S.I. 1999/671.

    (a) paragraph 4(6) (which was superseded by paragraph 4 of Schedule 1 to the Social Security Contributions (Transfer of Functions, etc.) (Northern Ireland) Order 1999), and

    (b) paragraph 66(3) (which has not come into force).

S.I. 1997/664 (C. 23).

1993 c. 48.

33. In Schedule 2 (transfer of functions under subordinate legislation), the entry in the third column relating to the Pensions Act 1995 (Commencement No. 10) Order 1997 shall have effect, and be deemed always to have had effect, with the substitution for "Articles 4 and 13" of "In Article 4, paragraph (1), paragraph (2), except so far as relating to section 55(3) of the Pension Schemes Act 1993, to the making of regulations under section 64(1) of that Act and to section 64(3) and (5) to (9) of that Act, and paragraph (3) and Article 13".

Social Security Contributions (Transfer of Functions, etc.) (Northern Ireland) Order 1999 (S.I. 1999/671)

S.R. (N.I.) 1997 No. 192 (C. 10).

1993 c. 49.

34. In Schedule 2 to the Social Security Contributions (Transfer of Functions, etc.) (Northern Ireland) Order 1999 (transfer of functions under subordinate legislation), the entry in the third column relating to the Pensions (1995 Order) (Commencement No. 8) Order (Northern Ireland) 1997 shall have effect, and be deemed always to have had effect, with the substitution for "Articles 4 and 13" of "In Article 4, paragraph (1), paragraph (2), except so far as relating to section 51(3) of the Pension Schemes (Northern Ireland) Act 1993 and to the making of regulations under section 60(1) of that Act, and paragraph (3) and Article 13".

Transfer of certain functions under subordinate legislation: Great Britain

35. There are hereby transferred to the Commissioners of Inland Revenue—

S.I. 1979/591.

1999 c. 2.

    (a) all functions of the Secretary of State under the Social Security (Contributions) Regulations 1979 which are not transferred to the Commissioners of Inland Revenue by virtue of section 1(2) of, and Schedule 2 to, the Social Security Contributions (Transfer of Functions, etc.) Act 1999, except his functions under regulation 44 of those regulations,

S.I. 1984/380.

S.I. 1996/1172.

    (b) the functions of the Secretary of State under those provisions of the Occupational Pension Schemes (Contracting-out) Regulations 1984 ("the 1984 regulations") which remain in force by virtue of regulation 77(a) of the Occupational Pension Schemes (Contracting-out) Regulations 1996 ("the 1996 regulations"), including his functions under the modifications of section 60(4) and (5) of the Pension Schemes Act 1993 made by regulation 23(10)(a)(iii) of the 1984 regulations, but excluding—

(i) his functions under paragraph (2) of regulation 20 of the 1984 regulations so far as relating to any extension of the period first referred to in that paragraph by more than six months, and

(ii) his functions under regulations 23(4) and 23A(4) of the 1984 regulations,

(c) the functions of the Secretary of State under regulation 2 of the Occupational Pension Schemes (Contracted-out Protected Rights Premiums) Regulations 1987 (so far as remaining in force by virtue of regulation 77(b) of the 1996 regulations), and

S.I. 1987/1103.

(d) the functions of the Secretary of State under the Personal Pension Schemes (Personal Pension Protected Rights Premiums) Regulations 1987 ("the 1987 regulations") (so far as remaining in force by virtue of regulation 4(2) of the Personal and Occupational Pension Schemes (Miscellaneous Amendments) Regulations 1997), except—

S.I. 1987/1111.

S.I. 1997/786.

(i) his functions under paragraph (3) of regulation 5 of the 1987 regulations so far as relating to any extension of the period first referred to in that paragraph by more than six months, and

(ii) his functions under regulation 6(4) of the 1987 regulations.

Transfer of certain functions under subordinate legislation: Northern Ireland

36.—(1) There are hereby transferred to the Commissioners of Inland Revenue—

(a) all functions of the Department under the Social Security (Contributions) Regulations (Northern Ireland) 1979 which are not transferred to the Commissioners of Inland Revenue by virtue of Article 3(2) of, and Schedule 2 to, the Social Security Contributions (Transfer of Functions, etc.) (Northern Ireland) Order 1999, except the functions of the Department under regulation 44 of those regulations,

S.R. (N.I.) 1979 No. 186.

S.I. 1999/671.

(b) the functions of the Department under those provisions of the Occupational Pension Schemes (Contracting-out) Regulations (Northern Ireland) 1985 ("the 1985 regulations") which remain in force by virtue of regulation 78(a) of the Occupational Pension Schemes (Contracting-out) Regulations (Northern Ireland) 1996 ("the 1996 regulations"), including its functions under the modifications of section 56(4) and (5) of the Pension Schemes (Northern Ireland) Act 1993 made by regulation 22(10)(a) of the 1985 regulations, but excluding—

S.R. (N.I.) 1985 No. 259.

S.R. (N.I.) 1996 No. 493.

1993 c. 49.

(i) its functions under paragraph (2) of regulation 19 of the 1985 regulations so far as relating to any extension of the period first referred to in that paragraph by more than six months, and

(ii) its functions under regulations 22(4) and 22A(4) of the 1985 regulations,

(c) the functions of the Department under regulation 2 of the Occupational Pension Schemes (Contracted-out Protected Rights Premiums) Regulations (Northern Ireland) 1987 (so far as remaining in force by virtue of regulation 78(b) of the 1996 regulations), and

S.R. (N.I.) 1987 No. 281.

(d) the functions of the Department under the Personal Pension Schemes (Personal Pension Protected Rights Premiums) Regulations (Northern Ireland) 1987 ("the 1987 regulations") (so far as remaining in force by virtue of regulation 4(2) of the Personal and Occupational Pension Schemes (Miscellaneous Amendments) Regulations (Northern Ireland) 1997), except—

S.R. (N.I.) 1987 No. 289.

S.R. (N.I.) 1997 No. 160.

(i) its functions under paragraph (3) of regulation 5 of the 1987 regulations so far as relating to any extension of the period first referred to in that paragraph by more than six months, and

(ii) its functions under regulation 6(4) of the 1987 regulations.

(2) In sub-paragraph (1) "the Department" means the Department of Health and Social Services for Northern Ireland.

Savings

1999 c. 2.

37. Paragraphs 1 and 2 of Schedule 8 to the Social Security Contributions (Transfer of Functions, etc.) Act 1999 (general provisions relating to transfers of functions) shall have effect as if paragraphs 2, 3, 6, 21 and 35 of this Schedule were provisions of that Act specified in section 21(1) of that Act.

S.I. 1999/671.

38. Paragraphs 1 and 2 of Schedule 7 to the Social Security Contributions (Transfer of Functions, etc.) (Northern Ireland) Order 1999 (general provisions relating to transfers of functions) shall have effect as if paragraphs 10, 12 and 36 of this Schedule were provisions of that Order specified in Article 20(1) of that Order.

Section 84.

SCHEDULE 12

Consequential amendments

Part I

Amendments consequential on Parts III and IV

Supreme Court Act 1981 (c.54)

1. In paragraph 3 of Schedule 1 to the Supreme Court Act 1981, after paragraph (f) there is inserted—

"(fa) all proceedings relating to a debit or credit under section 29(1) or 49(1) of the Welfare Reform and Pensions Act 1999;".

Matrimonial and Family Proceedings Act 1984 (c.42)

2. The Matrimonial and Family Proceedings Act 1984 is amended as follows.

3. In section 17, for subsection (1) there is substituted—

"(1) Subject to section 20 below, on an application by a party to a marriage for an order for financial relief under this section, the court may—

(a) make any one or more of the orders which it could make under Part II of the 1973 Act if a decree of divorce, a decree of nullity of marriage or a decree of judicial separation in respect of the marriage had been granted in England and Wales, that is to say—

(i) any order mentioned in section 23(1) of the 1973 Act (financial provision orders); and

(ii) any order mentioned in section 24(1) of that Act (property adjustment orders); and

(b) if the marriage has been dissolved or annulled, make one or more orders each of which would, within the meaning of that Part of that Act, be a pension sharing order in relation to the marriage."

4. In section 21—

(a) the word "made", in both places, is omitted,

(b) after paragraph (b) there is inserted—

"(ba) section 24B(3) to (5) (provisions about pension sharing orders in relation to divorce and nullity);

(bb) section 24C (duty to stay pension sharing orders);

(bc) section 24D (apportionment of pension sharing charges);", and

(c) at the end there is inserted—

"(l) section 40A (appeals relating to pension sharing orders which have taken effect)."

Family Law (Scotland) Act 1985 (c.37)

5. The Family Law (Scotland) Act 1985 has effect subject to the following amendments.

6. In section 8, after subsection (3) there is inserted—

"(4) The court shall not, in the same proceedings, make both a pension sharing order and an order under section 12A(2) or (3) of this Act in relation to the same pension arrangement.

(5) Where, as regards a pension arrangement, the parties to a marriage have in effect a qualifying agreement which contains a term relating to pension sharing, the court shall not—

(a) make an order under section 12A(2) or (3) of this Act; or

(b) make a pension sharing order,

relating to the arrangement unless it also sets aside the agreement or term under section 16(1)(b) of this Act.

(6) The court shall not make a pension sharing order in relation to the rights of a person under a pension arrangement if there is in force an order under section 12A(2) or (3) of this Act which relates to benefits or future benefits to which he is entitled under the pension arrangement.

(7) In subsection (5) above—

(a) "term relating to pension sharing" shall be construed in accordance with section 16(2A) of this Act; and

(b) "qualifying agreement" has the same meaning as in section 28(3) of the Welfare Reform and Pensions Act 1999."

7. After section 8 there is inserted—

"Pension sharing orders: apportionment of charges.   8A. If a pension sharing order relates to rights under a pension arrangement, the court may include in the order provision about the apportionment between the parties of any charge under section 41 of the Welfare Reform and Pensions Act 1999 (charges in respect of pension sharing costs) or under corresponding Northern Ireland legislation."

8.—(1) Section 10 is amended as follows.

(2) In subsection (5)(b), for "scheme" there is substituted "arrangement".

(3) For subsection (8) there is substituted—

"(8) The Secretary of State may by regulations make provision about calculation and verification in relation to the valuation for the purposes of this Act of benefits under a pension arrangement or relevant state scheme rights."

(4) After that subsection there is inserted—

"(8A) Regulations under subsection (8) above may include—

(a) provision for calculation or verification in accordance with guidance from time to time prepared by a prescribed person; and

158   c. **30**   *Welfare Reform and Pensions Act 1999*

Sch. 12

(b) provision by reference to regulations under section 30 or 49(4) of the Welfare Reform and Pensions Act 1999."

(5) In subsection (9), after "subsection (8) above" there is inserted "may make different provision for different purposes and".

(6) Subsections (10) and (11) cease to have effect.

9.—(1) Section 12A is amended as follows.

(2) In subsection (1)(a), for "scheme" there is substituted "arrangement".

(3) In subsection (2), for "trustees or managers of the pension scheme" there is substituted "person responsible for the pension arrangement".

(4) In subsection (3), in paragraphs (a) and (c) for "trustees or managers of the pension scheme" there is substituted "person responsible for the pension arrangement" and in paragraph (a) for "have" there is substituted "has".

(5) In subsection (4)—

(a) for "trustees or managers" there is substituted "person responsible for the pension arrangement", and

(b) for "trustees' or managers' liability" there is substituted "liability of the person responsible for the pension arrangement".

(6) In subsection (5), for "trustees or managers" there is substituted "person responsible for the pension arrangement".

(7) In subsection (6)—

(a) for "trustees or managers of", wherever occurring, there is substituted "person responsible for",

(b) for "scheme", wherever occurring, there is substituted "arrangement", and

(c) in paragraph (b), for "have" there is substituted "has".

(8) In subsection (7)—

(a) for "trustees or managers" where first occurring there is substituted "person responsible for the pension arrangement",

(b) for "trustees or managers of" there is substituted "person responsible for", and

(c) for "scheme" there is substituted "arrangement".

(9) For subsection (10) there is substituted—

"(10) The definition of "benefits under a pension scheme" in section 27 of this Act does not apply to this section."

10. In section 13(2)(b), after "property" there is inserted ", or a pension sharing order,".

11.—(1) Section 16 is amended as follows.

(2) In subsection (2), for paragraph (b) there is substituted—

"(b) under subsection (1)(b) above, if the agreement does not contain a term relating to pension sharing, on granting decree of divorce or within such time as the court may specify on granting decree of divorce; or

(c) under subsection (1)(b) above, if the agreement contains a term relating to pension sharing—

(i) where the order sets aside the agreement or sets aside or varies the term relating to pension sharing, on granting decree of divorce; and

(ii) where the order sets aside or varies any other term of the agreement, on granting decree of divorce or within such time thereafter as the court may specify on granting decree of divorce."

(3) After that subsection there is inserted—

"(2A) In subsection (2) above, a term relating to pension sharing is a term corresponding to provision which may be made in a pension sharing order and satisfying the requirements set out in section 28(1)(f) or 48(1)(f) of the Welfare Reform and Pensions Act 1999."

12. In section 27(1), the following definitions are inserted at the appropriate places—

""benefits under a pension arrangement" includes any benefits by way of pension, including relevant state scheme rights, whether under a pension arrangement or not;"

""pension arrangement" means—

(a) any occupational pension scheme within the meaning of the Pension Schemes Act 1993;

(b) a personal pension scheme within the meaning of that Act;

(c) a retirement annuity contract;

(d) an annuity or insurance policy purchased or transferred for the purpose of giving effect to rights under an occupational pension scheme or a personal pension scheme;

(e) an annuity purchased or entered into for the purpose of discharging liability in respect of a pension credit under section 29(1)(b) of the Welfare Reform and Pensions Act 1999 or under corresponding Northern Ireland legislation;"

""person responsible for a pension arrangement" means—

(a) in the case of an occupational pension scheme or a personal pension scheme, the trustees or managers of the scheme;

(b) in the case of a retirement annuity contract or an annuity falling within paragraph (d) or (e) of the definition of "pension arrangement" above, the provider of the annuity;

(c) in the case of an insurance policy falling within paragraph (d) of the definition of that expression, the insurer;"

""relevant state scheme rights" means—

(a) entitlement, or prospective entitlement, to a Category A retirement pension by virtue of section 44(3)(b) of the Social Security Contributions and Benefits Act 1992 or under corresponding Northern Ireland legislation; and

(b) entitlement, or prospective entitlement, to a pension under section 55A of the Social Security Contributions and Benefits Act 1992 (shared additional pension) or under corresponding Northern Ireland legislation;"

""retirement annuity contract" means a contract or scheme approved under Chapter III of Part XIV of the Income and Corporation Taxes Act 1988;"

""trustees or managers" in relation to an occupational pension scheme or a personal pension scheme means—

1993 c. 48.

1992 c. 4.

1988 c. 1.

(a) in the case of a scheme established under a trust, the trustees of the scheme; and

(b) in any other case, the managers of the scheme;".

Income and Corporation Taxes Act 1988 (c.1)

13. In section 659D(2) of the Income and Corporation Taxes Act 1988, for "24(1)" there is substituted "28(1)".

Social Security Contributions and Benefits Act 1992 (c.4)

14. The Contributions and Benefits Act has effect subject to the following amendments.

15.—(1) Section 20 is amended as follows.

(2) In subsection (1), after paragraph (f) there is inserted—

"(fa) shared additional pensions;".

(3) In subsection (2), in the definition of "long-term benefit", after paragraph (d) there is inserted—

"(e) a shared additional pension;".

16. In section 21(1), after "41 below" there is inserted "or a shared additional pension under section 55A below".

17. In section 39(1), (2) and (3), for "45A" there is substituted "45B".

18. In section 43, at the end there is inserted—

"(6) For the purposes of this section, a pension under section 55A below is not a retirement pension."

19. In section 48A(4), for "45A" there is substituted "45B".

20. In section 48B(2) and (3), for "45A" there is substituted "45B".

21. In section 48C(4), for "45A" there is substituted "45B".

22. In section 54(1), at the end there is inserted "or to a shared additional pension".

Social Security Administration Act 1992 (c.5)

23. The Administration Act is amended as follows.

24. In section 150(1)—

(a) after paragraph (c) there is inserted—

"(ca) which are shared additional pensions;", and

(b) after paragraph (d) there is inserted—

"(da) which are the increases in the rates of shared additional pensions under section 55C of that Act;".

25.—(1) Section 155A is amended as follows.

(2) In subsection (1)(a)(i), after "retirement pension" there is inserted "or shared additional pension".

(3) In subsection (2), after "retirement pension" there is inserted ", a shared additional pension".

26. In section 163(2)—

  (a) after paragraph (a) there is inserted—

    "(aa) any administrative expenses of the Secretary of State in supplying information about benefits under Part II of that Act in accordance with regulations under section 23 of the Welfare Reform and Pensions Act 1999;", and

  (b) in paragraph (b), for "that Act" there is substituted "the Contributions and Benefits Act".

27. In section 165(5)(b), after "section 163(2)(a)" there is inserted "or (aa)".

Pension Schemes Act 1993 (c.48)

28. The Pension Schemes Act 1993 has effect subject to the following amendments.

29. In section 50(1)—

  (a) in paragraph (a), at the end there is inserted—

    "(iii) of safeguarded rights under the scheme;"

  (b) in paragraph (b), after "protected" there is inserted ", or safeguarded,".

30.—(1) Section 52 is amended as follows.

(2) In subsection (2A), at the end there is inserted—

    "(c) any persons who have safeguarded rights under the scheme or are entitled to any benefit giving effect to safeguarded rights under it."

(3) In subsection (3)(b), after "protected", in both places, there is inserted ", or safeguarded,".

31.—(1) Section 83 is amended as follows.

(2) In subsection (1), before "benefits", in both places, there is inserted "relevant".

(3) After that subsection there is inserted—

    "(1A) The following are relevant benefits for the purposes of subsection (1)—

    (a) any benefits payable otherwise than by virtue of rights which are attributable (directly or indirectly) to a pension credit, and

    (b) in the case of a salary related occupational pension scheme, any benefits payable by virtue of such rights, to the extent that the rights involve the member being credited by the scheme with notional pensionable service."

(4) At the end there is inserted—

    "(4) For the purposes of this section, an occupational pension scheme is salary related if—

    (a) it is not a money purchase scheme, and

    (b) it does not fall within a prescribed class."

32. In section 85, after "73(2)(b)" there is inserted "or 101D(2)(b)".

33. In section 93, after subsection (1) there is inserted—

"(1ZA) In subsection (1), references to accrued rights to benefit do not include rights which are attributable (directly or indirectly) to a pension credit."

34. In section 93A, after subsection (1) there is inserted—

"(1A) In subsection (1), the reference to benefits which have accrued does not include benefits which are attributable (directly or indirectly) to a pension credit."

35. In section 94, after subsection (1A) there is inserted—

"(1B) In subsection (1), references to benefits which have accrued do not include benefits which are attributable (directly or indirectly) to a pension credit."

36. In section 96, there is inserted at the end—

"(4) Where a member of an occupational pension scheme or a personal pension scheme—

    (a) is entitled to give a notice under section 101F(1) to the trustees or managers of the scheme, or

    (b) would be entitled to do so, but for section 101G(1),

he may not, if the scheme so provides, make an application to them under section 95 unless he also gives them a notice under section 101F(1)."

37.—(1) Section 98 is amended as follows.

(2) In subsection (5)—

    (a) after "part of the" there is inserted "relevant", and

    (b) for "any of the benefits mentioned in that section" there is substituted "benefits".

(3) In subsection (8), after "this section" there is inserted—

""relevant benefits" means any benefits not attributable (directly or indirectly) to a pension credit; and".

38.—(1) Section 100 is amended as follows.

(2) In subsection (1), for "subsection (2)" there is substituted "subsections (2) and (2A)".

(3) After subsection (2) there is inserted—

"(2A) If the making of the application depended on the giving of a notice under section 101F(1), the application may only be withdrawn if the notice is also withdrawn."

39.—(1) Section 129 is amended as follows.

(2) In subsection (1), after "Part IV," there is inserted "Chapters I and II of Part IVA,".

(3) In subsection (2), for "does" there is substituted "and Chapter II of Part IVA do".

40.—(1) Section 178 is amended as follows.

(2) In paragraph (a)—

    (a) the words "or of" are omitted, and

(b) at the end there is inserted ", section 25D of the Matrimonial Causes Act 1973, section 12A of the Family Law (Scotland) Act 1985 or Part III or IV of the Welfare Reform and Pensions Act 1999."

(3) In paragraph (b), after "Part IV," there is inserted "Chapter I of Part IVA,".

41. In section 181(1)—

   (a) after the definition of "occupational pension scheme" there is inserted—

   ""pension credit" means a credit under section 29(1)(b) of the Welfare Reform and Pensions Act 1999 or under corresponding Northern Ireland legislation;", and

   (b) after the definition of "rights" there is inserted—

   ""safeguarded rights" has the meaning given in section 68A;".

42. In section 183(3), for "and 97(1)" there is substituted ", 97(1) and 101I".

Pensions Act 1995 (c.26)

43. The Pensions Act 1995 has effect subject to the following amendments.

44. In section 3(2)(a)—

   (a) in sub-paragraph (ii), after "values)," there is inserted "Chapter II of Part IVA (pension credit benefit transfer values),", and

   (b) after that sub-paragraph there is inserted "or

   (iii) the following provisions of the Welfare Reform and Pensions Act 1999: section 33 (time for discharge of pension credit liability) and section 45 (information),".

45.—(1) Section 16 is amended as follows.

(2) In subsections (1)(a) and (6)(a), before "members" there is inserted "qualifying".

(3) In subsection (8)—

   (a) after "a", in the second place, there is inserted "qualifying", and

   (b) for "a member of the scheme", in the second place, there is substituted "such a member".

46. In section 17(4)(a), before "members" there is inserted "qualifying".

47.—(1) Section 18 is amended as follows.

(2) In subsections (1)(a) and (6)(a), before "members" there is inserted "qualifying".

(3) In subsection (7)—

   (a) after "a", in the second place, there is inserted "qualifying", and

   (b) for "a member of the scheme", in the second place, there is substituted "such a member".

48. In section 20(5), after "a", in the second place, there is inserted "qualifying".

49. In section 21(7)—

   (a) after "section" there is inserted—

SCH. 12

"(a) "qualifying member", in relation to a trust scheme, means a person who is an active, deferred or pensioner member of the scheme, and

(b)",

and

(b) before "members" there is inserted "qualifying".

50.—(1) Section 38 is amended as follows.

(2) In subsection (1), for the words from "that the scheme" to the end there is substituted—

"(a) that the scheme is not for the time being to be wound up but that no new members are to be admitted to it, or

(b) that the scheme is not for the time being to be wound up but that no new members, except pension credit members, are to be admitted to it."

(3) In subsection (2), the words from "but" to the end are omitted.

(4) After that subsection there is inserted—

"(2A) Subsection (2) does not authorise the trustees to determine—

(a) where there are accrued rights or pension credit rights to any benefit, that the benefit is not to be increased, or

(b) where the power conferred by that subsection is exercisable by virtue of a determination under subsection (1)(b), that members of the scheme may not acquire pension credit rights under it."

51. In section 51(6), after "a pension" there is inserted "which is attributable (directly or indirectly) to a pension credit or".

52. In section 53, after subsection (3) there is inserted—

"(3A) In subsections (1) and (2), the references to a person's pension do not include any pension which is attributable (directly or indirectly) to a pension credit."

53.—(1) Section 67 is amended as follows.

(2) In subsection (2), for "or accrued right," there is substituted "accrued right or pension credit right".

(3) In subsection (4)(a), for "or accrued rights," there is substituted "accrued rights or pension credit rights".

(4) For subsection (5) there is substituted—

"(5) Subsection (2) does not apply to the exercise of a power—

(a) for a purpose connected with debits under section 29(1)(a) of the Welfare Reform and Pensions Act 1999, or

(b) in a prescribed manner."

54. In section 68(2), for "and" at the end of paragraph (d) there is substituted—

"(da) to enable the scheme to accommodate persons with pension credits or pension credit rights, and".

55. In section 73, after subsection (3) there is inserted—

"(3A) No pension or other benefit which is attributable (directly or indirectly) to a pension credit may be regarded for the purposes of subsection (3)(a) as derived from the payment of voluntary contributions."

56. In section 74(3)(b), at the end there is inserted "or pension credit rights".

57.—(1) Section 91 is amended as follows.

(2) In subsection (1), for the words from ", or has" to "occupational pension scheme" there is substituted "to a pension under an occupational pension scheme or has a right to a future pension under such a scheme".

(3) In subsection (2), for the words from ", or" to "scheme" there is substituted "to a pension under an occupational pension scheme, or right to a future pension under such a scheme,".

(4) In subsection (5)—

  (a) for the words from ", or has" to "scheme" there is substituted "to a pension under an occupational pension scheme, or has a right to a future pension under such a scheme",

  (b) in paragraph (d), for "accrued right, to pension" there is substituted "right,", and

  (c) in paragraph (e), for "accrued right, to pension" there is substituted "right".

58.—(1) Section 92 is amended as follows.

(2) In subsection (1), for the words from ", or" to "scheme" there is substituted "to a pension under an occupational pension scheme or a right to a future pension under such a scheme".

(3) In subsection (4), for the words from "person entitled" to "accrued" there is substituted "pensioner, or prospective pensioner".

59.—(1) Section 93 is amended as follows.

(2) In subsection (1), for the words from ", or" to "scheme" there is substituted "to a pension under an occupational pension scheme or right to a future pension under such a scheme".

(3) In subsection (2)—

  (a) for "accrued right to a pension" there is substituted "right", and

  (b) for "accrued right to a pension under the scheme" there is substituted "right".

(4) In subsection (4), for "accrued right to a pension" there is substituted "right".

60. In section 99(2)—

  (a) in paragraph (b), after "values)," there is inserted "Chapter II of Part IVA (pension credit benefit transfer values),", and

  (b) at the end of that paragraph there is inserted—

    "(ba) section 33 (time for discharge of pension credit liability) or 45 (information) of the Welfare Reform and Pensions Act 1999,".

61.—(1) Section 124 is amended as follows.

(2) In subsection (1), in the definition of "member", for "or pensioner" there is substituted ", pensioner or pension credit".

(3) In that subsection, after the definition of "payment schedule" there is inserted—

> ""pension credit" means a credit under section 29(1)(b) of the Welfare Reform and Pensions Act 1999" or under corresponding Northern Ireland legislation,
>
> "pension credit member", in relation to an occupational pension scheme, means a person who has rights under the scheme which are attributable (directly or indirectly) to a pension credit,
>
> "pension credit rights", in relation to an occupational pension scheme, means rights to future benefits under the scheme which are attributable (directly or indirectly) to a pension credit,".

(4) After subsection (2) there is inserted—

> "(2A) In subsection (2)(a), the reference to rights which have accrued to or in respect of the member does not include any rights which are pension credit rights."

62.—(1) Section 166 is amended as follows.

(2) In subsection (4), for "scheme" there is substituted "arrangement".

(3) In subsection (5)(d), for "scheme" there is substituted "arrangement".

63. In section 167(4)—

(a) for "scheme", where first occurring, there is substituted "arrangement", and

(b) for the words from "("pension scheme"" to the end of the subsection there is substituted "("pension arrangement" having the meaning given in subsection (1) of section 27 of that Act, as it has effect for the purposes of subsection (5) of the said section 10)."

Family Law Act 1996 (c.27)

64. The Family Law Act 1996 has effect subject to the following amendments.

65.—(1) Schedule 2 is amended as follows.

(2) In paragraph 2, for "section 21" there is substituted "sections 21 and 21A".

(3) In the section set out in that paragraph, for the sidenote there is substituted "Financial provision orders, property adjustment orders and pension sharing orders."

(4) In that section, in paragraphs (c) and (d) of subsection (2), there is inserted at the end ", other than one in the form of a pension arrangement (within the meaning of section 25D below)".

(5) In that section, after subsection (2) there is inserted—

> "(3) For the purposes of this Act, a pension sharing order is an order which—
>
> (a) provides that one party's—
>
> > (i) shareable rights under a specified pension arrangement, or
> >
> > (ii) shareable state scheme rights,
>
> be subject to pension sharing for the benefit of the other party, and
>
> (b) specifies the percentage value to be transferred."

(6) In that section, subsections (3), (4) and (5) become (4), (5) and (6).

(7) In that section, after subsection (6) (new numbering) there is inserted—

"(7) In subsection (3)—

(a) the reference to shareable rights under a pension arrangement is to rights in relation to which pension sharing is available under Chapter I of Part IV of the Welfare Reform and Pensions Act 1999, or under corresponding Northern Ireland legislation, and

(b) the reference to shareable state scheme rights is to rights in relation to which pension sharing is available under Chapter II of Part IV of the Welfare Reform and Pensions Act 1999, or under corresponding Northern Ireland legislation."

(8) In that section, subsection (6) becomes subsection (8).

(9) After paragraph 6 there is inserted—

"Pension sharing orders: divorce and nullity

6A. For section 24B substitute—

"Pension sharing orders: divorce.

24B.—(1) On an application made under this section, the court may at the appropriate time make one or more pension sharing orders.

(2) The "appropriate time" is any time—

(a) after a statement of marital breakdown has been received by the court and before any application for a divorce order or for a separation order is made to the court by reference to that statement;

(b) when an application for a divorce order has been made under section 3 of the 1996 Act and has not been withdrawn;

(c) when an application for a divorce order has been made under section 4 of the 1996 Act and has not been withdrawn;

(d) after a divorce order has been made.

(3) The court shall exercise its powers under this section, so far as is practicable, by making on one occasion all such provision as can be made by way of one or more pension sharing orders in relation to the marriage as it thinks fit.

(4) This section is to be read subject to any restrictions imposed by this Act and to section 19 of the 1996 Act.

Restrictions affecting section 24B.

24BA.—(1) No pension sharing order may be made under section 24B above so as to take effect before the making of a divorce order in relation to the marriage.

(2) The court may not make a pension sharing order under section 24B above at any time while the period for reflection and consideration is interrupted under section 7(8) of the 1996 Act.

(3) No pension sharing order may be made under section 24B above by virtue of a statement of marital breakdown if, by virtue of section 5(3) or 7(9) of the 1996 Act (lapse of divorce process), it has ceased to be possible—

(a) for an application to be made by reference to that statement, or

(b) for an order to be made on such an application.

(4) No pension sharing order may be made under section 24B above after a divorce order has been made, except—

(a) in response to an application made before the divorce order was made, or

(b) on a subsequent application made with the leave of the court.

(5) A pension sharing order under section 24B above may not be made in relation to a pension arrangement which—

(a) is the subject of a pension sharing order in relation to the marriage, or

(b) has been the subject of pension sharing between the parties to the marriage.

(6) A pension sharing order under section 24B above may not be made in relation to shareable state scheme rights if—

(a) such rights are the subject of a pension sharing order in relation to the marriage, or

(b) such rights have been the subject of pension sharing between the parties to the marriage.

(7) A pension sharing order under section 24B above may not be made in relation to the rights of a person under a pension arrangement if there is in force a requirement imposed by virtue of section 25B or 25C below which relates to benefits or future benefits to which he is entitled under the pension arrangement.

(8) In this section, "period for reflection and consideration" means the period fixed by section 7 of the 1996 Act.

Pension sharing orders: nullity of marriage.

24BB.—(1) On or after granting a decree of nullity of marriage (whether before or after the decree is made absolute), the court may, on an application made under this section, make one or more pension sharing orders in relation to the marriage.

(2) The court shall exercise its powers under this section, so far as is practicable, by making on one occasion all such provision as can be made by way of one or more pension sharing orders in relation to the marriage as it thinks fit.

(3) Where a pension sharing order is made under this section on or after the granting of a decree of nullity of marriage, the order is not to take effect unless the decree has been made absolute.

(4) This section is to be read subject to any restrictions imposed by this Act.

Restrictions affecting section 24BB.

24BC.—(1) A pension sharing order under section 24BB above may not be made in relation to a pension arrangement which—

(a) is the subject of a pension sharing order in relation to the marriage, or

(b) has been the subject of pension sharing between the parties to the marriage.

(2) A pension sharing order under section 24BB above may not be made in relation to shareable state scheme rights if—

(a) such rights are the subject of a pension sharing order in relation to the marriage, or

(b) such rights have been the subject of pension sharing between the parties to the marriage.

(3) A pension sharing order under section 24BB above may not be made in relation to the rights of a person under a pension

arrangement if there is in force a requirement imposed by virtue of section 25B or 25C below which relates to benefits or future benefits to which he is entitled under the pension arrangement."

66.—(1) Schedule 8 is amended as follows.

(2) In paragraph 9—

    (a) in sub-paragraph (2)—

        (i) for "or 24A" there is substituted ", 24A or 24B", and

        (ii) for "to 24A" there is substituted "to 24BB", and

    (b) in sub-paragraph (3), after paragraph (a) there is inserted—

      "(aa) for "or 24B" substitute ", 24B or 24BB";".

(3) In paragraph 10, in sub-paragraph (2), for "24A" there is substituted "24BB".

(4) For paragraph 11 there is substituted—

    "11. In each of sections 25B(3) and 25C(1) and (3), for "section 23" substitute "section 22A or 23".

    11A. In section 25D—

      (a) in each of subsections (1)(a) and (2)(a) and (ab), for "section 23" substitute "section 22A or 23", and

      (b) in subsection (3), in the definition of "shareable state scheme rights", for "section 21A(1)" substitute "section 21(3)"."

(5) In paragraph 16, in sub-paragraph (2), at the end there is inserted—

    "(f) after paragraph (f) there is inserted—

      "(fa) a pension sharing order under section 24B which is made at a time when no divorce order has been made, and no separation order is in force, in relation to the marriage;"

    (g) in paragraph (g), for "24B" substitute "24BB"."

(6) In that paragraph, after sub-paragraph (3) there is inserted—

    "(3A) In subsection (4A), after "paragraph" insert "(de), (ea), (fa) or"."

(7) In that paragraph, in sub-paragraph (4), for the words from "subsection (4)" to the end of the first of the inserted subsections there is substituted "subsection (4A) insert—", the second of the inserted subsections is renumbered "(4AA)" and after that subsection there is inserted—

    "(4AB) No variation of a pension sharing order under section 24B above shall be made so as to take effect before the making of a divorce order in relation to the marriage."

(8) In that paragraph, after sub-paragraph (4) there is inserted—

    "(4A) In subsection (4B), after "order" insert "under section 24BB above"."

(9) In that paragraph, after sub-paragraph (7) there is inserted—

    "(8) After subsection (7F) insert—

      "(7FA) Section 24B(3) above applies where the court makes a pension sharing order under subsection (7B) above as it applies where the court makes such an order under section 24B above."

    (9) In subsection (7G)—

      (a) for "Subsections (3) to (5) of section 24B" substitute "Section 24BA(5) to (7)", and

(b) for "that section" substitute "section 24B above"."

(10) After that paragraph there is inserted—

"16A. After section 31A insert—

"Discharge of   31B. Where, after the making of a pension sharing order
pension sharing   under section 24B above in relation to a marriage, a separation
orders on making   order is made in relation to the marriage, the pension sharing
of separation   order is discharged.""
order.

(11) In paragraph 19, in sub-paragraph (3)—

(a) after "24A" there is inserted ", 24B", and

(b) after "property adjustment order," there is inserted "any pension sharing order,".

(12) In paragraph 21—

(a) after "24,", in the first place, there is inserted "24B,", and

(b) for "24,", in the second place, there is substituted "24BB,".

(13) After paragraph 25 there is inserted—

"25A. In section 52(2)(aa), for "section 21A" substitute "section 21"."

(14) In paragraph 32, in sub-paragraph (2), for the words from "the words" to the end there is substituted "paragraph (a) substitute—

"(a) make one or more orders each of which would, within the meaning of Part II of the 1973 Act, be a financial provision order in favour of a party to the marriage or a child of the family or a property adjustment order in relation to the marriage;"."

(15) In that paragraph, in sub-paragraph (3), for "21(a)" there is substituted "21(1)(a)".

(16) In that paragraph, after sub-paragraph (3) there is inserted—

"(3A) For section 21(1)(ba) substitute—

"(ba) sections 24BA(5) to (7) (provisions about pension sharing orders in relation to divorce);

(baa) section 24BC(1) to (3) (provisions about pension sharing orders in relation to nullity);".

(3B) In section 21(3), for "section 23" substitute "section 22A or 23"."

(17) At the end of Part I insert—

"The Welfare Reform and Pensions Act 1999

43A. In section 24 of the Welfare Reform and Pensions Act 1999 (charges by pension arrangements in relation to earmarking orders), for "section 23" substitute "section 22A or 23"."

PART II

OTHER CONSEQUENTIAL AMENDMENTS

Bankruptcy (Scotland) Act 1985 (c.66)

67. The Bankruptcy (Scotland) Act 1985 has effect subject to the following amendments.

68. In section 35(1), in paragraph (a) for "under the said section 8(2) for the transfer of property by him" substitute "a court has, under the said section 8(2), made an order for the transfer of property by him or made a pension sharing order".

69. After section 36C there is inserted—

"Recovery of excessive contributions in pension-sharing cases.

36D.—(1) For the purposes of section 34 of this Act, a pension-sharing transaction shall be taken—

    (a) to be a transaction, entered into by the transferor with the transferee, by which the appropriate amount is transferred by the transferor to the transferee; and

    (b) to be capable of being an alienation challengeable under that section only so far as it is a transfer of so much of the appropriate amount as is recoverable.

(2) For the purposes of section 35 of this Act, a pension-sharing transaction shall be taken—

    (a) to be a pension sharing order made by the court under section 8(2) of the Family Law (Scotland) Act 1985; and

    (b) to be an order capable of being recalled under that section only so far as it is a payment or transfer of so much of the appropriate amount as is recoverable.

(3) For the purposes of section 36 of this Act, a pension-sharing transaction shall be taken—

    (a) to be something (namely a transfer of the appropriate amount to the transferee) done by the transferor; and

    (b) to be capable of being an unfair preference given to the transferee only so far as it is a transfer of so much of the appropriate amount as is recoverable.

(4) Where—

    (a) an alienation is challenged under section 34;

    (b) an application is made under section 35 for the recall of an order made in divorce proceedings; or

    (c) a transaction is challenged under section 36,

if any question arises as to whether, or the extent to which, the appropriate amount in the case of a pension-sharing transaction is recoverable, the question shall be determined in accordance with subsections (5) to (9).

(5) The court shall first determine the extent (if any) to which the transferor's rights under the shared arrangement at the time of the transaction appear to have been (whether directly or indirectly) the fruits of contributions ("personal contributions")—

    (a) which the transferor has at any time made on his own behalf, or

    (b) which have at any time been made on the transferor's behalf,

to the shared arrangement or any other pension arrangement.

(6) Where it appears that those rights were to any extent the fruits of personal contributions, the court shall then determine the extent (if any) to which those rights appear to have been the fruits of personal contributions whose making has unfairly prejudiced the transferor's creditors ("the unfair contributions").

(7) If it appears to the court that the extent to which those rights were the fruits of the unfair contributions is such that the transfer of the appropriate amount could have been made out

of rights under the shared arrangement which were not the fruits of the unfair contributions, then the appropriate amount is not recoverable.

(8) If it appears to the court that the transfer could not have been wholly so made, then the appropriate amount is recoverable to the extent to which it appears to the court that the transfer could not have been so made.

(9) In making the determination mentioned in subsection (6) the court shall consider in particular—

(a) whether any of the personal contributions were made for the purpose of putting assets beyond the reach of the transferor's creditors or any of them; and

(b) whether the total amount of any personal contributions represented, at the time the pension sharing arrangement was made, by rights under pension arrangements is an amount which is excessive in view of the transferor's circumstances when those contributions were made.

(10) In this section and sections 36E and 36F—

"appropriate amount", in relation to a pension-sharing transaction, means the appropriate amount in relation to that transaction for the purposes of section 29(1) of the Welfare Reform and Pensions Act 1999 (creation of pension credits and debits);

"pension-sharing transaction" means an order or provision falling within section 28(1) of the Welfare Reform and Pensions Act 1999 (orders and agreements which activate pension-sharing);

"shared arrangement", in relation to a pension-sharing transaction, means the pension arrangement to which the transaction relates;

"transferee", in relation to a pension-sharing transaction, means the person for whose benefit the transaction is made;

"transferor", in relation to a pension-sharing transaction, means the person to whose rights the transaction relates.

Recovery orders.   36E.—(1) In this section and section 36F of this Act, "recovery order" means—

(a) a decree granted under section 34(4) of this Act;

(b) an order made under section 35(2) of this Act;

(c) a decree granted under section 36(5) of this Act,

in any proceedings to which section 36D of this Act applies.

(2) Without prejudice to the generality of section 34(4), 35(2) or 36(5) a recovery order may include provision—

(a) requiring the person responsible for a pension arrangement in which the transferee has acquired rights derived directly or indirectly from the pension-sharing transaction to pay an amount to the permanent trustee,

(b) adjusting the liabilities of the pension arrangement in respect of the transferee,

(c) adjusting any liabilities of the pension arrangement in respect of any other person that derive, directly or indirectly, from rights of the transferee under the arrangement,

(d) for the recovery by the person responsible for the pension arrangement (whether by deduction from any amount which that person is ordered to pay or otherwise) of costs incurred by that person in complying in the debtor's case with any requirement under section 36F(1) or in giving effect to the order.

(3) In subsection (2), references to adjusting the liabilities of a pension arrangement in respect of a person include (in particular) reducing the amount of any benefit or future benefit to which that person is entitled under the arrangement.

(4) The maximum amount which the person responsible for an arrangement may be required to pay by a recovery order is the smallest of—

(a) so much of the appropriate amount as, in accordance with section 36D of this Act, is recoverable,

(b) so much (if any) of the amount of the unfair contributions (within the meaning given by section 36D(6)) as is not recoverable by way of an order under section 36A of this Act containing provision such as is mentioned in section 36B(1)(a), and

(c) the value of the debtor's rights under the arrangement acquired by the transferee as a consequence of the transfer of the appropriate amount.

(5) A recovery order which requires the person responsible for an arrangement to pay an amount ("the restoration amount") to the permanent trustee must provide for the liabilities of the arrangement to be correspondingly reduced.

(6) For the purposes of subsection (5), liabilities are correspondingly reduced if the difference between—

(a) the amount of the liabilities immediately before the reduction, and

(b) the amount of the liabilities immediately after the reduction,

is equal to the restoration amount.

(7) A recovery order in respect of an arrangement—

(a) shall be binding on the person responsible for the arrangement, and

(b) overrides provisions of the arrangement to the extent that they conflict with the provisions of the order.

Recovery orders: supplementary.

36F.—(1) The person responsible for a pension arrangement under which the transferee has, at any time, acquired rights by virtue of the transfer of the appropriate amount shall, on the permanent trustee making a written request, provide the trustee with such information about the arrangement and the rights under it of the transferor and transferee as the permanent trustee may reasonably require for, or in connection with, the making of an application for a recovery order.

(2) Nothing in—

(a) any provision of section 159 of the Pension Schemes Act 1993 or section 91 of the Pensions Act 1995 (which prevent assignation and the making of orders which restrain a person from receiving anything which he is prevented from assigning),

(b) any provision of any enactment (whether passed or made before or after the passing of the Welfare Reform and Pensions Act 1999) corresponding to any of the provisions mentioned in paragraph (a), or

(c) any provision of the arrangement in question corresponding to any of those provisions,

applies to a court exercising its power to make a recovery order.

(3) Regulations may, for the purposes of the recovery provisions, make provision about the calculation and verification of—

(a) any such value as is mentioned in section 36E(4)(c);

(b) any such amounts as are mentioned in section 36E(6)(a) and (b).

(4) The power conferred by subsection (3) includes power to provide for calculation or verification—

(a) in such manner as may, in the particular case, be approved by a prescribed person; or

(b) in accordance with guidance—

(i) from time to time prepared by a prescribed person, and

(ii) approved by the Secretary of State.

(5) References in the recovery provisions to the person responsible for a pension arrangement are to—

(a) the trustees, managers or provider of the arrangement, or

(b) the person having functions in relation to the arrangement corresponding to those of a trustee, manager or provider.

(6) In this section—

"prescribed" means prescribed by regulations;

"the recovery provisions" means this section and sections 34, 35, 36 and 36E of this Act;

"regulations" means regulations made by the Secretary of State.

(7) Regulations under the recovery provisions may—

(a) make different provision for different cases;

(b) contain such incidental, supplemental and transitional provisions as appear to the Secretary of State necessary or expedient.

(8) Regulations under the recovery provisions shall be made by statutory instrument subject to annulment in pursuance of a resolution of either House of Parliament."

Insolvency Act 1986 (c.45)

70. The Insolvency Act 1986 is amended as follows.

71. After section 342C there is inserted—

"Recovery of excessive contributions in pension-sharing cases.

342D.—(1) For the purposes of sections 339, 341 and 342, a pension-sharing transaction shall be taken—

> (a) to be a transaction, entered into by the transferor with the transferee, by which the appropriate amount is transferred by the transferor to the transferee; and
>
> (b) to be capable of being a transaction entered into at an undervalue only so far as it is a transfer of so much of the appropriate amount as is recoverable.

(2) For the purposes of sections 340 to 342, a pension-sharing transaction shall be taken—

> (a) to be something (namely a transfer of the appropriate amount to the transferee) done by the transferor; and
>
> (b) to be capable of being a preference given to the transferee only so far as it is a transfer of so much of the appropriate amount as is recoverable.

(3) If on an application under section 339 or 340 any question arises as to whether, or the extent to which, the appropriate amount in the case of a pension-sharing transaction is recoverable, the question shall be determined in accordance with subsections (4) to (8).

(4) The court shall first determine the extent (if any) to which the transferor's rights under the shared arrangement at the time of the transaction appear to have been (whether directly or indirectly) the fruits of contributions ("personal contributions")—

> (a) which the transferor has at any time made on his own behalf, or
>
> (b) which have at any time been made on the transferor's behalf,

to the shared arrangement or any other pension arrangement.

(5) Where it appears that those rights were to any extent the fruits of personal contributions, the court shall then determine the extent (if any) to which those rights appear to have been the fruits of personal contributions whose making has unfairly prejudiced the transferor's creditors ("the unfair contributions").

(6) If it appears to the court that the extent to which those rights were the fruits of the unfair contributions is such that the transfer of the appropriate amount could have been made out of rights under the shared arrangement which were not the fruits of the unfair contributions, then the appropriate amount is not recoverable.

(7) If it appears to the court that the transfer could not have been wholly so made, then the appropriate amount is recoverable to the extent to which it appears to the court that the transfer could not have been so made.

(8) In making the determination mentioned in subsection (5) the court shall consider in particular—

> (a) whether any of the personal contributions were made for the purpose of putting assets beyond the reach of the transferor's creditors or any of them, and

(b) whether the total amount of any personal contributions represented, at the time the pension-sharing transaction was made, by rights under pension arrangements is an amount which is excessive in view of the transferor's circumstances when those contributions were made.

(9) In this section and sections 342E and 342F—

"appropriate amount", in relation to a pension-sharing transaction, means the appropriate amount in relation to that transaction for the purposes of section 29(1) of the Welfare Reform and Pensions Act 1999 (creation of pension credits and debits);

"pension-sharing transaction" means an order or provision falling within section 28(1) of the Welfare Reform and Pensions Act 1999 (orders and agreements which activate pension-sharing);

"shared arrangement", in relation to a pension-sharing transaction, means the pension arrangement to which the transaction relates;

"transferee", in relation to a pension-sharing transaction, means the person for whose benefit the transaction is made;

"transferor", in relation to a pension-sharing transaction, means the person to whose rights the transaction relates.

Orders under section 339 or 340 in respect of pension-sharing transactions.

342E.—(1) This section and section 342F apply if the court is making an order under section 339 or 340 in a case where—

(a) the transaction or preference is, or is any part of, a pension-sharing transaction, and

(b) the transferee has rights under a pension arrangement ("the destination arrangement", which may be the shared arrangement or any other pension arrangement) that are derived, directly or indirectly, from the pension-sharing transaction.

(2) Without prejudice to the generality of section 339(2) or 340(2), or of section 342, the order may include provision—

(a) requiring the person responsible for the destination arrangement to pay an amount to the transferor's trustee in bankruptcy,

(b) adjusting the liabilities of the destination arrangement in respect of the transferee,

(c) adjusting any liabilities of the destination arrangement in respect of any other person that derive, directly or indirectly, from rights of the transferee under the destination arrangement,

(d) for the recovery by the person responsible for the destination arrangement (whether by deduction from any amount which that person is ordered to pay or otherwise) of costs incurred by that person in complying in the transferor's case with any requirement under section 342F(1) or in giving effect to the order,

(e) for the recovery, from the transferor's trustee in bankruptcy, by the person responsible for a pension arrangement, of costs incurred by that person in complying in the transferor's case with any requirement under section 342F(2) or (3).

(3) In subsection (2), references to adjusting the liabilities of the destination arrangement in respect of a person include (in particular) reducing the amount of any benefit or future benefit to which that person is entitled under the arrangement.

(4) The maximum amount which the person responsible for the destination arrangement may be required to pay by the order is the smallest of—

(a) so much of the appropriate amount as, in accordance with section 342D, is recoverable,

(b) so much (if any) of the amount of the unfair contributions (within the meaning given by section 342D(5)) as is not recoverable by way of an order under section 342A containing provision such as is mentioned in section 342B(1)(a), and

(c) the value of the transferee's rights under the destination arrangement so far as they are derived, directly or indirectly, from the pension-sharing transaction.

(5) If the order requires the person responsible for the destination arrangement to pay an amount ("the restoration amount") to the transferor's trustee in bankruptcy it must provide for the liabilities of the arrangement to be correspondingly reduced.

(6) For the purposes of subsection (5), liabilities are correspondingly reduced if the difference between—

(a) the amount of the liabilities immediately before the reduction, and

(b) the amount of the liabilities immediately after the reduction,

is equal to the restoration amount.

(7) The order—

(a) shall be binding on the person responsible for the destination arrangement, and

(b) overrides provisions of the destination arrangement to the extent that they conflict with the provisions of the order.

Orders under section 339 or 340 in pension-sharing cases: supplementary.

342F.—(1) On the transferor's trustee in bankruptcy making a written request to the person responsible for the destination arrangement, that person shall provide the trustee with such information about—

(a) the arrangement,

(b) the transferee's rights under it, and

(c) where the destination arrangement is the shared arrangement, the transferor's rights under it,

as the trustee may reasonably require for, or in connection with, the making of applications under sections 339 and 340.

(2) Where the shared arrangement is not the destination arrangement, the person responsible for the shared

arrangement shall, on the transferor's trustee in bankruptcy making a written request to that person, provide the trustee with such information about—

(a) the arrangement, and

(b) the transferor's rights under it,

as the trustee may reasonably require for, or in connection with, the making of applications under sections 339 and 340.

(3) On the transferor's trustee in bankruptcy making a written request to the person responsible for any intermediate arrangement, that person shall provide the trustee with such information about—

(a) the arrangement, and

(b) the transferee's rights under it,

as the trustee may reasonably require for, or in connection with, the making of applications under sections 339 and 340.

(4) In subsection (3) "intermediate arrangement" means a pension arrangement, other than the shared arrangement or the destination arrangement, in relation to which the following conditions are fulfilled—

(a) there was a time when the transferee had rights under the arrangement that were derived (directly or indirectly) from the pension-sharing transaction, and

(b) the transferee's rights under the destination arrangement (so far as derived from the pension-sharing transaction) are to any extent derived (directly or indirectly) from the rights mentioned in paragraph (a).

(5) Nothing in—

1993 c. 48.
1995 c. 26.

(a) any provision of section 159 of the Pension Schemes Act 1993 or section 91 of the Pensions Act 1995 (which prevent assignment and the making of orders which restrain a person from receiving anything which he is prevented from assigning),

(b) any provision of any enactment (whether passed or made before or after the passing of the Welfare Reform and Pensions Act 1999) corresponding to any of the provisions mentioned in paragraph (a), or

(c) any provision of the destination arrangement corresponding to any of those provisions,

applies to a court exercising its powers under section 339 or 340.

(6) Regulations may, for the purposes of sections 339 to 342, sections 342D and 342E and this section, make provision about the calculation and verification of—

(a) any such value as is mentioned in section 342E(4)(c);

(b) any such amounts as are mentioned in section 342E(6)(a) and (b).

(7) The power conferred by subsection (6) includes power to provide for calculation or verification—

(a) in such manner as may, in the particular case, be approved by a prescribed person; or

(b) in accordance with guidance—

> > (i) from time to time prepared by a prescribed
person, and
> > (ii) approved by the Secretary of State.

> (8) In section 342E and this section, references to the person
responsible for a pension arrangement are to—

> > (a) the trustees, managers or provider of the
arrangement, or
> > (b) the person having functions in relation to the
arrangement corresponding to those of a trustee,
manager or provider.

> (9) In this section—

> "prescribed" means prescribed by regulations;

> "regulations" means regulations made by the Secretary
of State.

> (10) Regulations under this section may—

> > (a) make different provision for different cases;

> > (b) contain such incidental, supplemental and transitional
provisions as appear to the Secretary of State
necessary or expedient.

> (11) Regulations under this section shall be made by
statutory instrument subject to annulment in pursuance of a
resolution of either House of Parliament."

72. In section 384(1) (meaning of "prescribed" in the second Group of Parts),
after "Subject to the next subsection" insert "and sections 342C(7) and 342F(9)
in Chapter V of Part IX".

Income and Corporation Taxes Act 1988 (c.1)

73. The Income and Corporation Taxes Act 1988 is amended as follows.

74. In section 172(3) (exceptions from tax), for "earnings threshold" substitute
"secondary threshold".

75. In section 617(2) (social security benefits and contributions), after
paragraph (ae) insert—

> "(af) payments made under regulations under section 79 of the Welfare
Reform and Pensions Act 1999 or under any corresponding enactment
having effect with respect to Northern Ireland;".

Social Security Contributions and Benefits Act 1992 (c.4)

76. The Contributions and Benefits Act has effect subject to the following
amendments.

77.—(1) Section 122(1) (interpretation of Parts I to VI etc.) is amended as
follows.

(2) In the definition of "current", after "limits" insert "and primary and
secondary thresholds".

(3) In the definition beginning with "lower earnings limit"—

(a) for "and "earnings threshold"" substitute ""primary threshold" and
"secondary threshold""; and

(b) for "the earnings" substitute "the primary or secondary".

78.—(1) Paragraph 1 of Schedule 1 (supplementary provisions relating to contributions) is amended in accordance with sub-paragraphs (2) to (5).

(2) For "earnings threshold" (wherever occurring) substitute "secondary threshold".

(3) For "lower earnings limit" (wherever occurring) substitute "primary threshold".

(4) Omit sub-paragraphs (4) and (5).

(5) After sub-paragraph (9) add—

"(10) In relation to earners paid otherwise than weekly, any reference in this paragraph to—

(a) the primary or the secondary threshold, or

(b) the upper earnings limit,

shall be construed as a reference to the equivalent of that threshold or limit prescribed under section 5(4) above."

(6) In paragraph 6 of that Schedule—

(a) in sub-paragraph (5), for "section 159A" substitute "section 4A, 159A"; and

(b) in sub-paragraph (6), after "relating" insert "to relevant payments or benefits within the meaning of section 4A above or (as the case may be)".

Social Security Administration Act 1992 (c.5)

79. The Administration Act has effect subject to the following amendments.

80. After section 140E insert—

"Financing of other expenditure.

140EE.—(1) The Secretary of State may make to a local authority such payments as he thinks fit in respect of expenses incurred by the authority in connection with the carrying out of any relevant function—

(a) by the authority,

(b) by any person providing services to the authority, or

(c) by any person authorised by the authority to carry out that function.

(2) In subsection (1) "relevant function" means any function conferred by virtue of section 2A, 2C or 7A above.

(3) The following provisions, namely—

(a) in section 140B, subsections (1), (3), (4), (5)(b), (7)(b) and (8), and

(b) section 140C,

apply in relation to a payment under this section as in relation to a payment of subsidy.

(4) The Secretary of State may (without prejudice to the generality of his powers in relation to the amount of subsidy) take into account the fact that an amount has been paid under this section in respect of costs falling within section 140B(4A)(a) above."

81. In section 170(5) (enactments conferring functions in respect of which Social Security Advisory Committee is to advise)—

(a) in the definition of "the relevant enactments", after paragraph (ad) insert—

"(ae) sections 60, 72 and 79 of the Welfare Reform and Pensions Act 1999;"; and

(b) in the definition of "the relevant Northern Ireland enactments", after paragraph (ad) insert—

"(ae) any provisions in Northern Ireland which correspond to sections 60, 72 and 79 of the Welfare Reform and Pensions Act 1999;".

82. In section 189 (regulations and orders—general), after subsection (7) insert—

"(7A) Without prejudice to the generality of any of the preceding provisions of this section, regulations under any of sections 2A to 2C and 7A above may provide for all or any of the provisions of the regulations to apply only in relation to any area or areas specified in the regulations."

83. In section 190 (Parliamentary control of orders and regulations), in subsection (1) (instruments subject to the affirmative procedure), before the "or" at the end of paragraph (a) insert—

"(aa) the first regulations to be made under section 2A;".

Social Security Contributions and Benefits (Northern Ireland) Act 1992 (c.7)

84. The Social Security Contributions and Benefits (Northern Ireland) Act 1992 has effect subject to the following amendments.

85.—(1) Section 121(1) (interpretation of Parts I to VI etc.) is amended as follows.

(2) In the definition of "current", after "limits" insert "and primary and secondary thresholds".

(3) In the definition beginning with "lower earnings limit"—

(a) for "and "earnings threshold"" substitute ""primary threshold" and "secondary threshold""; and

(b) for "the earnings" substitute "the primary or secondary".

86.—(1) Paragraph 1 of Schedule 1 (supplementary provisions relating to contributions) is amended in accordance with sub-paragraphs (2) to (5).

(2) For "earnings threshold" (wherever occurring) substitute "secondary threshold".

(3) For "lower earnings limit" (wherever occurring) substitute "primary threshold".

(4) Omit sub-paragraphs (4) and (5).

(5) After sub-paragraph (9) add—

"(10) In relation to earners paid otherwise than weekly, any reference in this paragraph to—

(a) the primary or the secondary threshold, or

(b) the upper earnings limit,

shall be construed as a reference to the equivalent of that threshold or limit prescribed under section 5(4) above."

(6) In paragraph 6 of that Schedule—

    (a) in sub-paragraph (5), for "section 155A" substitute "section 4A, 155A"; and

    (b) in sub-paragraph (6), after "relating" insert "to relevant payments or benefits within the meaning of section 4A above or (as the case may be)".

Social Security Act 1998 (c.14)

87. In Schedule 2 to the Social Security Act 1998 (decisions against which no appeal lies), after paragraph 5 insert—

"Work-focused interviews

5A. A decision terminating or reducing the amount of a person's benefit made in consequence of any decision made under regulations under section 2A of the Administration Act (work-focused interviews)."

<table>
<tr><td>Section 88.</td><td colspan="3" align="center">SCHEDULE 13
Repeals
Part I
Pensions: miscellaneous</td></tr>
</table>

Chapter	Short title	Extent of repeal
1993 c. 48.	Pension Schemes Act 1993.	In section 28(1), paragraph (aa) (but not the final "and"). In section 55(2A), the words following paragraph (e). In section 73(2)(a)(ii), the words "or a self-employed pension arrangement" and "or arrangement". In section 96(2)(a), sub-paragraph (iii) and the word "or" preceding it. Section 159(5). In section 181(1), the definition of "self-employed pension arrangement".
1993 c. 49.	Pension Schemes (Northern Ireland) Act 1993.	In section 51(2A), the words following paragraph (e).
1995 c. 26.	Pensions Act 1995.	In section 8(4), the word "or" at the end of paragraph (a). In section 58(6)(a), the words "continue to". In section 83(3)(a), "90 per cent. of". Section 91(3). In section 92(2), paragraph (b) and the word "or" preceding it.

Chapter	Short title	Extent of repeal
1995 c. 26.— *contd.*	Pensions Act 1995.—*contd.*	In section 94(3), paragraphs (c) and (e) and the word "and" preceding paragraph (e). Section 95. In section 142, subsections (2) and (3), and in subsection (4), paragraph (b) and the word "and" preceding it. In Schedule 5, paragraph 80(f).
1998 c. 46.	Scotland Act 1998.	In section 126(1), in the definition of "occupational pension scheme", "personal pension scheme" and "public service pension scheme", the words "but as if the reference to employed earners in the definition of personal pension scheme were to any earners,".

Part II

Pensions on divorce etc

Chapter	Short title	Extent of repeal
1973 c. 18.	Matrimonial Causes Act 1973.	Section 25B(2). In section 25D(2), paragraphs (c) and (d) and the words after paragraph (e).
1984 c. 42.	Matrimonial and Family Proceedings Act 1984.	In section 21, the word "made", in both places.
1985 c. 37.	Family Law (Scotland) Act 1985.	Section 10(10) and (11). Section 12A(8)(b).
1996 c. 27.	Family Law Act 1996.	Section 9(8). Sections 16 and 17.

Part III

Pension sharing

Chapter	Short title	Extent of repeal
1971 c. 56.	Pensions (Increase) Act 1971.	In section 8(1)(a), the words from "(either" to "person)".
1993 c. 48.	Pension Schemes Act 1993.	In section 178(a), the words "or of".

Chapter	Short title	Extent of repeal
1995 c. 26.	Pensions Act 1995.	In section 3(2)(a), the word "or" at the end of sub-paragraph (i). In section 38(2), the words from "but" to the end. In Schedule 3, paragraph 45(a).

PART IV

ABOLITION OF SEVERE DISABLEMENT ALLOWANCE

Chapter	Short title	Extent of repeal
1988 c. 1.	Income and Corporation Taxes Act 1988.	In section 617(1)(a), the words "severe disablement allowance,".
1992 c. 4.	Social Security Contributions and Benefits Act 1992.	Section 63(b). Sections 68 and 69. In section 93(a), sub-paragraph (ii) and the word "or" preceding it. In section 93(b), the words "or allowance" each time they occur. In section 122(1), in the definition of "relevant loss of faculty", paragraph (a). Section 129(2)(a)(ii) and (2B)(a)(iii). Section 150(1)(d). In Schedule 4, in Part III, paragraphs 2 and 3, and in Part IV, paragraph 8. In Schedule 6, in paragraph 1, the words "68 or", and in sub-paragraph (b), the words from "except" to "68 above," and paragraphs 4 and 5. In Schedule 9, paragraph 5. In Schedule 11, in paragraph 2, sub-paragraph (d)(iii) and the word "or" preceding it.
1992 c. 5.	Social Security Administration Act 1992.	In section 45(1), the words "and severe disablement allowance". In section 45(1)(a), the words "in relation to industrial injuries benefit,". In section 45(1)(b), the words "in relation to both benefits,".

Chapter	Short title	Extent of repeal
1992 c. 5.—*contd.*	Social Security Administration Act 1992.—*contd.*	In section 45(2), paragraph (d) and the word "or" preceding it. In section 46(1), the words "or severe disablement allowance". In section 47(9), the words "or severe disablement allowance, as the case may be,". In section 48(1)(c), the words "or, in a case relating to severe disablement allowance, at the prescribed time". In section 130(1), paragraph (e) and the word "or" preceding it. In section 132(1), paragraph (d) and the word "or" preceding it.
1994 c. 18.	Social Security (Incapacity for Work) Act 1994.	Section 9(1) to (3). In Schedule 1, paragraph 18. In Schedule 2, in the third column, the entry relating to section 68 of the Social Security Contributions and Benefits Act 1992.
1998 c. 14.	Social Security Act 1998.	In section 77(8), subsection (c).
1999 c. 10.	Tax Credits Act 1999.	In Schedule 1, paragraph 2(d).

PART V

BENEFITS: MISCELLANEOUS

Chapter or reference	Short title or title	Extent of repeal or revocation
1988 c. 1.	Income and Corporation Taxes Act 1988.	In section 617, in subsection (1)(a) the words "widow's payments,", and subsection (6).
1992 c. 4.	Social Security Contributions and Benefits Act 1992.	Section 20(1)(e)(i). In section 21, in subsection (2) the entry relating to maternity allowance, and in subsection (4) the words ", other than maternity allowance,". In Schedule 3, in Part I, paragraph 3. In Schedule 4, in Part I, the entry relating to maternity allowance.

Chapter or reference	Short title or title	Extent of repeal or revocation
1993 c. 48.	Pension Schemes Act 1993.	In Schedule 8, paragraph 24.
S.I. 1994/1230.	Maternity Allowance and Statutory Maternity Pay Regulations 1994.	Regulations 2(1), (2) and (4) and 6(2).
1995 c. 18.	Jobseekers Act 1995.	In section 1(4), the word "and" at the end of the definition of "a contribution-based jobseeker's allowance".
1998 c. 14.	Social Security Act 1998.	In Schedule 7, paragraph 78.

PART VI
NATIONAL INSURANCE CONTRIBUTIONS ETC

Chapter	Short title	Extent of repeal
1992 c. 4.	Social Security Contributions and Benefits Act 1992.	In section 8(1), in each of paragraphs (a) and (b), the words "(or the prescribed equivalent)". In Schedule 1, paragraphs 1(4) and (5) and 8(2) and (3).
1992 c. 5.	Social Security Administration Act 1992.	Section 143A. In section 144, the words "or 143A" (in each place where they occur, including the sidenote). In section 190(1)(a), "143A,". In Schedule 7, in each of paragraphs 3(a) and 12, ", 143A".
1993 c. 48.	Pension Schemes Act 1993.	In section 181(1), the definition of "the prescribed equivalent".
1996 c. 18.	Employment Rights Act 1996.	In Schedule 1, paragraph 51(2).
1998 c. 14.	Social Security Act 1998.	In section 8(3), the words ", subject to section 21(4) below,". Section 51. Section 65(1). In Schedule 7, paragraph 16(b) and the word "and" preceding it, and paragraphs 57, 91 and 110(1)(a).
1999 c. 2.	Social Security Contributions (Transfer of Functions, etc.) Act 1999.	Section 3(3)(c). Section 8(4). In section 20(1), paragraph (b) and the word "and" preceding it.

Chapter	Short title	Extent of repeal
1999 c. 2.—*contd.*	Social Security Contributions (Transfer of Functions, etc.) Act 1999.—*contd.*	Section 20(5). In Schedule 1, paragraphs 4(6), 19(3) and (4) and 66(3). In Schedule 3, paragraphs 2, 5, 6, 8, 9, 39(4) and 47. In Schedule 8, paragraphs 3 and 4.

Part VII

National Insurance contributions etc: Northern Ireland

Chapter or reference	Short title or title	Extent of repeal or revocation
1992 c. 7.	Social Security Contributions and Benefits (Northern Ireland) Act 1992.	In section 8(1), in each of paragraphs (a) and (b), the words "(or the prescribed equivalent)". In Schedule 1, paragraphs 1(4) and (5) and 8(2) and (3).
1992 c. 8.	Social Security Administration (Northern Ireland) Act 1992.	In section 129, "143A,". Section 145(1)(a)(i) and (ii).
1993 c. 49.	Pension Schemes (Northern Ireland) Act 1993.	In section 176(1), the definition of "the prescribed equivalent".
S.I. 1996/1919 (N.I. 16).	Employment Rights (Northern Ireland) Order 1996.	In Schedule 1, the amendment of section 6(5) of the Social Security Contributions and Benefits (Northern Ireland) Act 1992.
S.I. 1998/1506 (N.I. 10).	Social Security (Northern Ireland) Order 1998.	In Article 9(3), the words ", subject to Article 21(4),". Articles 48 and 61(1). In Schedule 6, paragraph 39.
1999 c. 2.	Social Security Contributions (Transfer of Functions etc.) Act 1999.	In section 20(2), paragraph (b) and the word "and" preceding it.
S.I. 1999/671.	Social Security Contributions (Transfer of Functions, etc.) (Northern Ireland) Order 1999.	In Schedule 1, paragraphs 22(3) and (4), 24(3), 33(5) and 75(3). In Schedule 3, paragraphs 3, 6, 7, 9, 10, 38(4) and (5) and 49(3). In Schedule 5, paragraph 2(2). In Schedule 7, paragraphs 3 and 4.

Chapter or reference	Short title or title	Extent of repeal or revocation
1999 c. 10.	Tax Credits Act 1999.	In Schedule 2, paragraph 34. In Schedule 6, the entry relating to the Social Security Administration (Northern Ireland) Act 1992.

Printed in the UK by The Stationery Office Limited
under the authority and superintendence of Carol Tullo, Controller of
Her Majesty's Stationery Office and Queen's Printer of Acts of Parliament